More on Nolo.com

companion page at:

www.nolo.com/back-of-book/DEDU.html

When there's an important change to the law affecting this book, we'll
post updates. You'll also find articles and other related materials.

More Resources
from Nolo.com

Legal Forms, Books, & Software
Hundreds of do-it-yourself products—all written in plain English,
approved, and updated by our in-house legal editors.

Legal Articles
Get informed with thousands of free articles on everyday legal
topics. Our articles are accurate, up to date, and reader friendly.

Find a Lawyer
Want to talk to a lawyer? Use Nolo to find a lawyer who can
help you with your case.

NOLO
LAW for ALL

△△ NOLO The Trusted Name
(but don't take our word for it)

"In Nolo you can trust."
THE NEW YORK TIMES

"Nolo is always there in a jam as the nation's premier publisher of do-it-yourself legal books."
NEWSWEEK

"Nolo publications . . . guide people simply through the how, when, where and why of the law."
THE WASHINGTON POST

"[Nolo's] . . . material is developed by experienced attorneys who have a knack for making complicated material accessible."
LIBRARY JOURNAL

"When it comes to self-help legal stuff, nobody does a better job than Nolo . . ."
USA TODAY

"The most prominent U.S. publisher of self-help legal aids."
TIME MAGAZINE

"Nolo is a pioneer in both consumer and business self-help books and software."
LOS ANGELES TIMES

18th Edition

Deduct It!

Lower Your Small Business Taxes

Stephen Fishman, J.D.

NOLO
LAW for ALL

EIGHTEENTH EDITION	JANUARY 2022
Editor	AMY LOFTSGORDON
Cover & Book Design	SUSAN PUTNEY
Proofreading	SUSAN CARLSON GREENE
Index	UNGER INDEXING
Printing	SHERIDAN

ISSN: 1941-8248 (print)
ISSN: 2326-0076 (online)
ISBN: 978-1-4133-2924-7 (pbk)
ISBN: 978-1-4133-2925-4 (ebook)

Please note

Accurate, plain-English legal information can help you solve many of your own legal problems. But this text is not a substitute for personalized advice from a knowledgeable lawyer. If you want the help of a trained professional—and we'll always point out situations in which we think that's a good idea—consult an attorney licensed to practice in your state.

Acknowledgments

Many thanks to:

Amy Loftsgordon, Diana Fitzpatrick, and Lisa Guerin for their superb editing

Susan Putney for her outstanding book design

Dedication

This book is dedicated to my wife, Michele M. Horaney.

About the Author

Stephen Fishman has dedicated his career as an attorney and author to writing useful, authoritative, and recognized guides on taxes and business law for small businesses, entrepreneurs, independent contractors, and freelancers. He is the author of over 20 books and hundreds of articles, and has been quoted in the *New York Times*, *Wall Street Journal*, *Chicago Tribune*, and many other publications. Among his books are *Home Business Tax Deductions: Keep What You Earn*, *Every Landlord's Tax Deduction Guide*, *Tax Deductions for Professionals*, and *Working for Yourself: Law & Taxes for Independent Contractors, Freelancers & Gig Workers of All Types*.

Table of Contents

Introduction

Few of us ever test our powers of deduction, except when filling out an income tax form.

—Laurence J. Peter

If you are truly serious about preparing your child for the future, don't teach him to subtract—teach him to deduct.

—Fran Lebowitz

The goal of this book is to help you, the small business owner, pay less federal tax so you can keep more of your hard-earned dollars. The trick to paying lower taxes is to take advantage of every tax deduction available to you. A potentially huge array of deductions is available to businesses of all sizes, but you need to know they exist and understand how to use them.

Remember, the IRS will never complain if you don't take all the deductions you are entitled to. In fact, the majority of small businesses miss out on many deductions every year simply because they don't know about them—or because they neglect to keep the records necessary to back them up.

That's where this book comes in. We explain all the most valuable business deductions and show you how to deduct all or most of your business expenses. Learn how to take and properly document your travel, home office and operating expenses, depreciation, and other deductions. Even if you work with an accountant or another tax professional, you need to understand business deductions. With this book, you will learn how to keep better records, ask better questions, obtain better advice and—just as important—evaluate any information you get from tax professionals, websites, and other sources. If you do your taxes yourself, your need for knowledge is even greater. This book can be your guide—providing you with practical advice and information you need to rest assured that you are not missing out on valuable deductions.

Now more than ever, you'll need guidance when it comes to under-standing your taxes. In 2017, Congress enacted the most sweeping changes to the tax code in over 30 years when it passed the Tax Cuts and Jobs Act (TCJA), which took effect in 2018. Now, in an effort to stave off economic devastation in the wake of the coronavirus (COVID-19) pandemic, Congress has revised the nation's tax laws yet again, temporarily suspending many of the harshest provisions of the TCJA. We explain how these changes affect small business deductions including:

- tax treatment of the hugely popular Paycheck Protection Program (PPP) loans

- new rules for deducting net operating losses (see Chapter 1)
- changes to bonus and regular depreciation for improvements to nonresidential real property (see Chapter 5)
- new tax credits for employers who retain their payrolls and provide sick leave and family leave (see Chapter 11)
- new tax credits for self-employed business owners impacted by the COVID-19 pandemic (see Chapter 13)
- how employers can deduct pandemic-related payments to employees (see Chapter 11)
- temporary rules allowing penalty-free withdrawals from retirement accounts (see Chapter 12)
- rules for deducting business-related meals (see Chapter 14), and
- changes affecting charitable contributions by businesses (see Chapter 14).

This book is for anyone who owns a business, including self-employed businesspeople; sole proprietors; professionals who own their own practices; those engaged in part-time or sideline businesses; consultants, freelancers, and independent contractors; owner-employees of small corporations; partners in business partnerships; and members of limited liability companies. If you're an employee of a business you don't own, this book doesn't cover your situation. Nor is this book a tax preparation guide—it doesn't show you how to fill out your tax forms.

By the time you do your taxes, it might be too late to take deductions you could have claimed if you had planned the prior year's business spending wisely and kept proper records. To avoid this fate, you can (and should) use this book all year long to make April 15 as painless as possible.

Get Updates to This Book on Nolo.com

When important changes to the information in this book happen, we'll post updates online, on a page dedicated to this book:

www.nolo.com/back-of-book/DEDU.html

Tax Deduction Basics

The tax code is full of deductions for businesses—from automobile expenses to wages for employees. Before you can start taking advantage of these deductions, however, you need a basic understanding of how businesses pay taxes and how tax deductions work. This chapter gives you all the information you need to get started. It covers:

- how tax deductions work
- how businesses are taxed
- how to calculate the value of a tax deduction, and
- what businesses can deduct.

How Tax Deductions Work

A tax deduction (also called a tax "write-off") is an amount of money you are entitled to subtract from your gross income (all the money you make) to determine your taxable income (the amount on which you must pay tax). The more deductions you have, the lower your taxable income will be and the less tax you will have to pay.

Types of Tax Deductions

The three basic types of tax deductions are personal deductions, investment deductions, and business deductions. This book covers only business deductions—the large array of write-offs available to business owners.

Personal Deductions

For the most part, your personal, living, and family expenses are not tax deductible. For example, you can't deduct the food that you buy for yourself and your family. However, special categories of personal expenses may be deducted, subject to strict limitations. These include items such as home mortgage interest, state and local taxes (subject to an annual limit), charitable contributions, medical expenses above a threshold amount, interest on education loans, and alimony. This book does not cover these personal deductions.

Investment Deductions

Many people try to make money by investing money. For example, they might invest in real estate or play the stock market. These people incur all kinds of expenses, such as fees paid to money managers or financial planners, legal and accounting fees, and interest on money borrowed to buy investment property. In the past, these and other investment expenses (also called "expenses for the production of income") were tax deductible, subject to certain limitations. However, the Tax Cuts and Jobs Act eliminated many of these deductions for 2018 through 2025. Investment deductions are not covered in this book.

Business Deductions

People in business usually must spend money on their business—for office space, supplies, and equipment. Most business expenses are deductible, sooner or later, one way or another. And that's what this book is about: the many deductions available only to people who are in business (sole proprietors, independent contractors, and small business owners).

You Only Pay Taxes on Your Business Profits

The federal income tax law recognizes that you must spend money to make money. Virtually every business, however small, incurs some expenses. Even someone with a low overhead business (such as a freelance writer) must buy computer equipment and office supplies. Some businesses incur substantial expenses, even exceeding their income.

You are not legally required to pay tax on every dollar your business takes in (your gross business income). Instead, you owe tax only on the amount left over after your business's deductible expenses are subtracted from your gross income (this remaining amount is called your "net profit"). Although some tax deduction calculations can get a bit complicated, the basic math is simple: The more deductions you take, the lower your net profit will be, and the less tax you will have to pay.

> **EXAMPLE:** Karen, a sole proprietor, earned $100,000 this year from her consulting business. Fortunately, she doesn't have to pay income tax on the entire $100,000—her gross income. Instead, she can deduct from her gross income various business expenses, including a $5,000 home office deduction (see Chapter 7) and a $5,000 deduction for equipment expenses (see Chapter 5). She deducts these expenses from her $100,000 gross income to arrive at her net profit: $90,000. She pays income tax only on this net profit amount.

You Must Have a Legal Basis for Your Deductions

All tax deductions are a matter of legislative grace, which means that you can take a deduction only if it is specifically allowed by one or more provisions of the tax law. You usually do not have to indicate on your tax return which tax law provision gives you the right to take a particular deduction. If you are audited by the IRS, however, you'll have to provide a legal basis for every deduction the IRS questions. If the IRS concludes that your deduction wasn't justified, it will deny the deduction and charge you back taxes and, in some cases, penalties.

You Must Be in Business to Claim Business Deductions

Only businesses can claim business tax deductions. This concept probably seems simple, but it can get tricky. Even though you might believe you are running a business, the IRS might beg to differ. If your small-scale business doesn't turn a profit for several years in a row, the IRS might decide that you are engaged in a hobby rather than a business. This might not sound like a big deal, but it could have disastrous tax consequences: People engaged in hobbies are entitled to very limited tax deductions, while businesses can deduct all kinds of expenses. Fortunately, this unhappy outcome can be avoided by careful taxpayers. (See Chapter 2 for a detailed discussion on how to beat the hobby loss rule.)

How Businesses Are Taxed

If your business earns money (as you undoubtedly hope it will), you will have to pay taxes on those profits. How you pay those taxes will depend on how you have structured your business. So, before getting further into the details of tax deductions, it's important to understand what type of business you have formed (a sole proprietorship, partnership, limited liability company, or corporation) and how you will pay tax on your business's profit.

 RESOURCE
This section briefly summarizes some fairly complex areas of law. Although it covers the basic tax consequences of each business form, it does not explain how to choose the best structure for your business. If you need to decide how to organize a new business or want to know whether you should change your current business form, you can refer to *LLC or Corporation? Choose the Right Form for Your Business*, by Anthony Mancuso (Nolo).

Basic Business Forms

Every business, from a part-time operation you run from home while in your jammies to a Fortune 500 multinational company housed in a gleaming skyscraper, has a legal structure. If you're running a business right now, it has a legal form even if you made no conscious decision about how it should be legally organized.

The four basic legal structures for a business are sole proprietorship, partnership, limited liability company, and corporation. For tax purposes, corporations are either S corporations (corporations that have elected pass-through tax treatment) or C corporations (also called regular corporations). Every business falls into one of these categories—and your category will determine how your business's profits will be taxed.

Sole Proprietorship

A sole proprietorship is a one-owner business. You can't be a sole proprietor if two or more people own the business (unless you own the business with your spouse). Unlike the other business forms, a sole proprietorship has no legal existence separate from the business owner. It cannot sue or be sued, own property in its own name, or file its own tax returns. The business owner (proprietor) personally owns all of the assets of the business and controls its operation. If you're running a one-person business and you haven't incorporated or formed a limited liability company, you are a sole proprietor.

Partnership

A partnership is a form of shared ownership and management of a business. The partners contribute money, property, or services to the partnership; in return, they receive a share of the profits it earns, if any. The partners jointly manage the partnership business. A partnership automatically comes into existence whenever two or more people enter into business together to earn a profit and don't incorporate or form a limited liability company. Although many partners enter into written partnership agreements, no written agreement is required to form a partnership.

Corporation

Unlike a sole proprietorship or partnership, a corporation cannot simply spring into existence—it can only be created by filing incorporation documents with your state government. A corporation is a legal entity distinct from its owners. It can hold title to property, sue and be sued, have bank accounts, borrow money, hire employees, and perform other business functions.

For tax purposes, there are two types of corporations: S corporations (also called "small business corporations") and C corporations (also called "regular corporations"). The most important difference between the two types of corporation is how they are taxed. An S corporation pays no taxes itself—instead, its income or loss is passed on to its owners, who must pay personal income taxes on their share of the corporation's profits. A C corporation is a separate tax-paying entity that pays taxes on its profits. (See "Tax Treatment," below.)

Limited Liability Company

The limited liability company, or LLC, is the newest type of business form in the United States. An LLC is like a sole proprietorship or partnership in that its owners (called members) jointly own and manage the business and share in the profits. However, an LLC is also like a corporation, because its owners must file papers with the state to create the LLC, it exists as a separate legal entity, and its structure gives owners some protection from liability for business debts.

Tax Treatment

Your business's legal form will determine how it is treated for tax purposes. The two different ways business entities can be taxed are: The business itself can be taxed as a separate entity, or the business's profits and losses can be "passed through" to the owners, who include the profits or losses on their individual tax returns.

Pass-Through Entities: Sole Proprietorships, Partnerships, LLCs, and S Corporations

Sole proprietorships and S corporations are always pass-through entities. LLCs and partnerships are almost always pass-through entities as well—partnerships and multiowner LLCs are automatically taxed as partnerships when they are created. One-owner LLCs are automatically taxed like sole proprietorships. However, LLC and partnership owners have the option of choosing to have their entity taxed as a C corporation or an S corporation by filing an election with the IRS. The rules for spouses who co-own a business are different (see "Spouses Who Co-Own a Business," below).

A pass-through entity does not pay any taxes itself. Instead, the business's profits or losses are "passed through" to its owners, who include them on their own personal tax returns (IRS Form 1040). If a profit is passed through to the owner, that money is added to any other income the owner has, and the owner pays taxes on the total amount. If a loss is passed through, the owner can generally use it to offset income from other sources—for example, salary from a job, interest, investment income, or a spouse's income (as long as the couple files a joint tax return). The owner can subtract the business loss from this other income, which leaves a lower total subject to tax.

> EXAMPLE: Lisa is a sole proprietor who works part time as a personal trainer. During her first year in business, she incurs $10,000 in expenses and earns $5,000, giving her a $5,000 loss from her business. She reports this loss on IRS Schedule C, which she files with her personal income tax return (Form 1040). Because Lisa is a sole proprietor, she can deduct this $5,000 loss from any income she has, including her $100,000 annual salary from her engineering job. This saves her about $2,000 in total taxes for the year.

Owners of pass-through entities qualify for a pass-through income tax deduction of up to 20% of their business income under the Tax Cuts and Jobs Act. See Chapter 10 for a detailed discussion.

Although pass-through entities don't pay taxes, their income and expenses must still be reported to the IRS as follows:

- **Sole proprietors** must file IRS Schedule C, *Profit or Loss From Business (Sole Proprietorship)*, with their tax returns. This form lists all the proprietor's business income and deductible expenses.

- **Partnerships** are required to file an annual tax form (Form 1065, *U.S. Return of Partnership Income*) with the IRS. Form 1065 is not used to pay taxes. Instead, it is an "information return" that informs the IRS of the partnership's income, deductions, profits, losses, and tax credits for the year. Form 1065 also includes a separate part called Schedule K-1, in which the partnership lists each partner's share of the items listed on Form 1065. A separate Schedule K-1 must be provided to each partner. The partners report on their individual tax returns (Form 1040) their share of the partnership's net profit or loss as shown on Schedule K-1. Ordinary business income or loss is reported on Schedule E, *Supplemental Income and Loss.* However, certain items must be reported on other schedules—for example, capital gains and losses must be reported on Schedule D and charitable contributions on Schedule A.

- **S corporations** report their income and deductions much like a partnership. An S corporation files an information return (Form 1120-S) reporting the corporation's income, deductions, profits, losses, and tax credits for the year. Like partners, shareholders must be provided a Schedule K-1 listing their share of the items listed in the corporation's Form 1120-S. The shareholders file Schedule E with their personal tax returns (Form 1040) showing their share of corporation income or losses. Unlike with the other pass-through entities, S corporation owners ordinarily work as employees of their corporation. This can help them maximize the new 20% pass-through tax deduction (see Chapter 10 for more information).

- **An LLC** with only one member is treated like a sole proprietorship for tax purposes. The member reports profits, losses, and deductions on Schedule C—just like a sole proprietor. An LLC with two or more members is treated like a partnership for tax purposes unless the members elect to be taxed like a C corporation or an S corporation.

Regular C Corporations

A regular C corporation is the only business form that is not a pass-through entity. Instead, a C corporation is taxed separately from its owners. Like any other business, a C corporation is entitled to deduct its business expenses. It must then pay income taxes on its net income at the C corporation tax rate and file its own tax return with the IRS, using Form 1120 or Form 1120-A. You pay personal income tax on C corporation income only when it is distributed to you in the form of salary, bonuses, or dividends. Starting in 2018, the tax rate for regular C corporations was reduced from a top rate of 35% to a flat tax of 21% on all C corporation income. See IRS Publication 542, *Corporations* for more information.

C Corporation Versus Pass-Through Tax Treatment: How to Choose What's Best for Your Business

The Tax Cuts and Jobs Act reduced the tax rate for regular C corporations from a top rate of 35% to a flat tax of 21% on all C corporation income. For the first time in decades, corporate tax rates are substantially lower than the income tax rates paid by higher income individuals. At the same time, the new tax law created a brand new deduction for pass-through entities, allowing them to deduct 20% of the net income from their business—a huge tax savings. Which tax treatment should you choose? You will need to do some number crunching and analysis to figure that out but here are some things you'll want to consider.

20% Tax Deduction for Pass-Through Entities

Owners of pass-through entities are allowed to deduct up to 20% of the net income from the business—for example, if your net income from your sole proprietorship or LLC business is $100,000, you may be able to deduct as much as $20,000 from your income taxes. This effectively reduces your tax rate by 20%. For example, if you're in the 32% tax bracket, your effective tax rate would be 25.6%, not much more than the corporate rate. If you're in the 24% bracket (income up to $164,925 for singles and $329,850 for marrieds), your effective rate is just 19.2%.

C corporations do not qualify for this deduction. However, not all pass-through entities can use the deduction: Pass-through business owners who provide personal services may not take the deduction if their taxable income is over $429,800 (married) or $214,900 (single). See Chapter 10 for a detailed discussion. One factor in your decision will be whether you can use the pass-through deduction.

Double Taxation for Certain Corporate Payments

If you're the owner of a C corporation, any direct payment of your corporation's profits to you will be considered a dividend by the IRS and taxed twice. First, the corporation will pay corporate income tax on the profit at the 21% corporate rate on its own return, and then you'll pay personal income tax on what you receive from the corporation. This is called "double taxation."

C corporation dividends are usually taxed at capital gains rates. Higher income taxpayers must also pay a 3.8% Medicare tax on net dividend and investment income. The tax rates on dividends range from 15% to 23.8% for high income taxpayers. Thus, for example, if you pay tax on your corporation's dividends at the 15% rate, the total tax on every $100 distributed to you will amount to $32.85. The effective tax rate is 32.85%: 21% corporate tax rate + (79% x 15% capital gains rate) = 32.85%. And dividend payments are not deductible by the corporation.

There is no double taxation with pass-through entities. All income passes through to the owners who include the income on their personal tax returns. There is no separate taxation at the business entity level for any income earned by a pass-through entity.

Employee Tax Issues for Corporations

When you form a C corporation and actively work in the business, you must become your corporation's employee. You can get paid a reasonable salary for the work you do but you also must pay tax on that salary at your individual tax rate. The corporation gets to deduct employee salaries and benefits from its taxable income, so there is no double taxation on these payments, but there is no tax savings either.

There are tax benefits, however, that come with C corporation employee status. The tax law allows a C corporation to provide its employees with many types of fringe benefits that it can deduct from the corporation's income as a business expense. And employees need not include the value of the fringe benefits in their taxable income, effectively making these benefits tax free to them. This can result in substantial tax savings and benefits for employees and the corporation. Possible tax-free employee fringe benefits include: health, accident, and dental insurance for you and your family, disability insurance, reimbursement of medical expenses not covered by insurance, deferred compensation plans, working condition fringe benefits such as company-owned cars, and group term life insurance.

With pass-through entities, on the other hand, there are few tax-free employee benefits available to the owners.

The Bottom Line

There are so many factors involved that the only way to evaluate whether forming a C corporation might be a good idea is to have an accountant or tax pro crunch the numbers for you. As a general rule, a C corporation will only be advantageous if you can avoid double taxation by keeping a substantial amount of money in your corporation to expand your business and/or provide employee benefits, rather than distributing it as dividends. Money you keep in your C corporation business is taxed only once at the 21% rate. If your income is over $523,600 if you're single or $628,300 if married, you'll be in the top 37% personal income tax bracket and the 21% C corporation rate will be most beneficial. This is particularly true if you provide a personal service, because at these income levels you won't qualify for the pass-through deduction.

Spouses Who Co-Own a Business

Prior to 2007, spouses who co-owned a business were classified as a partnership for federal tax purposes (unless they formed a corporation or an LLC, or lived in a community property state—see below). Now, married couples in any state who own a business together may be able to elect to be taxed as sole proprietors. This does not reduce their taxes, but it does result in a much simpler tax return.

The rules for electing sole proprietor tax status differ depending on whether you live in a community property state or not. If a couple doesn't choose or qualify for sole proprietor status, their jointly owned business will be classified as a partnership for federal tax purposes, assuming they have not formed an LLC or a corporation. This means they must file a partnership tax return for the business. Each spouse should carry his or her share of the partnership income or loss from Form 1065, Schedule K-1, to their joint or separate Form 1040. Each spouse should also include his or her share of self-employment income on a separate Form 1040, Schedule SE.

Spouses in all states. Spouses in all states who jointly own and manage a business together can elect to be taxed as a "qualified joint venture" and treated as sole proprietors for tax purposes. To qualify as co–sole proprietors, the married couple must be the only owners of the business and they must both "materially participate" in the business—be involved with the business's day-to-day operations on a regular, continuous, and substantial basis. Working more than 500 hours during the year meets this requirement. It's likely that many couples will not be able to satisfy the material participation requirement.

A couple elects to be treated as a qualified joint venture by filing a joint tax return (IRS Form 1040). Each spouse files a separate Schedule C to report that spouse's share of the business's profits and losses, and a separate Schedule SE to report his or her share of self-employment tax. That way, each spouse gets credit for Social Security and Medicare coverage purposes. If, as is usually the case, each spouse owns 50% of the business, they equally share the business income or loss on their individual Schedule Cs. The couple must also share any deductions and credits according to their individual ownership interest in the business. If the business has employees, either spouse may report and pay the employment taxes due on any wages paid to the employees. The employer-spouse must report taxes due using the Employer Identification Number (EIN) of the sole proprietorship.

Spouses in community property states. Spouses in any of the nine community property states (Arizona, California, Idaho, Louisiana, Nevada, New Mexico, Texas, Washington, and Wisconsin) may elect qualified joint venture status as described above. However, couples in these states can also choose to classify their business as a sole proprietorship simply by filing a single Schedule C listing one spouse as the sole proprietor. For many couples, this is easier to do than the qualified joint venture status because there is no material participation requirement. The only requirements are that:

- The business is wholly owned by the husband and wife as community property.
- No person other than one or both spouses would be considered an owner for federal tax purposes.
- The business entity is not treated as a corporation. (Rev. Proc. 2002-69.)

One drawback to this election is that only one spouse (the one listed in the Schedule C) receives credit for Social Security and Medicare coverage purposes.

What If Your Spouse Is Your Employee?

Instead of being co-owners of a business, spouses can have an employer-employee relationship—that is, one spouse solely owns the business (usually as a sole proprietor) and the other spouse works as an employee. In this event, you don't have to worry about having to file a partnership tax return. One Schedule C would be filed in the name of the owner-spouse. The nonowner spouse's income would be employee salary subject to income tax and FICA (Social Security and Medicare) withholding. (See Chapter 11.)

As far as taxes go, this is an excellent way to organize a small business because the employer-spouse can provide the employee-spouse with tax-free employee fringe benefits such as health insurance, which can cover the entire family (see Chapter 13).

However, a spouse is considered an employee only if there is an employer/employee type of relationship—that is, the first spouse substantially controls the business in terms of management decisions and the second spouse is under the direction and control of the first spouse. If the second spouse has an equal say in the affairs of the business, provides substantially equal services to the business, and contributes capital to the business, that spouse cannot be treated as an employee.

The Value of a Tax Deduction

Most taxpayers, even sophisticated businesspeople, don't fully appreciate just how much money they can save with tax deductions. Only part of any deduction ends up back in your pocket as money saved. Because a deduction represents income on which you don't have to pay tax, the value of any deduction is the amount of tax you would have had to pay on that income had you not deducted it. So, a deduction of $1,000 won't save you $1,000—it will save you whatever you would otherwise have had to pay as tax on that $1,000 of income.

Federal and State Income Taxes

To determine how much income tax a deduction will save you, you must first figure out your income tax bracket. The United States has a progressive income tax system for individual taxpayers. The higher your income, the higher your tax rate. As a result of the enactment of the Tax Cuts and Jobs Act, there are seven different tax rates (called tax brackets), ranging from 10% of taxable income to 37%. (See the chart below.)

You move from one bracket to the next only when your taxable income exceeds the bracket amount. For example, if you are a single taxpayer, you pay 10% income tax on all your taxable income up to $9,950. If your taxable income exceeds that amount, the next tax rate (12%) applies to all your income over $9,950—but the 10% rate still applies to the first $9,950. If your income exceeds the 12% bracket amount, the next tax rate (22%) applies to the excess amount, and so on until the top bracket of 37% is reached.

The tax bracket in which the last dollar you earn for the year falls is called your "marginal tax bracket." For example, if you have $85,000 in taxable income, your marginal tax bracket is 22%. To determine how much federal income tax a deduction will save you, multiply the amount of the deduction by your marginal tax bracket. For example, if your marginal tax bracket is 22%, you will save 22¢ in federal income taxes for every dollar you are able to claim as a deductible business expense (22% × $1 = 22¢). This calculation is only approximate because an additional deduction may move you from one tax bracket to another and thus lower your marginal tax rate.

The following table lists the 2021 federal income tax brackets for single and married individual taxpayers.

2021 Federal Personal Income Tax Rates		
Rate	Married Filing Jointly	Individual Return
10%	0–$19,900	$0–$9,950
12%	$19,901–$81,050	$9,951–$40,525
22%	$81,051–$172,750	$40,526–$86,375
24%	$172,751–$329,850	$86,376–$164,925
32%	$329,851–$418,850	$166,926–$209,425
35%	$418,851–$628,300	$209,426–$523,600
37%	Over $628,300	Over $523,600

Income tax brackets are adjusted each year for inflation. For current brackets, see IRS Publication 505, *Tax Withholding and Estimated Tax*.

You can also deduct your business expenses from any state income tax you must pay. The average state income tax rate is about 6%, although eight states (Alaska, Florida, Nevada, South Dakota, Tennessee, Texas, Washington, and Wyoming) don't have an income tax and New Hampshire taxes only dividends and interest. You can find a list of all state income tax rates at the Federation of Tax Administrators website, at www.taxadmin.org.

Self-Employment Taxes

Everyone who works—whether a business owner or an employee—is required to pay Social Security and Medicare taxes. Employees pay one-half of these taxes through payroll deductions; the employer must pony up the other half and send the entire payment to the IRS. Business owners must pay all of these taxes themselves. Business owners' Social Security and Medicare contributions are called self-employment taxes.

Self-employment taxes consist of two separate taxes: the Social Security tax and the Medicare tax.

Social Security tax. The Social Security tax is a flat 12.4% tax on net self-employment income up to an annual ceiling that is adjusted for inflation each year. In 2021, the ceiling was $142,800 in net self-employment income. Thus, a self-employed person who had that much or more in net self-employment income would pay $17,707 in Social Security taxes.

Medicare tax. There are two Medicare tax rates: a 2.9% tax up to an annual ceiling—$200,000 for single taxpayers and $250,000 for married couples filing jointly. All income above the ceiling is taxed at a 3.8% rate. Thus, for example, a single taxpayer with $300,000 in net self-employment income would pay a 2.9% Medicare tax on the first $200,000 of income and a 3.8% tax on the remaining $100,000. This 0.9% Medicare tax increase applies to high-income employees as well as to the self-employed. Employees must pay a 2.35% Medicare tax on the portion of their wages over the $200,000/$250,000 thresholds (their one-half of 2.9% (1.45%) plus the 0.9%). In addition, Medicare taxes must be paid by high-income taxpayers on investment income. (See "Income-Producing Activities" in Chapter 2.) For both the self-employed and employees, the combined Social Security and Medicare tax is 15.3%, up to the Social Security tax ceiling.

However, the effective self-employment tax rate is lower. This is because you pay self-employment tax on only 92.35% of your net self-employment income, resulting in a 14.13% effective rate. Also, you may deduct half of your self-employment taxes from your net income for income tax purposes. These income tax savings result in an even lower effective self-employment tax rate. How much lower depends on your taxable income. But taxpayers who earn more than the $200,000/$250,000 threshold, can't deduct the 0.9% increase in Medicare tax from their income.

Like income taxes, self-employment taxes are paid on the net profit you earn from a business. Thus, deductible business expenses reduce the amount of self-employment tax you have to pay by lowering your net profit.

Total Tax Savings

When you add up your savings in federal, state, and self-employment taxes, you can see the true value of a business tax deduction. For example, if you're single and make $100,00, a business deduction can be worth as much as 24% (in federal income tax) + 15.3% (in self-employment taxes) + 6% (in state taxes—depending on which state you live in). That adds up to a whopping 45.3% savings. If you buy a $1,000 computer for your business and you deduct the expense, you save about $453 in taxes. In effect, the government is paying for almost half of your business expenses. This is why it's so important to know all the business deductions you are entitled to take—and to take advantage of every one.

> CAUTION
> **Don't buy stuff just to get a tax deduction.** Although tax deductions can be worth a lot, it doesn't make sense to buy something you don't need just to get a deduction. After all, you still have to pay for the item, and the tax deduction you get in return will only cover a portion of the cost. If you buy a $1,000 computer, you'll probably be able to deduct less than half of the cost. That means you're still out more than $500—money you've spent for something you don't need. On the other hand, if you really do need a computer, the deduction you're entitled to is like found money—and it might help you buy a better computer than you could otherwise afford.

What Businesses Can Deduct

Business owners can deduct several broad categories of business expenses:
- start-up expenses
- operating expenses
- capital expenses, and
- inventory costs.

There is also a new 20% pass-through tax deduction available to pass-through business entities (any business entity other than a regular C corporation). This section provides an introduction to each of these deduction categories (they are covered in greater detail in later chapters).

!   CAUTION
    You must keep track of your expenses. You can deduct only those expenses that you actually incur. You need to keep records of these expenses to (1) know for sure how much you actually spent, and (2) prove to the IRS that you really spent the money you deducted on your tax return, in case you are audited. Accounting and bookkeeping are discussed in detail in Chapter 15.

Start-Up Expenses

The first money you will have to shell out will be for your business's start-up expenses. These include most of the costs of getting your business up and running, like license fees, advertising costs, attorney and accounting fees, travel expenses, market research, and office supplies expenses. You may deduct up to $5,000 in start-up costs the first year a new business is in operation. You may deduct amounts of more than $5,000 over the next 15 years.

> **EXAMPLE:** Cary, a star hairdresser at a popular salon, decides to open his own hairdressing business. Before Cary's new salon opens for business, he has to rent space, hire and train employees, and pay for an expensive pre-opening advertising campaign. These start-up expenses cost Cary $25,000. Cary may deduct $5,000 of his $25,000 in start-up expenses the first year he's in business. He may deduct the remaining $20,000 in equal amounts over the next 15 years.

Operating Expenses

Operating expenses are the ongoing day-to-day costs a business incurs to stay in business. They include such things as rent, utilities, salaries, supplies, travel expenses, car expenses, and repairs and maintenance. These expenses (unlike start-up expenses) are currently deductible—that is, you can deduct them all in the same year when you pay them. (See Chapter 4 for more on deducting operating expenses.)

> **EXAMPLE:** After Cary's salon opens, he begins paying $5,000 a month for rent and utilities. This is an operating expense that is currently deductible. When Cary does his taxes, he can deduct from his income the entire $60,000 that he paid for rent and utilities for the year.

Capital Expenses

Capital assets are things you buy for your business that have a useful life of more than one year, such as land, buildings, equipment, vehicles, books, furniture, machinery, and patents you buy from others. These costs, called capital expenses, are considered to be part of your investment in your business, not day-to-day operating expenses.

The cost of business real estate—buildings and building components—must always be deducted over many years, a process called depreciation. Commercial real estate is depreciated over 39 years. However, the cost of personal property used in business—computers, for example—can usually be deducted in a single year using 100% bonus depreciation (available through 2022) or Section 179 of the tax code. Bonus depreciation and Section 179 are discussed in detail in Chapter 5.

> **EXAMPLE:** Cary spent $5,000 on fancy barber chairs for his salon. Because the chairs have a useful life of more than one year, they are capital assets that he will either have to depreciate over several years or deduct in one year under Section 179 or using 100% bonus depreciation.

Certain capital assets, such as land and corporate stock, never wear out. Capital expenses related to these costs are not deductible; the owner must wait until the asset is sold to recover the cost. (See Chapter 5 for more on this topic.)

Pass-Through Tax Deduction

Business owners (other than those who have formed a C corporation) may qualify for a special pass-through tax deduction in effect for 2018 through 2025. This enables them to deduct from their income taxes up to 20% of their net business income. There are certain limitations and requirements that must be met to qualify for this 20% pass-through deduction. (See Chapter 10 for more information.)

> **EXAMPLE:** Cary, a sole proprietor, earned $100,000 in net profit from his hair salon during the year (and had $120,000 in taxable income). By claiming the pass-through deduction, he may deduct from his income taxes 20% of this amount, or $20,000.

Frequently Asked Questions About Tax Deductions

- **Do I have to pay cash for an item to get a deduction?** No. You may deduct the entire amount you pay for a deductible expense whether you pay by cash, check, credit card, or loan. (See Chapter 4.)
- **Do I need a receipt to take a business expense deduction?** Yes and no. You can claim whatever deductions you want, regardless of whether you have proof of the expense. If you are audited, however, you must be able to prove that you are entitled to the deduction. If you don't have receipts, you may be able to use other records to prove you shelled out those costs. (See Chapter 15.)

Inventory

Inventory includes almost anything you make or buy to resell to customers. It doesn't matter whether you manufacture the goods yourself or buy finished goods from someone else and resell the items to customers. Inventory doesn't include tools, equipment, or other items that you use in your business; it refers only to items that you buy or make to sell.

Before 2018, you had to deduct inventory costs separately from all other business expenses—you deducted inventory costs as you sold the inventory. However, starting in 2018, smaller businesses have the option to deduct inventory (1) as nonincidental materials and supplies, or (2) in accordance with their accounting method, enabling some cash method businesses to deduct inventory in the year it's paid for. (See Chapter 6 for more on deducting inventory.)

Businesses That Lose Money

Unfortunately, businesses don't always earn a profit. If your losses exceed your income from all sources for the year, you have a "net operating loss" (NOL). NOLs are particularly likely to occur when businesses are first starting out or when economic conditions are bad. The COVID-19 pandemic resulted in many NOLs in 2020 and likely in 2021 as well. In response, the Coronavirus Aid Relief and Economic Security Act (CARES Act) enacted by Congress in 2020 loosened the strict rules for claiming NOLs that the Tax Cuts and Jobs Act imposed. As a result, there are three separate sets of rules for deducting NOLs, depending on when they occur.

If your business lost money during 2018 through 2020, your loss could provide you with a refund of all or part of previous years' taxes in as little as 90 days—a quick infusion of cash that should be very helpful.

What Is an NOL?

If your business deductions exceed your business income, you have a tax loss for the year. If, like most small business owners, you're a sole proprietor, you may deduct any loss your business incurs from your other income for the year—for example, income from a job, investment income, or your spouse's income (if you file a joint return). If your business is operated as an LLC, an S corporation, or a partnership, your share of the business's losses are passed through the business to your individual return and deducted from your other personal income in the same way as a sole proprietor. However, if you operate your business through a C corporation, you can't deduct a business loss on your personal return. It belongs to your corporation. After deducting your tax loss from other income, any remaining loss is called a net operating loss (NOL).

> **EXAMPLE:** Jason incurred $30,000 in losses from his sole proprietorship business for the year and earned $10,000 from a part-time job. His NOL is $20,000.

NOLs for 2017 and Earlier

For NOLs occurring during 2017 and earlier, business owners could "carry a loss back"—that is, they could apply a NOL to past tax years by filing an application for a refund or amended return. This enabled them to get a refund for all or part of the taxes they paid in past years. NOLs could generally be carried back two years, and then carried forward 20 years. Moreover, NOLs could reduce taxable income to zero in the carryback or carryforward years. You also had the option to elect to only carry an NOL forward to future years.

> **EXAMPLE:** Assume that Jason from the previous example incurred his $20,000 NOL in 2017. He could carry it back to 2015 and obtain a refund of the tax he paid that year. If he does not fully use the NOL, it is carried forward to 2016 and then to 2018 and future years. He also had the option of waiving the carryback and carrying the $20,000 forward to 2017, where it could offset up to 100% of his income. Any unused amount would be carried forward up to 20 years.

NOLs for 2018 Through 2020

The Tax Cuts and Jobs Act (TCJA) radically changed NOL deductions starting in 2018. However, Congress temporarily changed these rules in response to the COVID-19 pandemic.

The TCJA eliminated all carrybacks of NOLs starting in 2018. Instead, taxpayers were only allowed to deduct them in any number of future years. Moreover, an NOL could only offset up to 80% of taxable income (before the pass-through deduction) for any year.

> **EXAMPLE:** Assume that Jason from the previous examples incurred his $20,000 NOL in 2018. Because of the TCJA, he could not carry it back to 2016 and obtain a refund of the tax he paid that year. He could only carry it forward to 2019 where it could only offset a maximum of 80% of his income. Any remaining amount had to be deducted in 2020 and later.

Due to the economic devastation caused by the COVID-19 pandemic, Congress amended the rules for 2018 through 2020 to make it easier to deduct NOLs. For these years, an NOL may be carried back five years and then carried forward indefinitely until used up. Ordinarily, you must carry an NOL back to the earliest year within the carryback period in which there is taxable income, then to the next earliest year, and so on. Also, NOLs for these years may offset 100% of taxable income to reduce the tax liability to zero.

> **EXAMPLE:** Assume that Jason from the previous examples incurred his $20,000 NOL in 2020. He may carry it back to 2015 to reduce his taxable income for that year and obtain a refund of up to 100% of the tax he paid. If he has any NOL amount remaining, it is applied to 2016 through 2019 in turn. Any remaining NOL is applied to 2021 and any number of future years. Alternatively, Jason could elect only to carry his NOL forward to 2021 and future years.

You didn't have to carry back an NOL for 2018 through 2020 for five years if you didn't want to. You could elect to apply the NOL only to future years by attaching a statement to your tax return for the year. For 2018 and 2019 NOLs, you had to make this election on your 2020 tax return. You must attach a separate statement for each year for which you are waiving the NOL carryback, and state that you elect to apply Revenue Procedure 2020-24.

NOLs for 2021 and Later

The NOL rules initially put in place in 2018 by the TCJA and then postponed for 2018 through 2020, return for 2021, and later. Thus, for 2021 and later years, you may only deduct NOLs for the current year and any number of future years. You may not carry them back to deduct in past years. In addition, NOLs for these years may only offset up to 80% of taxable income (before the pass-through deduction) for any year.

Annual Dollar Limit on NOL Deductions

Another change made by the Tax Cuts and Jobs Act was to limit deductions of "excess business losses" by individual business owners during 2018 through 2025. Married taxpayers filing jointly could deduct no more than $519,000 per year in total business losses. Individual taxpayers could deduct no more than $259,000. Unused losses had to be deducted in any number of future years as part of the taxpayer's NOL carryforward. Congress eliminated this dollar limitation for losses incurred during 2018 through 2020. Thus, taxpayers with very large losses for any of these years could deduct them in full.

The excess business loss limit returned for 2021 and was extended through 2026. For 2021, NOLs are limited to $262,000 for individual taxpayers and $524,000 for married taxpayers filing jointly. Losses over these amounts must be carried forward and deducted in future years.

Claiming an NOL Refund

You can take advantage of an NOL only after you've completed and filed your tax return for the year involved. The return will show the amount of the NOL.

There are two ways to claim a refund for prior years' taxes due to an NOL. The quickest way is to file IRS Form 1045, *Application for Tentative Refund*. If you file Form 1045, the IRS is required to send your refund within 90 days. Additionally, the IRS makes only a limited examination of the claim for omissions and computational errors. Ordinarily, you must file Form 1045 within one year after the end of the year in which the NOL arose.

The other way to deduct an NOL is to amend your tax return for the year involved by filing IRS Form 1040-X, *Amended U.S. Individual Income Tax Return*. You have three years after the end of the tax year to file Form 1040-X.

RESOURCE

Need to know more about NOLs? Refer to IRS Publication 536, *Net Operating Losses (NOLs) for Individuals, Estates, and Trusts*, for more information. You can download it from the IRS website at www.irs.gov.

Are You Really in Business?

One of the most powerful weapons in the IRS arsenal is the hobby loss rule. Under this rule, only taxpayers who operate a bona fide business can take business deductions. To the IRS, a business is a venture operated to make money and run in a professional, businesslike manner. In contrast, the IRS may classify a venture that consistently loses money and/or looks more like a personal pursuit than a business as a "hobby." If the IRS decides that you are indulging a hobby rather than operating a business, you will face disastrous tax consequences.

The hobby loss rule prevents taxpayers from entering into losing propositions primarily to incur expenses that they could deduct from their other income. It also prevents you from deducting the expenses you incur for activities you engage in primarily for recreation or other nonbusiness purposes. The IRS has identified the following activities as possible hobbies: auto racing, craft sales, bowling, stamp collecting, dog breeding, yacht charter, art, horse breeding, farming, gambling, fishing, horse racing, photography, writing, working as an entertainer, airplane charter, motocross racing, and direct sales. This is a nonexclusive list.

What Is a Business?

For tax purposes, a business is any activity in which you regularly engage primarily to earn a profit. You don't have to show a profit every year to qualify as a business. As long as your primary purpose is to make money, you should qualify as a business (even if you show a loss some years). Your business can be full time or part time, as long as you work at it regularly and continuously. And you can have more than one business at the same time. However, if your primary purpose is something other than making a profit—for example, to incur deductible expenses or just to have fun— the IRS may find that your activity is a hobby rather than a business.

The IRS has established two tests to determine whether someone is in business. One is a simple mechanical test that looks at whether you have earned a profit in three of the last five years. The other is a more complex test designed to determine whether you act like a business.

Profit Test

If your venture earns a profit in three of any consecutive five years, the IRS must presume that you have a profit motive. The IRS can still claim that your activity is a hobby, but it will have to prove that you lack a profit motive some other way. In practice, the IRS usually doesn't attack ventures that pass the profit test unless the numbers have clearly been manipulated just to meet the standard.

To show a profit, your gross income from an activity must be more than the tax deductions you took for it. Careful year-end planning can help your business show a profit for the year. If clients owe you money, for example, you can press for payment before the end of the year. You can also put off paying expenses or buying new equipment until the new year.

The presumption that you are in business applies to your third profitable year. It then extends to all subsequent years within that five-year period beginning with your first profitable year.

> **EXAMPLE:** Tom began to work as a self-employed graphic designer in 2016. Due to economic conditions and the difficulty of establishing a new business, his income varied dramatically from year to year. However, as the chart below shows, he managed to earn a profit in three of the first five years that he was in business.
>
> | Year | Losses | Profits |
> |------|--------|---------|
> | 2016 | $10,000 | |
> | 2017 | | $5,500 |
> | 2018 | $6,000 | |
> | 2019 | | $9,000 |
> | 2020 | | $18,000 |
>
> If the IRS audits Tom's taxes for 2020, it must presume that he was in business during that year because he earned a profit during three of the five consecutive years ending with 2020. The presumption that Tom is in business extends through 2022, five years after his first profitable year (2017).

The IRS doesn't have to wait for five years after you start your activity to decide whether it is a business or hobby—it can audit you and classify your venture as a business or hobby at any time. However, you can give yourself some breathing room by filing IRS Form 5213, which requires the IRS to postpone its determination until you've been in business for at least five years.

Although this may sound like a good idea, filing the election only alerts the IRS to the fact that you might be a good candidate to audit on the hobby loss issue after five years. It also adds two years to the statute of limitations—the period in which the IRS can audit you and assess a tax deficiency. For this reason, almost no one ever files Form 5213. Also, you can't wait five years and then file the election once you know that you will pass the profit test. You must make the election within three years after the due date for the tax return for the first year you were in business—that is, within three years after the first April 15 following your first business year. So if you started doing business in 2021, you would have to make the election by April 15, 2025 (three years after the April 15, 2022 due date for your 2021 tax return).

There is one situation in which it might make sense to file Form 5213. If the IRS has already told you that you will be audited, you may want to file the election to postpone the audit for two years. However, you can do this only if the IRS audit notice is sent to you within three years after the due date for your first business tax return. If you're notified after this time, it's too late to file the election. In addition, you must file your election within 60 days after you receive an IRS audit notice, whenever it is given, or you'll lose the right to make the election.

Behavior Test

If you keep incurring losses and can't satisfy the profit test, don't panic. Millions of business owners are in the same boat. The sad fact is that many businesses don't earn profits every year or even for many years in a row. Indeed, more than four million sole proprietors file a Schedule C tax form each year showing a loss from their business, yet the IRS does not categorize all of these ventures as hobbies.

You can continue to treat your activity as a business and fully deduct your losses, even if you have yet to earn a profit. However, you should take steps to demonstrate that your business isn't a hobby, in case you ever face an audit. You want to be able to convince the IRS that earning a profit—not having fun or accumulating tax deductions—is your primary motive for doing what you do. This will be particularly difficult if you're engaged in an activity that could objectively be considered fun—such as creating artwork, photography, or writing—but it can be done. People who have incurred losses for seven, eight, or nine years in a row have been able to convince the IRS that they were running businesses.

How does the IRS figure out whether you really want to earn a profit? IRS auditors can't read your mind to establish your motives, and they certainly aren't going to take your word for it. Instead, they look at whether you behave as though you want to make money.

Factors the IRS Considers

The IRS looks at the following objective factors to determine whether you are behaving like a person who wants to earn a profit (and, therefore, should be classified as a business). You don't have to satisfy all of these factors to pass the test—the first three listed below (acting like a business, expertise, and time and effort expended) are the most important by far. Studies demonstrate that taxpayers who meet these three factors are always found to be in business, regardless of how they do on the rest of the criteria. (See "How to Pass the Behavior Test," below, for tips on satisfying these factors.) The factors considered are:

- **Whether you act like a business.** Among other things, acting like a business means you keep good books and other records and carry on your activities in a professional manner.
- **Your expertise.** People who are in business to make money usually have some knowledge and skill relevant to the business.
- **The time and effort you spend.** Businesspeople work regularly and continuously at their businesses. You don't have to work full time, but you must work regularly.
- **Your track record.** Having a track record of success in other businesses— whether or not they are related to your current business—helps show that you are trying to make money in your most recent venture.

- **Your history of profit and losses.** Even if you can't satisfy the profit test described above, earning a profit in at least some years helps show that you're in business. This is especially true if you're engaged in a business that tends to be cyclical—that is, where one or two good years are typically followed by one or more bad years.
- **Your profits.** Earning a substantial profit, even after years of losses, can help show that you are trying to make a go of it. On the other hand, earning only small or occasional yearly profits when you have years of large losses and/or a large investment in the activity tends to show that you aren't in it for the money.
- **Your business assets.** Your profit includes money you make through the appreciation (increase in value) of your business assets. Even if you don't make any profit from your business's day-to-day operations, you can still show a profit motive if you stand to earn substantial profits when you sell your assets. Of course, this rule applies only to businesses that purchase assets that increase in value over time, such as land or buildings.
- **Your personal wealth.** The IRS figures that you probably have a profit motive—and are running a real business—if you don't have a substantial income from other sources. After all, you'll need to earn money from your venture to survive. On the other hand, the IRS may be suspicious if you have substantial income from other sources (particularly if the losses from your venture generate substantial tax deductions).
- **The nature of your activity.** If your venture is inherently fun or recreational, the IRS may doubt that you are in it for the money. This means that you'll have a harder time convincing the IRS that you're in business if your venture involves activities such as artwork, photography, or writing; antique or stamp collecting; or training and showing dogs or horses (for example). However, these activities can still be businesses, if they are carried on in a businesslike manner.

How to Pass the Behavior Test

Almost anyone can pass the behavior test, but it takes time, effort, and careful planning. Focus your efforts on the first three factors listed above.

As noted earlier, a venture that can meet these three criteria will always be classified as a business. Here are some tips that will help you satisfy these crucial factors—and ultimately ace the behavior test.

Act Like a Businessperson

First and foremost, you must show that you carry on your activity in a businesslike manner. Doing the things outlined below will not only help you with the IRS, it will also help you actually earn a profit someday (or at least help you figure out that your business will not be profitable).

- **Keep good business records.** Keeping good records of your expenses and income from your activity is the single most important thing you can do to show that you're in business. Without good records, you'll never have an accurate idea of where you stand financially. Lack of records shows that you don't really care whether you make money or not—and it is almost always fatal in an IRS audit. You don't necessarily need an elaborate set of books; a simple record of your expenses and income will usually suffice. (See Chapter 15 for a detailed discussion of record keeping.)
- **Keep a separate checking account.** Open up a separate checking account for your business. This will help you keep your personal and business expenses separate—another factor that shows you're running a business.
- **Create a business plan.** Draw up a business plan with a realistic profit and loss forecast: a projection of how much money your business will bring in, your expenses, and how much profit you expect to make. The forecast should cover the next five or ten years. It should show you earning a profit some time in the future (although it doesn't have to be within five years). Both the IRS and the courts are usually impressed by good business plans. In one case, for example, a court found that a sailboat chartering operation that incurred losses for three straight years was a business because the owner made a detailed, realistic profit and loss forecast showing that the charter service would be profitable in 12 to 15 years. (*Pryor v. Commissioner,* TC Memo 1991-109.)

RESOURCE

Need help drawing up a business plan? If you are really serious about making money, you will need a business plan. A business plan is useful not only to show the IRS that you are running a business, but also to convince others— such as lenders and investors—that they should support your venture financially. For detailed guidance on putting together a business plan, see *How to Write a Business Plan*, by Mike McKeever (Nolo).

- **Get business cards and letterhead.** It may seem like a minor matter but obtaining business stationery and business cards shows that you think you are in business. Hobbyists ordinarily don't have such things. You can use software programs to create your own inexpensive stationery and cards.
- **Create a website.** Most businesses have some sort of website that, at a minimum, provides contact information. Lack of a website indicates you're not serious about being in business.
- **Obtain all necessary business licenses and permits.** Getting the required licenses and permits for your activities will show that you are acting like a business. For example, an inventor attempting to create a wind-powered ethanol generator was found to be a hobbyist partly because he failed to get a permit to produce alcohol from the Bureau of Alcohol, Tobacco, Firearms, and Explosives.
- **Obtain a separate phone line for your home office.** If you work at home, obtain a separate phone line for your business (which may be a cellphone). This helps separate the personal from the professional and reinforces the idea that you're in business.
- **Join professional organizations and associations.** Taking part in professional groups and organizations will help you make valuable contacts and obtain useful advice and expertise. This helps to show that you're serious about making money.

Expertise

If you're already an expert in your field, you're a step ahead of the game. But if you lack the necessary expertise, you can develop it by attending educational seminars and similar activities and/or consulting with other experts. Keep records of your efforts (for example, a certificate for completing a training course or your notes documenting your attendance at a seminar or convention).

Work Steadily

You don't have to work full time to show that you're in business. It's fine to hold a full-time job and work at your sideline business only part of the time. However, you must work regularly and continuously rather than sporadically. You may establish any schedule you want, as long as you work regularly. For example, you could work at your business an hour every day, or one day a week, as long as you stick to your schedule.

Although there is no minimum amount of time you must work, you'll have a hard time convincing the IRS that you're in business if you work less than five or ten hours a week. Keep a log showing how much time you spend working. Your log doesn't have to be fancy—you can just mark down your hours and a summary of your activities each day on your calendar or appointment book.

 CAUTION
You won't find out whether you have a hobby or a business until you get audited. You may mistakenly presume that you are in business, only to learn five or six years later that the IRS has a different opinion. If that happens, you could owe the IRS for all of the improper deductions you took during those years, as well as miscalculated taxes and penalties. Obviously, these costs can be quite expensive. Be sure to keep good records to bolster your position that you are running a business.

Tax Consequences of Being a Hobbyist

You do not want what you consider business activities to be deemed a hobby by the IRS. Because hobbies are not businesses, hobbyists cannot take the tax deductions to which businesspeople are entitled. However, for decades hobbyists were allowed to deduct their hobby-related expenses up to the amount of income the hobby earned during the year.

Hobby expenses were deductible as a personal miscellaneous itemized deduction on IRS Schedule A. This meant they could be deducted only by taxpayers who itemized their personal deduction, and only if, and to the extent, they exceeded 2% of the hobbyist's adjusted gross income (total income minus business expenses and a few other expenses). This was not a very generous deduction, but it was better than nothing.

Unfortunately for people who earn income from hobbies, the Tax Cuts and Jobs Act completely eliminated the itemized deduction for hobby expenses, along with all other miscellaneous itemized deductions. The prohibition on deducting these expenses is in effect for 2018 through 2025. This means that taxpayers may not deduct any expenses they earn from hobbies during these years, but they still have to report and pay tax on any income they earn from their hobby! The only exception is that hobbyists may deduct the cost of goods they sell or the cost of materials and supplies they use to make things they sell. (IRS Reg. 1.183-1(e).) For example, a hobbyist painter may deduct the cost of canvas, paints, and brushes from income earned from selling paintings. And a hobbyist Amway, Herbalife, or Mary Kay seller may deduct the cost of the products he or she sells.

> **EXAMPLE:** Charles runs a yacht charter business using his personal yacht. During 2021, he incurred $10,000 in expenses and earned $5,000 in income from the activity. The IRS determines that this activity is a hobby. As a result, his $10,000 in expenses cannot be deducted but he must still report and pay income tax on the $5,000 in income he earned from his hobby.

Start-Up Expenses

E veryone knows that it costs money to get a new business up and running or to buy an existing business. What many people don't know is that these costs (called "start-up expenses") are subject to special tax rules. This chapter explains what types of expenditures are start-up expenses and how you can deduct these costs as quickly as possible.

What Are Start-Up Expenses?

To have business deductions, you must actually be running a business. (See Chapter 2 for more about businesses versus hobbies.) This common-sense rule can lead to problems if you want to start or buy a new business. The money you spend to get your business up and running is not a business operating expense because your business hasn't yet begun.

Instead, business start-up expenses are capital expenses because you incur them to acquire an asset (a business) that will benefit you for more than one year. Normally, you can't deduct these types of capital expenses until you sell or otherwise dispose of the business. However, a special tax rule allows you to deduct up to $5,000 in start-up expenses the first year you are in business, and then deduct the remainder, if any, in equal amounts over the next 15 years. (I.R.C. § 195.) Without this special rule for business start-up expenses, these costs (capital expenses) would not be deductible until you sold or otherwise disposed of your business.

Once your business begins, the same expenses that were start-up expenses before your business began become currently deductible business operating expenses. For example, rent you pay for office space *after* your business starts is a currently deductible operating expense, but rent you pay *before* your business begins is a start-up expense.

Obviously, you want to spend no more than $5,000 on start-up expenses so you don't have to wait 15 years to get all your deductions. There are ways you can avoid spending more than the $5,000 threshold amount.

TIP
Your business must start to have start-up expenses. If your business never gets started, many of your expenses will not be deductible. So think carefully before spending your hard-earned money to investigate starting a new business venture. (See "Organizational Expenses," below.)

Starting a New Business

Most of the funds you spend investigating whether, where, and how to start a new business, as well as the cost of actually creating it, are deductible business start-up expenses. The tax law is much more generous with deductions for start-up costs if you are creating a new business than if you are buying an existing business. (See "Buying an Existing Business," below.)

Common Start-Up Expenses

Here are some common types of deductible start-up expenses:
- the cost of investigating what it will take to create a successful business, including research on potential markets, products, labor supply, and transportation facilities
- advertising costs, including advertising for your business opening
- costs for employee training before the business opens
- travel expenses related to finding a suitable business location
- expenses related to obtaining financing, suppliers, customers, or distributors
- licenses, permits, and other fees
- fees paid to lawyers, accountants, consultants, and others for professional services, and
- operating expenses incurred before the business begins, such as rent, telephone, utilities, office supplies, and repairs.

Costs That Are Not Start-Up Expenses

Some costs related to opening a business are not considered start-up expenses. Many of these costs are still deductible, but different rules and restrictions apply to the way they are deducted.

Expenses That Wouldn't Qualify as Business Operating Expenses

You can only deduct as start-up expenses those costs that would be currently deductible as business operating expenses after your business begins. This means the expenses must be ordinary, necessary, directly related to the business, and reasonable in amount. (See Chapter 4 for a discussion of business operating expenses.) For example, you can't deduct the cost of pleasure travel or entertainment *unrelated* to your business. These expenses would not be deductible as operating expenses by an ongoing business, so you can't deduct them as start-up expenses either.

Inventory

The largest expense many people incur before they start their business is for inventory—that is, buying the goods they will sell to customers. For example, a person opening a florist shop has to buy an inventory of flowers to sell. The cost of purchasing this inventory is not treated as a start-up expense. Instead, you deduct inventory costs as you sell the inventory or as it's purchased. (See Chapter 6 for more on deducting inventory costs.)

Long-Term Assets

Long-term assets are things you purchase for your business that will last for more than one year, such as computers, office equipment, cars, and machinery. Long-term assets you buy before your business begins are not considered part of your start-up costs. Instead, you treat these purchases like any other long-term asset you buy after your business begins: You must either depreciate the item over several years or deduct the cost in one year, using bonus depreciation or Section 179. (Chapter 5 explains how to deduct long-term assets.) However, you can't take regular or bonus depreciation or Section 179 deductions until after your business begins.

Research and Development Costs

The tax law includes a special category for research and development expenses. These are costs a business incurs to discover something new (in the laboratory or experimental sense), such as a new invention, formula, prototype, or process. They include laboratory and computer supplies, salaries, rent, utilities, other overhead expenses, and equipment rental, but not the purchase of long-term assets. Research and development costs are currently deductible under Section 174 of the Internal Revenue Code, even if you incur them before the business begins operations.

Taxes and Interest

Any tax and interest that you pay before your business begins is not a start-up expense. Instead, these costs are currently deductible as business operating expenses once your business begins. There are a few exceptions to this rule. Sales tax you pay for long-term assets for your business is added to the cost of the asset for purposes of regular or bonus depreciation or the Section 179 deduction. (See Chapter 5.) And money you borrow to buy an interest in an S corporation, a partnership, or an LLC must be allocated among the company's assets. (See Chapter 14.)

Organizational Costs

Costs you incur to form a partnership, an LLC, or a corporation are not part of your start-up costs. However, they are deductible in the same amounts as start-up expenses under a separate tax rule.

Education Expenses

You cannot deduct education expenses you incur to qualify for a new business or profession. For this reason, courts have held that IRS agents could not deduct the cost of going to law school, because a law degree would qualify them for a new business—being a lawyer. (*Jeffrey L. Weiler*, 54 TC 398 (1970).)

Buying an Existing Business

Different rules apply if you buy an existing business rather than creating a new one. If you are buying a business, you can only deduct as start-up expenses the costs you incur to decide *whether* to purchase a business and *which* business you should buy. The money you pay to actually purchase the existing business is not a start-up expense. Nor is this cost currently a deductible business expense. Instead, it is a capital expense that becomes part of the tax basis of your business. If and when you sell the business, you will be able to deduct this amount from any profit you make on the sale before taxes are assessed.

You don't have to make an offer, sign a letter of intent, or enter into a binding legal agreement to purchase an existing business for your expenses to cease being start-up expenses. You just have to make up your mind to purchase a specific business and focus on acquiring it. (Rev. Rul. 1999-23.)

EXAMPLE: Sean, a wealthy and successful entrepreneur, wants to buy an existing business. He hires Duane, an investment banker, to help him. Duane conducts research on several industries and evaluates publicly available financial information for several businesses. Eventually, Duane focuses on the trucking industry. Duane evaluates several businesses within the industry, including the Acme Trucking Company and several of Acme's competitors. Sean decides he would like to buy Acme and hires accountant Al to conduct an in-depth review of its books and records to determine a fair acquisition price. Sean then enters into an acquisition agreement with Acme to purchase all its assets. The fees Sean paid to Duane are start-up expenses because they were paid to help Sean determine whether to purchase an existing business and which business to buy. The fees Sean paid to Al are not start-up expenses, because they were incurred to help Sean purchase a specific existing business: the Acme Trucking Company.

Expanding an Existing Business

What if you already have a business and decide to expand your operation? The cost of expanding an existing business is considered a business operating expense, not a start-up expense. As long as these costs are ordinary and necessary, they are currently deductible.

> **EXAMPLE:** Sam runs a dry cleaning store. He pays $2,000 for legal, accounting, licensing, and advertising costs to expand to two new locations. These costs are currently deductible as ordinary and necessary operating expenses.

However, this rule applies only when the expansion involves a business that is the same as—or similar to—the existing business. The costs of expanding into a new business are start-up costs, not operating expenses.

> **EXAMPLE:** Assume that Sam decides to start a Greek restaurant. This business is unrelated to his existing dry-cleaning business. Therefore, the ordinary and necessary expenses he incurs before the restaurant begins are start-up costs.

When Does a Business Begin?

The date when your business begins for tax purposes marks an important turning point. Operating expenses you incur once your business starts are currently deductible, while expenses you incur before this crucial date may have to be deducted over many years.

A new business begins for tax purposes when it starts to function as a going concern and performs the activities for which it was organized. (*Richmond Television Corp. v. U.S.*, 345 F.2d 901 (4th Cir. 1965).) The IRS says that a venture becomes a going concern when it acquires all of the assets necessary to perform its intended functions and puts those assets to work. In other words, your business begins when you start doing business, whether or not you are actually earning any money.

This is usually not a difficult test to apply. Here are the rules that apply to some common types of businesses.

Retail Businesses

Retail businesses that sell tangible products to customers begin when the business is ready to offer its product for sale to the public. It is not necessary to actually make any sales. For example, a restaurant owner's business begins when the restaurant's doors open and the restaurant is ready to serve food to customers. If no diners show up and the restaurant doesn't actually sell any food for a week, the start date is not affected. Once the restaurant is ready to offer its food for sale to the public, it's in business.

Manufacturers

A manufacturing or other production-related business begins when it starts using its assets to produce saleable products. The products don't have to be completed, nor do sales have to be solicited or made. For example, a company organized to manufacture bowling trophies would begin when it acquired all the workspace, personnel, material, and equipment it needs to make the trophies and starts using them to manufacture the product. If it takes several days to assemble a completed trophy (and to find someone willing to buy it), that doesn't matter—the company begins when the process of making the trophy starts.

Knowledge Workers

Writers, artists, photographers, graphic designers, computer programmers, and similar knowledge workers might not think of themselves as manufacturers, but the courts do. For example, courts have held that a writer's business begins when the writer starts working on a writing project. (*Gestrich v. Commissioner*, 681 F.2d 805 (3d Cir. 1982).) Just like a manufacturing business, a writer's business begins when the necessary materials are in place and the work starts—not when the work is finished or sold. Similarly, an inventor's business begins when the inventor starts working on an invention in earnest, not when the invention is completed, patented, or sold.

Service Providers

If your business involves providing a service to customers or clients—for example, accounting, consulting, financial planning, law, medicine, or dentistry—your business begins when you first offer your services to the public. No one has to hire you; you just have to be available for hire. For example, a dentist's business begins when the dentist opens a dental office and is ready to perform dental work on patients.

An Existing Business

If you buy an existing business, your business is deemed to begin for tax purposes when the purchase is completed—that is, when you take over ownership.

Proving When Your Business Began

Because your business start date is so important for tax purposes, you should be able to prove to the IRS exactly when it began. There are many ways you can do this. Being able to show the IRS a copy of an advertisement or website for your business is a great way to prove you were open for business. You can also distribute brochures or other promotional materials. You don't have to advertise to show you are open for business—simply handing out business cards is sufficient. Give your first business cards to friends and associates who could testify for you if you're audited by the IRS. Establish your office to show you are ready to take on clients or customers. Take a digital photo (which will be date stamped).

If you're selling a product, you can start with a small inventory. Keep invoices and other documents showing the date you purchased the inventory. Take digital pictures of your equipment and inventory.

If you are making a product, your business begins when you have all the equipment and materials ready to start production. Keep invoices and other documents showing when you obtained these items.

Claiming the Deduction

If you have more than $50,000 of start-up expenses in one year, you are not entitled to the full $5,000 first-year deduction. You must reduce your first-year $5,000 deduction by the amount that your start-up expenditures exceed the $50,000 annual threshold. For example, if you have $53,000 in start-up expenses, you may only deduct $2,000 the first year. If you have $55,000 or more in start-up expenses, you get no current deduction for start-up expenses. Instead, you must deduct the whole amount over the first 180 months (15 years) you're in business. That is the minimum amortization period; you can choose a longer period if you wish (almost no one does).

You are automatically deemed to have made the election for the year in which your business began. All you must do is list your start-up costs as "Other expenses" on your Schedule C (or other appropriate return if you are not a sole proprietor). You don't have to specifically identify the deducted amounts as start-up expenditures for the election to be effective. However, if you have more than $5,000 in start-up expenses, you must amortize (deduct) the excess over 180 months. To do so, you must complete and attach IRS Form 4562 to your tax return for the first tax year you are in business.

If you don't want to deduct your start-up expenses the first year, you can forgo the deemed election by clearly capitalizing your start-up expenses instead. You must do this on your federal income tax return for the tax year in which your business began. Your return must be filed on time (including any extensions) and this election is irrevocable.

If Your Business Doesn't Last 15 Years

Not all businesses last for 15 years. In fact, most small businesses don't last this long. If you had more than $5,000 in start-up expenses and are in the process of deducting the excess amount, you don't lose the value of your deductions if you sell or close your business before you have had a chance to deduct all of your start-up expenses. You can deduct any leftover start-up expenses as ordinary business losses. (I.R.C. § 195(b)(2).) This means that you might be able to deduct them from any income you have that year, deduct them in future years, or deduct them from previous years' taxes.

If you sell your business or its assets, your leftover start-up costs will be added to your tax basis in the business. This is just as good as getting a tax deduction. If you sell your business at a profit, the remaining start-up costs will be subtracted from your profits before taxes are assessed, which reduces your taxable gain. If you sell at a loss, the start-up costs will be added to the money you lost—because this shortfall is deductible, a larger loss means lower taxes.

Organizational Expenses

If you decide to go into business, you might want to form some type of business entity, such as a corporation, partnership, or limited liability corporation. (See Chapter 1 for a discussion of different possible business structures.) The costs of forming an entity to run your business are deductible. These organizational expenses are not considered start-up expenses, although they are deducted in much the same way.

If you form a corporation, you can deduct the cost of creating the corporation, including legal fees for drafting articles of incorporation, bylaws, minutes of organizational meetings, and other organizational documents, and accounting fees for setting up the corporation and its books. You can also deduct state incorporation fees and other filing fees. However, you may not deduct the cost of transferring assets to the corporation or fees associated with issuing stock or securities—for example, commissions and printing costs. These are capital expenses.

If you form a partnership or an LLC with two or more members, you may deduct the cost of negotiating and drafting a partnership or an LLC agreement, accounting services to organize the partnership, and LLC filing fees.

Organizational expenses are deducted in the same way as start-up costs. You may deduct the first $5,000 the first year you are in business, and any excess over the first 180 months. However, your first-year deduction is reduced by the amount by which your organizational expenditures exceed $50,000. You must file IRS Form 4562, *Depreciation and Amortization*, with your tax return.

CAUTION
If you form a single-member LLC, don't spend more than $5,000 in organizational expenses. Because single-member LLCs are considered disregarded entities for tax purposes, the IRS doesn't allow these entities to deduct organizational expenses over $5,000. Instead any expenses over that amount must be capitalized, which means they would not be deductible until the LLC is dissolved. (Treasury Regs. §§ 1.263(a)-5(d)(1) and (3).) So, if you're forming a single-member LLC, it's best to avoid spending over $5,000 in organizational expenses, which generally should not pose a problem.

CHAPTER

4

Business Operating Expenses

This chapter covers the basic rules for deducting business operating expenses—the bread and butter expenses virtually every business incurs for things like rent, supplies, and salaries. If you don't maintain an inventory or buy expensive equipment, these day-to-day costs will probably be your largest category of business expenses (and your largest source of deductions).

Requirements for Deducting Operating Expenses

Because so many different kinds of business operating expenses exist, the tax code couldn't possibly list them all. Instead, if you want to deduct an item as a business operating expense, you must make sure the expenditure meets certain requirements. If it does, it will qualify as a deductible business operating expense. To qualify, the expense must be:

- ordinary and necessary
- a current expense
- directly related to your business, and
- reasonable in amount. (I.R.C. § 162.)

Your Business Must Have Begun

You must be *carrying on* a business to have deductible operating expenses. Costs you incur before your business is up and running are not currently deductible operating expenses, even if they are ordinary and necessary. However, up to $5,000 in start-up expenses may be deducted the first year you're in business, with the remainder deducted over the next 15 years. (See Chapter 3 for a discussion of start-up expenses.)

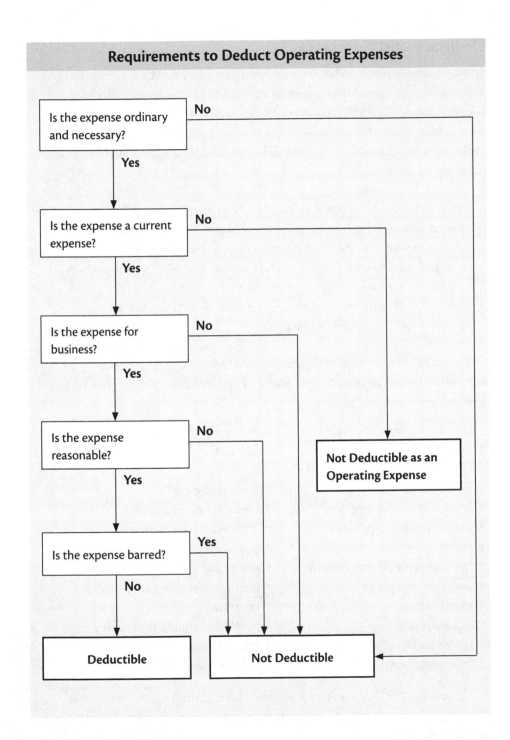

Ordinary and Necessary

The first requirement is that the expense must be ordinary and necessary. This means that the cost is common and "helpful and appropriate" for your business. (*Welch v. Helvering*, 290 U.S. 111 (1933).) The expense doesn't have to be indispensable to be necessary; it need only help your business in some way—even if it's minor. A one-time expenditure can be ordinary and necessary.

> **EXAMPLE:** Connie, a dentist, buys a television and installs it in her dental office waiting room so patients can watch TV while waiting for their appointments. Although having a TV in her waiting room is not an indispensable item for Connie's dental business, it is helpful; some patients might prefer to see Connie instead of another dentist because they can watch TV while they wait. Therefore, the TV is an ordinary and necessary expense for Connie's dental practice.

It's usually fairly easy to figure out whether an expense passes the ordinary and necessary test. Some of the most common types of operating expenses include:

- rent for an outside office
- employee salaries and benefits
- equipment rental
- business websites
- legal and accounting fees
- car and truck expenses
- travel expenses
- business-related meal expenses
- supplies and materials
- publications
- subscriptions
- repair and maintenance expenses
- business taxes
- interest on business loans
- licenses
- banking fees
- advertising costs
- home office expenses
- business-related education expenses
- postage
- professional association dues
- business liability and property insurance
- health insurance for employees
- office utilities, and
- software used for business.

Generally, the IRS won't second-guess your claim that an expense is ordinary and necessary, unless the item or service clearly has no legitimate business purpose.

EXAMPLE: An insurance agent claimed a business deduction for part of his handgun collection because he had to go to "unsafe job sites" to settle insurance claims, and there was an unsolved murder in his neighborhood. The tax court disallowed the deduction explaining, "A handgun simply does not qualify as an ordinary and necessary business expense for an insurance agent, even a bold and brave Wyatt Earp type with a fast draw who is willing to risk injury or death in the service of his clients." (*Samp v. Commissioner,* TC Memo 1981-1986.)

Current Expense

Only current expenses are deductible as business operating expenses. Current expenses are costs for items that will benefit your business for less than one year. These are the costs of keeping your business going on a day-to-day basis, including money you spend on items or services that get used up, wear out, or become obsolete in less than one year. A good example of a current expense is your business's monthly office rent, which benefits your business for one month. In contrast, buying an office building for your business would be a capital expense (not a current expense) because the phone will benefit your business for more than one year. Other common current expenses include office supplies, repairs, and monthly rent.

Current expenses are currently deductible—that is, they are fully deductible in the year in which you incur them. Because all business operating expenses are current expenses, they are also all currently deductible. However, the annual deductions for some operating expenses (notably home offices) are limited to the amount of profits you earn from the business in that year. (See Chapter 7 for more on the home office deduction.) Items you buy for your business that last for more than one year (capital expense items) must be depreciated over several years or deducted in one year using bonus depreciation or Section 179. (See Chapter 5 for more on deducting long-term assets.)

Business Related

An expense must be directly related to your business to be deductible as a business operating expense. This means that you cannot deduct personal expenses. For example, the cost of a personal computer is a deductible operating expense only if you use the computer for business purposes; it is not deductible if you use it to play computer games (unless you're a computer game designer).

If you buy something for both personal and business use, you can deduct only the business portion of the expense. For example, if you buy a cellphone and use it half of the time for business calls and half of the time for personal calls, you can deduct only half of the cost of the phone as a business expense.

A business expense for one person can be a personal expense for another, and vice versa. For example, a professional screenwriter could probably deduct the cost of going to movies—he needs to see movies for his screenwriting business. But a salesperson could not deduct this type of expense.

The chart below provides some examples of expenses that courts have found to be (and not to be) business related.

Deductible Business Expenses	Nondeductible Personal Expenses
Dental expenses a professional actor incurred when his teeth were knocked out while making a boxing movie. (*Denny v. Commissioner*, 33 BTA 738 (1935).) *Reason: The expense was directly attributable to his occupation as an actor.*	Money an author paid to prostitutes while researching a book on legal brothels. (*Vitale v. Commissioner*, TC Memo 1999-131.) *Reason: The expenditures were "so personal in nature as to preclude their deductibility."*
Flowers the president of a loan company sent to employees while they were in the hospital. (*Blackwell v. Commissioner*, TC Memo 1956-184.) *Reason: The expense benefited the company, not the president personally.*	A bar mitzvah reception for a rabbi's son. (*Feldman v. Commissioner*, 86 TC 458 (1986).) *Reason: The reception was a personal, family event, not a business meeting or business entertainment.*
High-protein foods a person with a rare blood type ate to maintain the quality of her blood so she could regularly sell it to a serological company. (*Green v. Commissioner*, 74 TC 1229 (1980).) *Reason: The expenses were incurred for her business as a seller of blood plasma.*	Parking fees a college professor paid to park on campus. (*Greenway v. Commissioner*, TC Memo 1980-97.) *Reason: The fees were part of the professor's commuting expenses and therefore were personal.*

Many expenses have both a personal and business component, which can make it difficult to tell if an expense is business related. Because of this, the business-related requirement is usually the most challenging factor in determining whether an expense qualifies as a deductible business operating expense.

Even the most straightforward costs can present difficulties. For example, it's usually easy to tell whether postage is a personal or business expense. If you mail something for your business, it's a business expense; if you mail something unrelated to your business, it's a personal expense. But even here, questions might arise. For example, should a doctor be allowed to deduct the postage for postcards he sends to his patients while he is on vacation in Europe? (Yes—the tax court said the postage was deductible as an advertising expense; *Duncan v. Commissioner*, 30 TC 386 (1958).)

The IRS has created rules and regulations for some of the more common operating expenses that often involve a difficult crossover of personal and business. Some of these rules help by laying out guidelines for when an expense is and isn't deductible. Others impose record-keeping and other requirements to prevent abuses by dishonest taxpayers. Most of the complexity in determining whether an expense is deductible as a business operating expense involves understanding and applying these special rules and regulations.

The expenses that present the most common problems (and are subject to the most comprehensive IRS rules and regulations) include:
- home office expenses (see Chapter 7)
- meals (see Chapter 14)
- travel (see Chapter 9)
- car and truck expenses (see Chapter 8)
- business gifts (see Chapter 14)
- bad debts (see Chapter 14)
- employee benefits (see Chapter 12)
- interest payments (see Chapter 14)
- health insurance (see Chapter 13)
- casualty losses (see Chapter 14)
- taxes (see Chapter 14), and
- education expenses (see Chapter 14).

Through these rules and regulations, the IRS provides guidance on the following types of questions:

- If you rent an apartment and use part of one room as a business office, should you be allowed to deduct all or a portion of the rent as a business operating expense? How much of the room has to be used as an office (and for what period of time) for it to be considered used for business rather than personal purposes? (See Chapter 7 for information on the home office deduction.)
- Can you deduct the money you spend on a nice suit to wear to your office? (See Chapter 14 for information about deducting business clothing.)
- Can you deduct the cost of driving from home to your business office? (See Chapter 8 for rules about deducting commuting expenses.)

Reasonable

Subject to some important exceptions, there is no limit on how much you can deduct, as long as the amount is reasonable and you don't deduct more than you spend. As a rule of thumb, an expense is reasonable unless there are more economical and practical ways to achieve the same result. If the IRS finds that your deductions are unreasonably large, it will disallow them or at least disallow the portion it finds unreasonable.

Whether a deduction is reasonable depends on the circumstances. In one case, the IRS found that it was unreasonable for an aircraft controller to spend more than $17,000 to buy a plane to learn to fly, when she could have learned to fly just as well (but far more cheaply) by renting a plane. (*Behm v. Commissioner*, 53 TC 427 (1987).) On the other hand, it was reasonable for a shopping center developer to pay to keep a charter plane on 24-hour standby when the plane had to be available at a moment's notice to transport prospective tenants to a building site. (*Palo Alto Town & Country Village, Inc. v. Commissioner*, 565 F.2d 1388 (9th Cir. 1977).)

Certain areas are hot buttons for the IRS—especially car and travel expenses. There are strict rules requiring you to fully document these deductions. (See Chapters 8 and 9 for more on car and travel expenses.) The reasonableness issue also comes up when a business pays excessive salaries to employees to obtain a large tax deduction. For example, a business owner might hire his 12-year-old son to answer phones and pay him $50 an hour—clearly an excessive wage for this type of work.

For some types of operating expenses, the IRS limits how much you can deduct. These include:

- the home office deduction, which is limited to the profit from your business (although you can carry over and deduct any excess amount in future years) (see Chapter 7)
- business meals, which are ordinarily 50% deductible, but a 100% deduction is allowed for restaurant meals during 2021–2022 (see Chapter 14)
- travel expenses, which are limited depending on the length of your trip and the time you spent on business while away (see Chapter 9), and
- business gifts, which are subject to a $25 maximum per individual per year (see Chapter 14).

Operating Expenses That Are Not Deductible

Even though they might be ordinary and necessary, some types of operating expenses are not deductible under any circumstances. In some cases, this is because Congress has declared that it would be morally wrong or otherwise contrary to sound public policy to allow people to deduct these costs. In other cases, Congress simply doesn't want to allow the deduction. These nondeductible expenses include:

- fines and penalties paid to the government for violation of any law— for example, tax penalties, parking tickets, or fines for violating city housing codes (I.R.C. § 162(f))
- illegal bribes or kickbacks to private parties or government officials (I.R.C. § 162(c))
- lobbying expenses or political contributions (businesses used to be able deduct up to $2,000 per year to influence local legislation (not including hiring professional lobbyists; the Tax Cuts and Jobs Act eliminated this deduction for 2018 and later)

- two-thirds of any damages paid for violation of the federal antitrust laws (I.R.C. § 162(g))
- bar or professional examination fees
- charitable donations by any business other than a C corporation (these donations are only deductible as personal expenses; see Chapter 14)
- country club, social club, or athletic club dues (see Chapter 14)
- federal income taxes you pay on your business income (see Chapter 14), and
- certain interest payments (see Chapter 14).

Entertainment Deduction Eliminated

For decades, taxpayers were allowed to partly deduct entertainment, amusement, and recreation costs if the purpose was to generate income or provide some other specific business benefit. The Tax Cuts and Jobs Act eliminated all such deductions starting in 2018. (I.R.C. § 274(a).) So, you can no longer deduct entertainment expenses like club or skiing outings, theater or sporting event tickets, entertainment at night clubs, or hunting, fishing, or vacation trips. However, a few types of entertainment remain deductible; see Chapter 14.

Operating Expenses Paid With Paycheck Protection Program Loans

The Paycheck Protection Program (PPP) was one of the most popular economic relief programs during the COVID-19 pandemic. In 2020 and 2021, millions of business owners obtained PPP loans from the Small Business Administration (SBA). A business with fewer than 500 full-time employees could borrow up to 2.5 times its average monthly payroll costs for 2019 or 2020, up to $10 million. Self-employed people without employees could borrow up to $20,833. Businesses whose receipts fell by 25% or more between comparable quarters in 2019 and 2020 could obtain a second PPP loan.

What made PPP loans so popular is that the SBA forgave the loan if the borrower spent at least 60% of the loan on employee payroll and maintained their employee head count for a specified period. Self-employed borrowers qualified for PPP loan forgiveness simply by using the loan to pay themselves. When a loan is forgiven, it doesn't have to be repaid. So, forgiven PPP loans are essentially government grants to businesses.

Forgiven PPP Loans Are Tax Free

Under normal tax rules, when a lender forgives a loan, the amount becomes taxable income—that is, it must be included in the borrower's income, and the borrower must pay income tax on it. However, Congress enacted a special tax rule, making forgiven PPP loans completely tax free for the businesses that received them. PPP borrowers don't have to list the PPP loans in their business tax returns. Lenders that process PPP loans do not have to file with the IRS, or furnish to borrowers, a Form 1099-C reporting the PPP loans.

Deductions for Expenses Paid With Forgiven PPP Loans

Under normal tax rules, businesses that use tax-free government money to pay expenses can't also deduct those expenses from their taxes—a form of "double dipping." For example, if you used a $10,000 forgiven PPP loan to pay employee payroll and other expenses like office rent, you could not deduct $10,000 for those same expenses on your tax return.

The IRS originally wanted to apply the normal rules to forgiven PPP loans and make expenses paid with them not deductible. However, this plan caused an uproar in the business community. So, Congress enacted a special tax rule allowing businesses to deduct all expenses paid with forgiven PPP loans. The IRS has fully implemented this rule (Revenue Ruling 2021-02), so you can safely deduct any business expenses you paid with PPP loan proceeds.

These same rules apply to Economic Injury Disaster Loan (EIDL) advances of up to $10,000 from the SBA.

Tax Reporting

It's very easy to deduct operating expenses from your income taxes. You simply keep track of everything you buy (or spend money on) for your business during the year, including the amount spent on each item. Then you record the expenses on your tax return. If you are a sole proprietor or an owner of a one-person limited liability company (LLC), you do this on IRS Schedule C, *Profit or Loss From Business (Sole Proprietorship)*. To make this task easy, Schedule C lists common current expense categories—you just need to fill in the amount for each category. For example, if you spend $1,000 for business advertising during the year, you would fill in this amount in the box for the advertising category. You add up all of your current expenses on Schedule C and deduct the total from your gross business income to determine your net business income—the amount on which you are taxed.

If you are a member of a limited liability company with more than one owner, a partner in a partnership, or an S corporation owner, the process is very similar, except you don't use Schedule C. Multimember LLCs and partnerships file IRS Form 1065, *U.S. Return of Partnership Income,* and their owners' share of expenses is reported on Schedule K-1. S corporations use Form 1120-S, *U.S. Income Tax Return for an S Corporation*. Each partner, LLC member, and S corporation shareholder's share of these deductions passes through the entity and is deducted on the owner's individual tax return on Schedule E. Regular C corporations file their own corporate tax returns.

Deducting Long-Term Assets

D o you like to go shopping? How would you like to get a 43% discount on what you buy? Sound impossible? It's not. Consider this example: Sid and Sally each buy the same $2,000 computer at their local computer store. Sid uses his computer to play games and balance his personal checkbook. Sally uses her computer in her graphic design business. Sid's net cost for his computer—that is, his cost after he pays his taxes for the year—is $2,000. Sally's net cost for her computer is $1,140.

Why the difference in cost? Because Sally uses her computer for business, she is allowed to deduct its cost from her income, which saves her $860 in federal and state taxes. Thanks to tax laws designed to help people who own businesses, Sally gets a 43% discount on the computer.

This chapter explains how you can take advantage of these tax laws whenever you purchase long-term property for your business. You will need to be aware of, and follow, some tax rules that at times might seem complicated. But it's worth the effort. After all, by allowing these deductions, the government is effectively offering to help pay for your equipment and other business assets. All you have to do is take advantage of the offer.

What Is a Long-Term Asset?

Whether an item is a long-term asset or not depends on its useful life. The useful life of an asset is not its physical life, but rather the period during which it may reasonably be expected to be useful in your business —and the IRS, not you, makes this call. Anything you buy that will benefit your business for more than one year is a capital expense. For businesses, this typically includes items such as buildings, equipment, vehicles, books, furniture, machinery, and patents you buy from others. These are all long-term assets. Long-term assets are also called capital expenses—the terms are used interchangeably in this book. Anything you purchase that will benefit your business for less than one year is a current expense, not a long-term asset.

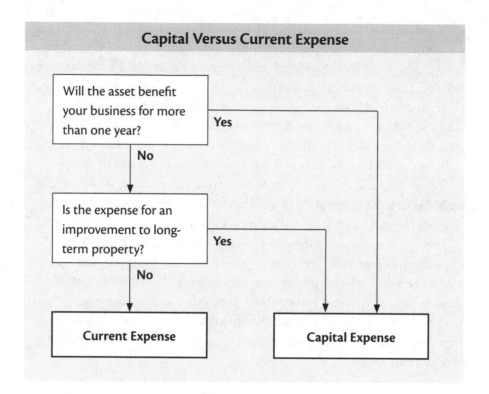

Capital Versus Current Expense

The difference between current and capital expenses is important for tax purposes because current expenses (also called "operating expenses") can always be deducted in the year you pay for them (assuming you're a cash basis taxpayer). In contrast, the cost of long-term assets may have to be deducted over several years. How the cost of a long-term asset may be deducted depends on whether it is personal property or real property. The cost of personal property may usually be deducted in a single year, unless you opt to deduct it over several years through depreciation. Real property must always be depreciated over many years, although some real property improvements can be deducted in one year.

TIP

Inventory is treated differently. This chapter covers the tax treatment of things you buy to use in your business. It does not cover the cost of items you buy or make to sell to others. (See Chapter 6 for more on inventory.)

Deducting Inexpensive Property: The De Minimis Safe Harbor and Materials and Supplies Deduction

IRS regulations permit you to deduct relatively inexpensive property without worrying about the complex depreciation rules. Because of the low cost involved, you are not required to treat this property as a capital asset. Instead, you are allowed to treat it as a business operating expense that you can automatically deduct in a single year, the same as office rent or utilities. The two ways to do this are:

- the "de minimis" safe harbor, or
- the materials and supplies deduction.

These deductions can be particularly helpful for smaller businesses that don't purchase a lot of expensive equipment or other property. Indeed, you may be able to currently deduct all the long-term property you buy for your business by taking advantage of these rules alone. Lots of things are great about these methods of deducting long-term property:

- They're simple and easy to use.
- They allow you to remove such assets from your books, balance sheet, and tax returns, and there is no need to keep them on depreciation schedules or list them on IRS Form 4562, *Depreciation and Amortization*—this simplifies your tax and business records.
- Unlike the Section 179 deduction, assets deducted with these methods are not subject to recapture if the property is later used over 50% of the time for personal use (recapture requires you to recognize as ordinary income the increased deductions you took under Section 179).

We'll start with the de minimis safe harbor because you will likely not use the materials and supplies deduction if you use the safe harbor.

The De Minimis Safe Harbor

Businesses may use the de minimis safe harbor to currently deduct in one year the cost of long-term property items that cost up to $2,500 apiece. (IRS Reg. 1.263(a)-1(f).) This rule gets its name because it applies to relatively small amounts ("de minimis" is Latin for minor or inconsequential) and businesses that use it are safe from the IRS. However, although $2,500 might not seem like a lot to the IRS, this deduction can really add up because there is no limit on how many items costing up to $2,500 apiece can be deducted each year.

To use this deduction, you must file an annual election with your tax return—something that is easy to do. When you make this election, it applies to all expenses you incur that qualify for the de minimis safe harbor. You cannot pick and choose which items you want to include. You must also include items that would otherwise be deductible as materials and supplies.

The de minimis safe harbor can't be used to deduct the cost of land, inventory (items held for sale to customers), certain spare parts for machinery or other equipment, or amounts that you pay for property that you produce or acquire for resale.

You can use the de minimis safe harbor to deduct the cost of property you don't use 100% of the time for business. Your deduction is limited to the dollar amount of your business use percentage.

EXAMPLE: Sheila purchases a $2,000 computer she uses 50% of the time for her Web design business and 50% of the time for personal purposes. She may deduct $1,000 of the cost using the de minimis safe harbor.

However, to determine whether property qualifies for the de minimis safe harbor, you look at its total cost, without subtracting the personal use percentage.

EXAMPLE: Assume that Sheila from the above example purchases a $3,000 computer she uses 50% of the time for business. She may not deduct the computer under the safe harbor because it cost more than $2,500.

What if you sell property you deducted using the de minimis safe harbor? You'll have taxable gain because your adjusted basis in the property will be zero. The entire amount of gain you realize from the sale is treated like ordinary business income—that is, it goes on your Schedule C and is taxed at your normal individual tax rates not lower capital gain rates. Remember, when you use the de minimis safe harbor it means that the property involved is treated as an operating expense, not a capital asset. The gain is also subject to self-employment (Social Security and Medicare) tax—this is a 15.3% tax up to an annual income ceiling.

De Minimis Safe Harbor Versus Bonus Depreciation

As a result of the Tax Cuts and Jobs Act, you can fully deduct much the same expenses in a single year using 100% bonus depreciation (through 2022) as you can deduct using the de minimis safe harbor. However, the great virtue of the de minimis safe harbor is its simplicity. All expenses deducted with the safe harbor are currently deducted as business operating expenses. Unlike with bonus depreciation, you don't need to list your safe harbor expenses on IRS Form 4562, *Depreciation and Amortization*. Nor do you have to create or maintain depreciation schedules for property items or include them in your accounting records as assets.

Bonus depreciation has some advantages over the de minimis safe harbor however. First, there is no $2,500 per-item ceiling on bonus depreciation. Also, if you sell property for which you took 100% bonus depreciation, you only pay income tax on your gain, not self-employment tax. This is not the case when you use the de minimis safe harbor, as described below.

Moreover, property deducted with the safe harbor won't count for purposes of taking the pass-through deduction. At higher income levels ($164,900 for singles and $329,800 for marrieds (2021)), this deduction can be limited wholly or partly to 2.5% of the cost of a business owner's depreciable property. This would not include property you've deducted using the safe harbor but it does include property deducted with bonus depreciation. (See Chapter 10 for a full discussion of the pass-through tax deduction.) For this reason, if you want to maximize your pass-through deduction, you may wish to avoid using the de minimis safe harbor and use bonus depreciation instead.

You elect to use the safe harbor each year, and you can choose to use it in some years and not others. Alternatively, you could reduce the dollar amount of your de minimis safe harbor election. $2,500 per item is the maximum amount allowed under the safe harbor (unless you have a financial statement; see below). But you can elect to deduct a smaller amount—for example, $1,000 or $500 per item, and use bonus depreciation to deduct more expensive items.

EXAMPLE: John used the de minimis safe harbor to fully deduct in one year the $1,000 camera he purchased for his real estate business. His adjusted basis in the camera after the sale is $0. He sells the camera for $500 one year later. He has a $500 taxable gain ($500 sale price – $0 adjusted basis = $500). He adds the $500 to his income on his Schedule C. He must pay both income tax and self-employment tax on his gain.

Maximum De Minimis Amount

Unless you have an applicable financial statement for your business (something few small businesses have—see below), you may use the de minimis safe harbor only for property whose cost does not exceed $2,500 per invoice, or $2,500 per item as substantiated by the invoice. If the cost exceeds $2,500 per invoice (or item), no part of the cost may be deducted using the de minimis safe harbor. The de minimis limit was initially $500, but the IRS increased it to $2,500. If you have an applicable financial statement, then you may increase the per-item or per-invoice amount up to $5,000.

EXAMPLE: Alice purchases the following items for her consulting business from a local computer supply store:
- a computer for $2,000
- an office chair for $1,000, and
- an office desk for $3,000.

Alice's total bill is $6,000. However, she applies the de minimis safe harbor rule item by item as shown on the invoice. Each item is less than the $2,500 de minimis safe harbor limit, except the desk. So, Alice may immediately deduct $3,000 of the total using the safe harbor. She can't use the safe harbor to deduct the $3,000 cost of the desk. Instead, she may deduct the desk in one year using Section 179 or depreciate it over five years.

Be sure to save all your receipts and invoices for property you deduct using the de minimis safe harbor.

Since the $2,500 de minimis limit is based on the cost of an item as shown on the invoice, you might be tempted to artificially break an item down into separate costs on the invoice, each of which is less than the limit. However, the IRS does not allow this. You cannot break into separate components property that you would normally buy as a single unit.

EXAMPLE: Alice from the example above purchased an office desk for $3,000. She instructs the office supply store to separately bill her $250 for each of four desk drawers and $2,000 for the remainder of the desk. Because an office desk is normally purchased along with its drawers as a single unit, the IRS adds the cost of each component to determine that the actual cost is $3,000. So, the desk does not qualify for the de minimis safe harbor.

In determining whether the cost of an item exceeds the $2,500 (or $5,000) threshold, you must include all additional costs included on the same invoice with the property—for example, delivery or installation fees. If the additional costs on a single invoice apply to several items, you must divide the costs among them in a reasonable way. IRS regulations give you three options: (1) equal division for each item, (2) specific identification (for example, if the installation costs apply only to one item), or (3) weighted average based on the property's relative cost.

EXAMPLE: Alexander pays $6,000 for three microscopes for his medical lab. They cost $2,000 each, and he also paid a single $750 fee for installation. He can treat the installation cost as $250 per microscope ($750 ÷ 3). This results in a total price of $2,250 for each microscope. Because this is less than the $2,500 de minimis limit, he can currently deduct the entire $6,750 cost using the de minimis safe harbor.

Do You Have an Applicable Financial Statement?

If you have an applicable financial statement for your business, you may increase your de minimis amount to $5,000 per item—twice the $2,500 limit for businesses without such statements. The most common type of applicable financial statement is a certified financial statement prepared by a CPA. These usually cost at least several thousand dollars, so few small businesses have them. A financial statement (other than a tax return) filed with the SEC or another state or federal agency (not including the IRS) can also qualify—for example, a Form 10-K or an Annual Statement to Shareholders. Only larger corporations or businesses that are publicly traded usually file such statements.

Qualifying for the Safe Harbor

To qualify for the de minimis expensing safe harbor, a taxpayer must:

- establish before the first day of the tax year (January 1 for calendar year taxpayers) an accounting procedure requiring it to expense amounts paid for property either (1) costing less than a certain dollar amount, and/or (2) with an economic useful life of 12 months or less, and
- actually treat such amounts as currently deductible expenses on its books and records.

If you have an "applicable financial statement" and wish to qualify to use the $5,000 de minimis limit, your accounting procedure must be in writing and signed before January 1 of the tax year. If you don't have such a statement and qualify only for the $2,500 limit, you do not need to put your procedure in writing (although you still may do so). But it should still be in place before January 1 of the tax year. Here is an example of a written procedure for a taxpayer without an applicable financial statement:

De Minimis Safe Harbor Procedure

Effective January 1, 20xx, XYZ hereby adopts the following policy regarding certain expenditures: Amounts paid to acquire or produce tangible personal property will be expensed, and not capitalized, in the year of purchase if: (1) The property costs less than $2,500, or (2) the property has a useful life of 12 months or less.

Claiming the Safe Harbor

To take advantage of the de minimis safe harbor, you must file an election with your tax return each year, using the following format:

Section 1.263(a)-1(f) De Minimis Safe Harbor Election

Taxpayer's name:

Taxpayer's address:

Taxpayer's identification number:

The taxpayer is hereby making the de minimis safe harbor election under Section 1.263(a)-1(f).

The Materials and Supplies Deduction

Items that fall within the definition of materials and supplies in IRS regulations may be currently deducted. However, many small businesses won't need (or be able) to use this deduction because these items can usually be deducted using the de minimis safe harbor.

"Materials and supplies" are tangible property used or consumed in your business operations that fall within any of the following categories:

- any item of tangible personal property that cost $200 or less
- any item of personal property with an economic useful life of 12 months or less (no cost limit), or
- components acquired to maintain or repair a unit of tangible property—that is, spare parts (no cost limit).

The cost of such items may be deducted the year the item is used or consumed in your business—which may be later than the year purchased. To use this deduction, you are supposed to keep records of when such items are used or consumed in your business—something few small business owners do in practice. For this reason, this deduction may be useless for most small businesses. Fortunately, they can use the de minimis safe harbor discussed above instead to deduct materials and supplies.

Incidental Materials and Supplies

"Incidental" materials and supplies are personal property items that are carried on hand and for which no record of consumption is kept or for which beginning and ending inventories are not taken. In other words, these are inexpensive items not worth keeping track of. Examples include pens, paper, staplers, toner, and trash baskets. Costs of incidental materials and supplies are deductible in the year they are paid for, not when the items are used or consumed in the business.

> EXAMPLE: John, a professional writer, purchases two packs of pens and three boxes of paper clips he plans to use for his writing activity over the next two years. The cost was minimal and he does not keep inventory of each pen or paper clip. These are incidental compared to his business and deductible the year he paid for them.

Interaction With De Minimis Safe Harbor

If you elect to use the de minimis safe harbor discussed above, and any materials and supplies also qualify for the safe harbor, you must deduct the amounts paid for them under the safe harbor in the tax year the amounts are paid or incurred. (IRS Reg. § 1.263(a)-1(f)(3)(ii).) So, if you use the de minimis safe harbor, you can largely ignore the materials and supplies deduction. This is to your advantage since the de minimis safe harbor has a $2,500 limit for most businesses, as opposed to the $200 materials and supplies limit for property with a useful life of over one year. Moreover, the de minimis safe harbor permits you to deduct the cost of items the year they are purchased, instead of when they are actually used or consumed in your business.

One exception where the materials and supplies deduction could prove useful, even where a de minimis safe harbor election is made, is for components used to repair property. If the components cost more than $2,500, the de minimis safe harbor can't be used. But the materials and supplies deduction can be used, no matter how much the components cost because there is no dollar limit on deducting such components using the materials and supplies deduction. The deduction may be taken in the year when the components are actually used in the course of a repair or maintenance.

Deducting Long-Term Personal Property: Bonus Depreciation, Section 179, Regular Depreciation

If you can't use the de minimis safe harbor or the material and supplies deduction, the other options you have for deducting long-term personal property are bonus depreciation, Section 179 expensing, and regular depreciation. You get to decide which of these methods to use, as long as the property is eligible for that method. Bonus depreciation and Section 179 enable you to deduct the full cost of personal property in a single year. Regular depreciation, on the other hand, forces you to spread your deduction out over several years.

Regardless of which method you choose, the following general rules apply whenever you deduct long-term property using bonus depreciation, Section 179 expensing, or regular depreciation. There are other additional rules discussed later that apply to each of the three methods that might make property eligible under one method and not another. The rules discussed below do not apply to the de minimis safe harbor or the material and supplies deduction.

Property Eligible to Deduct

Long-term personal property consists of virtually any tangible property you buy for your business other than land, land improvements, buildings, and building components. For example, it includes computers and other electronic equipment, office furniture, and vehicles (subject to special rules covered in Chapter 8). Personal property also includes computer software you purchase (buy "off the shelf").

You are allowed to deduct the cost of long-term personal property that you use for business that wears out, deteriorates, or gets used up over time. This does not include:

- property that doesn't wear out, including stocks, securities, or gold
- property you use solely for personal purposes
- property purchased and disposed of in the same year
- inventory, or
- collectibles that appreciate in value over time, such as antiques and artwork.

If you use this property in your business, you get no tax deduction while you own it. But if you sell it, you get to deduct its tax basis (see below) from the sales price to calculate your taxable profit. If the basis exceeds the sales price, you'll have a deductible loss on the property. If the price exceeds the basis, you'll have a taxable gain.

> **EXAMPLE:** Amy bought a digital camera for her architecture business in January for $3,000 and sold it in December of the same year for $1,000. It was purchased and disposed of in the same year so it can't be depreciated or expensed. Instead, the property's basis (its original cost) is deducted from the sale price. This results in a loss of $2,000, which is a deductible business loss.

You also may not deduct property that you do not own. For example, you get no bonus or regular depreciation or Section 179 expensing deduction for property you lease. The person who owns the property—the lessor—gets to deduct its cost. (However, you may deduct your lease payments as current business expenses.) Leasing may be preferable to buying and depreciating equipment that wears out or becomes obsolete quickly. (See "Leasing Long-Term Assets," below.)

Mixed-Use Property

To deduct long-term personal property, you must use it in your business. You can't deduct an asset you use solely for personal purposes.

> **EXAMPLE:** Jill, a freelance writer, bought a computer for $3,000. She used it to play games, manage her checkbook, and surf the Internet for fun. In other words, she used it only for personal purposes. The computer is not deductible.

However, you need not use an asset 100% of the time for business to claim a deduction. You can use it for personal purposes part of the time. In this event, your deduction is reduced by the percentage of your personal use. This will, of course, reduce the amount of your deduction.

> **EXAMPLE:** Miranda buys a $4,000 video camera for her wedding video business. She uses the camera 75% of the time for business and 25% for personal use. Her deduction is reduced by 25%, so Miranda can deduct only $3,000 of the camera's $4,000 cost.

If you use property for both business and personal purposes, you must keep a diary or log with the dates, times, and reasons the property was used to distinguish business from personal use. Moreover, special rules apply if you use cars and other types of listed property less than 50% of the time for business.

When to Take Your Deduction

You may deduct personal long-term property the year it is placed in service—that is, when it's ready and available for use in your business. As long as it is available for use, you don't have to actually use the property for business during the year to deduct it.

> **EXAMPLE:** Tom, a publicist, purchased a $3,000 copy machine for his office. He had the device ready for use in his office on December 31, 2021, but he didn't actually use it until January 2, 2022. Tom may take a deduction for the copier for 2021 because it was available for use that year.

CAUTION

You must actually be in business to deduct long-term assets. In other words, you cannot deduct a long-term asset until your business is up and running. This is one important reason why it is a good idea to postpone large property purchases until your business has begun. (See Chapter 3 for a detailed discussion of tax deductions for business start-up expenses.)

How Much You Can Deduct

You are allowed to deduct your total investment in a long-term asset you buy for your business, up to your business use percentage of the property (however, there are dollar limits on the Section 179 deductions). In tax lingo, your investment is called your "basis" or "tax basis."

Usually, your basis in long-term property is whatever you paid for it. This includes not only the purchase price, but also sales tax, delivery charges, installation, and testing fees, if any. You may deduct the entire cost, no matter how you paid for the property—in cash, with a credit card, or with a bank loan.

> EXAMPLE: The ABC Web Design Co. buys ten computers for its office. They are used 100% for business. ABC pays $20,000 cash, $1,800 in sales tax, and $500 for delivery and installation. Its basis in the property is $22,300.

You must subtract the amount of your deductions from the property's basis. This new basis is called the adjusted basis because it reflects adjustments from your starting basis. When your adjusted basis is reduced to zero, you can no longer deduct any of the property's cost.

> EXAMPLE: The ABC Web Design Co. (from the above example) bought ten computers. Its starting basis was $22,300. It deducts the entire cost using bonus depreciation. The computers' adjusted basis is zero, and ABC gets no more deductions for the property.

Disposing of Long-Term Property

Long-term personal property doesn't last forever, and you probably don't want to use it forever anyway. Sooner or later, you'll get rid of this property. If you sell long-term property, your gain or loss on the sale is determined by subtracting the property's adjusted basis from the sales price.

Any regular or bonus depreciation or Section 179 expensing that you claimed on personal property (also called Section 1245 property) is taxed as ordinary income to the extent of your taxable gain. This ordinary income does not go on your Schedule C, where it would be subject to the self-employment tax. Instead, it goes on IRS Form 4797, *Sales of Business Property*, because it is income from the sale of a business asset. Any excess gain—that is, gain over the amount of depreciation and/or expensing claimed—is taxed at capital gains rates, which are usually lower than ordinary income tax rates.

> **EXAMPLE:** Jack purchased a $10,000 computer system in 2020 and uses it 100% for his Bitcoin mining business. He deducts the entire amount using bonus depreciation. He's in the 37% top income tax bracket, so he saves $3,700 in income tax in 2020 due to his deduction. The 100% bonus depreciation deduction leaves Jack with an adjusted basis of zero in the computer. Two years later, Jack sells the system for $5,000, resulting in a taxable gain of $5,000 ($5,000 − zero basis = $5,000). The entire $5,000 gain is taxed as ordinary income, since this is less than the bonus depreciation Jack claimed. He pays $5,000 x 37% = $1,850 in tax on his gain.

If you abandon long-term business property instead of selling it, you may deduct its adjusted basis as a business loss. Of course, if your adjusted basis in the property is zero, you get no deduction. You abandon property when you voluntarily and permanently give up possessing and using it with the intention of ending your ownership and without passing it on to anyone else. Loss from abandonment of business property is fully deductible as an ordinary loss, even if the property is a capital asset.

For more information on the tax implications of selling or otherwise disposing of business property, refer to IRS Publication 544, *Sales and Other Dispositions of Assets*.

Listed Property

The IRS imposes special rules on certain personal property items that can easily be used for personal as well as business purposes. These items, called "listed property," include cars and other passenger vehicles below 6,000 pounds; motorcycles, boats, and airplanes; and any other property generally used for entertainment, recreation, or amusement—for example, digital cameras. Computers and cellphones used to be listed property but are no longer.

As long as you use listed property more than 50% of the time for business, you may deduct its cost just like any other long-term business property. However, if you use listed property 50% or less of the time for business, you can deduct it only by using the slowest method of regular depreciation: straight-line depreciation. (See "Depreciation Rules for Listed Property," below, for more details.)

Bonus Depreciation

Bonus depreciation enables you to deduct in a single year a specified percentage of a long-term asset's cost. For property placed into service starting September 28, 2017 through December 31, 2022, the percentage is a whopping 100%—in other words, you can deduct in one year the entire cost of property using bonus depreciation. This makes bonus depreciation the go-to method for deducting personal property during these five-plus years.

Unlike the de minimis safe harbor, bonus depreciation is not limited to items that cost $2,500 ($5,000 for businesses with financial statements). Nor is it limited to your annual net income, as is the case with Section 179 expensing discussed below. You can deduct any amount of eligible property using bonus depreciation, even it results in your business incurring a loss for tax purposes.

Bonus depreciation is optional—you don't have to take it if you don't want to. But if you want to get the largest depreciation deduction you can in the year you buy personal property for your business, you will want to take advantage of it whenever possible.

Property That Qualifies for Bonus Depreciation

You can use bonus depreciation to deduct any property you acquire by purchase that has a depreciation period of 20 years or less—this includes all types of tangible personal business property and off-the-shelf software (but not custom software). The property may be used or new, but you must not have used it before acquiring it. Thus, you can't convert property you previously used for personal use to business use and deduct the cost with bonus depreciation.

You can use bonus depreciation only for property that you purchase—not for leased property or property you inherit or receive as a gift. You also can't use it for property that you buy from a relative or a corporation or an organization that you control. Special rules apply to cars. (See Chapter 8 for more about deducting car expenses.)

Bonus depreciation cannot be used for:
- land
- permanent structures attached to land (except for certain improvements, see below)
- inventory (see Chapter 6)
- intangible property, such as patents, copyrights, and trademarks, or
- property used outside the United States.

You can use bonus depreciation to deduct listed property only if you use the property at least 51% of the time for business use. For example, you may deduct a video camera with bonus depreciation only if you use it over 50% of the time for your business, not for personal use. If your business use falls below 51% during the asset's depreciation period (usually 5 or 7 years) you have to give back the bonus depreciation you claimed the first year—a process called recapture (see below).

Calculating the Bonus Amount

You use bonus depreciation to figure out your depreciation deduction for the first year that you own an asset. You figure the deduction by multiplying the depreciable basis of the asset by the applicable bonus percentage. For property placed in service starting September 28, 2017 through December 31, 2022, the bonus percentage is 100%. You get the full 100% deduction no matter what month during the year you place the property into service. This differs from regular depreciation rules, where property bought later in the year may be subject to a smaller deduction for the first year.

> EXAMPLE: Stan, a printer, purchased and placed into service a new printing press for his business in March 2021. The press cost $10,000 plus $1,000 in shipping costs and $2,000 in installation costs. He deducts the equipment with 100% bonus depreciation, which allows him to deduct the full $13,000 cost for 2021.

The amount you can deduct is initially based on the property's cost. The cost includes the amount you paid for the property, plus sales tax, delivery, and installation charges. It doesn't matter if you pay cash or finance the purchase with a credit card or bank loan. However, if you pay for property with both cash and a trade-in, the value of the trade-in is not deductible with bonus depreciation. You must depreciate the amount of the trade-in.

If you use property solely for business like in the above example, you can deduct 100% of the cost (subject to the other limitations discussed below). However, if you use property for both business and personal purposes, you must reduce your deduction by the percentage of the time that you use the property for personal purposes.

> EXAMPLE: Max buys a $4,000 computer. The year he buys it, he uses it for his consulting business 75% of the time, and for personal purposes 25% of the time. He may currently deduct 75% of the computer's cost (or $3,000) using bonus depreciation. The remaining $1,000 is not deductible because the 25% personal use of the computer is not a business expense.

Class-Wide Requirement

If you use bonus depreciation, you must use it for all assets that fall within the same class. You may not pick and choose the assets you want to apply it to within a class. For example, if you buy a car and take bonus depreciation, you must take bonus depreciation for any other property you buy that year within the same class. Cars are five-year property, so you must take bonus depreciation that year for any other five-year property—for example, computers and office equipment. (See the "Depreciation Periods" chart, below, for a list of the various classes of property.)

Opting Out of the Bonus

The bonus depreciation deduction is applied automatically to all taxpayers who qualify for it. However, the deduction is optional. You don't have to take it if you don't want to. You can elect not to take the deduction by attaching a note to your tax return. It might be advantageous to do this if you expect your income to go up substantially in future years, placing you in a higher tax bracket.

CAUTION

When you opt out, you do so for the entire class of assets. It's very important to understand that if you opt out of the bonus, you must do so for the entire class of assets, not just one asset within a class. This is the same rule that applies when you decide to take the bonus.

Bonus Depreciation Percentages

As the following chart shows, the bonus depreciation percentages vary over the years. The 100% bonus depreciation amount is scheduled to remain in effect for property placed into service through December 31, 2022. The bonus amount will then phase down each year in 20% increments.

Year Property Placed In Service	Bonus Depreciation Percentage
1/1/2015 through 9/27/2017 (new property only)	50%
9/28/2017 through 2022	100%
2023	80%
2024	60%
2025	40%
2026	20%
2027 and later	0%

Section 179 Expensing

Section 179 of the tax code is similar to bonus depreciation in that it allows you to deduct in one year the entire cost of personal property you use in your business (as well as certain real property improvements, see below). This is called "first-year expensing" or "Section 179 expensing." ("Expensing" is an accounting term that means currently deducting a long-term asset.)

Section 179 may be used to deduct much the same property as bonus depreciation. However, during 2018 through 2022, Section 179 will likely not be used much by businesses because they can deduct 100% of the cost of the same property using bonus depreciation. Section 179 has the following disadvantages that make it less desirable than bonus depreciation.

First, you can only use Section 179 for property you use over 50% of the time for business (this isn't the case with bonus depreciation, except for listed property). If your use of the property falls below 50% you have to give back your Section 179 deduction through recapture (see below). There is no such recapture with bonus depreciation except for listed property.

In addition, you can't use Section 179 to deduct in one year more than your net taxable business income for that year (not counting the Section 179 deduction but including your spouse's salary and business income). Amounts that are not deductible are carried forward and can be deducted in future years. So, Section 179 may never result in a loss whereas there is no such limitation on bonus depreciation.

There is also an annual limit on the amount of property that can be deducted with Section 179. For 2021, the limit is $1,050,000. The limit is phased out if the amount of qualifying property you place into service during the year exceeds $2,620,000. The annual deduction limit applies to all of your businesses combined, not to each business you own and run. If you're a partner in a partnership, member of a limited liability company (LLC), or shareholder in an S corporation, the limit applies both to the business entity and to each owner personally.

Unlike bonus depreciation, Section 179 expensing doesn't apply classwide. Thus, you may pick and choose which assets you wish to deduct using Section 179 within the same asset class. This is a potential advantage. Section 179 deductions are not automatic. You must claim a Section 179 deduction on your tax return by completing IRS Form 4562, Part I, and checking a specific box. If you neglect to do this, you may lose your deduction.

Deducting Repairs and Improvements

The general rule is that repairs to business property are a currently deductible business operating expense, while improvements are a capital expense that must be depreciated over several years. However, there are exceptions to the rule. It's often possible to fully deduct the cost of improvements to personal property in one year using one of the following methods:

- 100% bonus depreciation (available 2018 through 2022)
- Section 179 expensing (for property used over 50% for business), or
- the de minimis safe harbor (for property that costs up to $2,500).

For example, you could use any of these methods to currently deduct the cost of buying and installing a new engine in a business vehicle—an expense that is an improvement.

However, repairs are still better than improvements for tax purposes. Since a repair is a business operating expense, you get to deduct the full amount in the year the repair expense is incurred and there will be no tax impact when you later sell the property. If you sell personal property used for business at a profit (more than its adjusted tax basis), it is taxed at low capital gains rates (15% or 20% if you owned the property over one year).

In contrast, when you deduct an expense through regular depreciation, bonus depreciation, or Section 179 expensing and sell personal property at a profit, you must pay tax on your regular or bonus depreciation or Section 179 deductions at your ordinary income tax rates (as much as 37%). This is called "recapture." Also, repairs don't have to be tracked on depreciation schedules or reported to the IRS on special tax forms, as is the case with depreciable improvements.

Under IRS repair regulations adopted in 2014, an expense is an improvement if it:

- makes an asset better than it was before (a "betterment" in tax jargon)
- restores it to operating condition, or
- adapts it to a new use.

Expenses that don't result in a betterment, restoration, or adaptation are currently deductible repairs. Unfortunately, there are no bright-line rules that explain exactly how much an asset must be altered to constitute an improvement. Instead, you have to look at all the facts and circumstances and make a judgment call to determine whether an expense results in a betterment, restoration, or adaptation of a business asset. For more guidance, see the detailed and extremely helpful FAQs the IRS has created at www.irs.gov/businesses/small-businesses-self-employed/tangible-property-final-regulations.

Additionally, IRS regulations permit you to fully deduct in one year as an operating expense the costs of routine maintenance to keep business property in ordinarily efficient operating condition. This "routine maintenance safe harbor" applies to:

- inspection, cleaning, and testing, and
- replacing damaged or worn parts with comparable and commercially available replacement parts.

Maintenance automatically qualifies for this treatment if, when you placed the asset into service, you reasonably expected to perform such maintenance more than once during its class life—that is, the time period over which it must be depreciated. (See the list of class lives in the "Depreciation Periods" chart later in this chapter.) There is no recapture involved when you use this safe harbor. See "Building Improvements," below for more information on deducting the cost of improvements.

Regular Depreciation

The traditional method of getting back the money you spend on long-term business assets is to deduct the cost a little at a time over several years (exactly how long is determined by the IRS). This process is called "depreciation."

Depreciation is a complicated subject. The IRS instruction booklet on the subject (Publication 946, *How to Depreciate Property*) is more than 100 pages long. For a comprehensive discussion of depreciation, read Publication 946. In this section, we cover the depreciation basics that all business owners should know.

> CAUTION
> **Regular depreciation is not optional.** Unlike bonus depreciation or the Section 179 deduction, regular depreciation is not optional. You must take a depreciation deduction if you qualify for it. If you fail to take it, the IRS will treat you as if you had taken it. This means that you could be subject to depreciation recapture when you sell the asset—even if you never took a depreciation deduction. This would increase your taxable income by the amount of the deduction you failed to take. So if you don't use bonus depreciation or Section 179, be sure to take the proper depreciation deductions for it. If you realize later that you failed to take a depreciation deduction that you should have taken, you may file an amended tax return to claim any deductions that you should have taken in prior years.

When to Use Regular Depreciation

With bonus depreciation, Section 179, and the de minimis safe harbor and materials and supplies deductions, you might not need to use regular depreciation for the foreseeable future. However, you may need to use regular depreciation to write off the cost of long-term assets that don't qualify for these methods. For example, you can't use any of those methods for:

- personal property items that you convert to business use

- intangible assets, such as patent, copyright, trademark, or business goodwill
- items purchased from a relative, or
- property inherited or received as a gift or inheritance.

Instead, with any such property or assets, you must use regular depreciation to deduct the cost.

Under some circumstances, it might be better to use depreciation and draw out your deduction over several years instead of getting your deductions all at once with the other methods. This might be the case where you have little or no business income in the current year and expect to have more in future years. In that case, you would be in a higher tax bracket in those later years so taking your depreciation deduction then would result in more tax savings.

How Regular Depreciation Works

With regular depreciation, you deduct the cost of property a little at a time over the depreciation period. The depreciation period (also called the "recovery period") is the time over which you must take your depreciation deductions for an asset. The tax code has assigned depreciation periods to all types of business assets, ranging from three to 39 years. These periods are somewhat arbitrary. However, property that can be expected to last a long time generally gets a longer recovery period than property that has a short life—for example, nonresidential real property has a 39-year recovery period, while software has only a three-year period. Most of the personal property that you buy for your business will probably have a five- or seven-year depreciation period.

The major depreciation periods are listed below. These periods are also called recovery classes, and all property that comes within a period is said to belong to that class. For example, computers have a five-year depreciation period and thus fall within the five-year class, along with automobiles and office equipment.

Depreciation Periods	
Depreciation Period	**Type of Property**
3 years	Computer software Tractor units for over-the-road use Any racehorse more than 2 years old when placed in service Any other horse more than 12 years old when placed in service
5 years	Automobiles, taxis, buses, and trucks Computers and peripheral equipment Office machinery (such as typewriters, calculators, and copiers) Any property used in research and experimentation Breeding cattle and dairy cattle Appliances, carpets, furniture, and so on used in a residential rental real estate activity
7 years	Office furniture and fixtures (such as desks, files, and safes) Agricultural machinery and equipment Any property that does not have a class life and has not been designated by law as being in any other class
10 years	Vessels, barges, tugs, and similar water transportation equipment Any single-purpose agricultural or horticultural structure Any tree or vine bearing fruits or nuts
15 years	Improvements made directly to land or added to it (such as shrubbery, fences, roads, and bridges) Any retail motor fuels outlet, such as a convenience store
20 years	Farm buildings (other than single-purpose agricultural or horticultural structures)
27.5 years	Residential rental property—for example, an apartment building
39 years	Nonresidential real property, such as a home office, office building, store, or warehouse

First-Year Depreciation

The IRS has established certain rules (called "conventions") that govern how many months of depreciation you can take for the first year in which you own an asset. Because of these rules, the actual period you depreciate property is one year longer than the statutory depreciation period, with only a partial deduction claimed for the first and last years. For example, five-year property must be depreciated over six years.

The basic rule is that, no matter what month and day of the year you buy an asset, you treat it as being placed in service on July 1— the midpoint of the year. This means that you get one half-year of depreciation for the first year that you own an asset.

You are not allowed to use the half-year convention if more than 40% of the long-term personal property that you buy during the year is placed in service during the last three months of the year. The 40% figure is determined by adding together the basis of all the depreciable property you bought during the year and comparing that with the basis of all of the property you bought during the fourth quarter only.

If you exceed the 40% ceiling, you must use the midquarter convention. You group all the property that you purchased during the year by the quarter it was bought and treat it as being placed in service at the midpoint of that quarter.

Depreciation Methods

There are several ways to calculate depreciation. However, most tangible property is depreciated using the Modified Accelerated Cost Recovery System, or MACRS. (A slightly different system, called ADS, applies to certain listed property (see "Depreciation Rules for Listed Property," below), property used outside the United States, and certain farm property and imported property.)

You can ordinarily use three different methods to calculate the depreciation deduction under MACRS: straight-line or one of two accelerated depreciation methods. Once you choose your method, you're stuck with it for the entire life of the asset. In addition, you must use the same method for all property of the same class that you purchase during the year.

With the straight-line method, you deduct an equal amount each year over the useful life of an asset. You can use the straight-line method to deduct any type of depreciable property, except for the first and last years. The following chart shows how much you deduct each year using the straight-line method for five-year property using the half-year convention.

Year	Depreciation Deduction (% of property basis)
1	10%
2	20%
3	20%
4	20%
5	20%
6	10%

There is nothing wrong with straight-line depreciation, but the tax law provides an alternative that most businesses prefer: accelerated depreciation. As the name implies, this method provides faster depreciation than the straight-line method. It does not increase your total depreciation deduction, but it permits you to take larger deductions in the first few years after you buy an asset. You make up for this by taking smaller deductions in later years.

The fastest and most commonly used form of accelerated depreciation is the double declining balance method. With this method you get double the deduction that you would get for the first full year under the straight-line method. You then get less in later years. This method may be used to depreciate all property within the three-, five-, seven-, and ten-year classes, excluding farm property. This covers virtually all the tangible personal property you buy for your business. The following chart shows how much you deduct each year using the double declining balance method for five-year property using the half-year convention.

Year	Depreciation Deduction (% of property basis)
1	20%
2	32%
3	19.20%
4	11.52%
5	11.52%
6	14.76%

Using accelerated depreciation is not necessarily a good idea if you expect your income to go up in future years and you will be in a higher tax bracket. There are also some restrictions on when you can use accelerated depreciation. For example, you can't use it for listed property that you use for business less than 50% of the time.

Depreciation Rules for Listed Property

As mentioned above, "listed property" is various types of personal property than can easily be used for nonbusiness purpose, including cars, light trucks, boats, airplanes; and any other property generally used for entertainment, recreation, or amusement—for example, digital cameras. If you use listed property for business more than 50% of the time, you may deduct its cost just like any other long-term business property (with bonus or regular depreciation or Section 179).

The IRS imposes special record-keeping rules on listed property. (See "Listed Property" in Chapter 15.) In addition, if you use listed property 50% or less of the time for business, you may not deduct the cost under Section 179 or use bonus depreciation or accelerated depreciation. Instead, you must use the slowest method of depreciation: straight-line depreciation. In addition, listed property other than cars and light trucks that is used less than 51% for business must be depreciated over a longer period.

If you start out using accelerated depreciation and/or bonus depreciation and in a later year your business use drops to 50% or less, you have to switch to the straight-line method and ADS period for that year and subsequent years. In addition, you are subject to depreciation recapture for the prior years—that is, you must calculate how much more depreciation you got in the prior years by using accelerated depreciation and/or bonus depreciation and count that amount as ordinary taxable income for the current year. This will, of course, increase your tax bill for the year. If you're a sole proprietor, you'll have to include this income on your Schedule C and pay both income tax and self-employment tax on it.

Deducting Real Property

Real property includes land and the buildings and other structures on land. Unlike personal property, the cost of real property generally cannot be deducted in one year with bonus depreciation or Section 179—but there is an exception for improvements to real property. Instead, real property (other than certain improvements) must be depreciated over many years.

Land

Land cannot be depreciated because it never wears out. However, this doesn't mean you don't get a tax deduction for land. When you sell it, you may deduct the cost of the land from the sale price to determine your taxable gain, if any. The cost of clearing, grading, landscaping, or demolishing buildings on land before it is placed into service is not depreciable. It is added to the tax basis of the land—that is, to its cost—and subtracted from the money you get when you sell the land.

Buildings

Unlike land, buildings do wear out over time and therefore may be depreciated. This means that when you buy property with buildings on it, you must separate out the cost of the buildings from the total cost of the property to calculate your depreciation.

As you might expect, the depreciation periods for buildings are quite long (after all, buildings usually last a long time). The depreciation period for nonresidential buildings is 39 years. Nonresidential buildings include office buildings, stores, workshops, and factories. Residential real property—an apartment building, for example—is depreciated over 27.5 years. Different periods apply to property purchased before 1993. For detailed guidance on how to depreciate residential real property, refer to *Every Landlord's Tax Deduction Guide*, by Stephen Fishman (Nolo).

You must use the slow straight-line method to depreciate real property. This means you'll only be able to deduct a small fraction of its value each year—1/39th of its value each year if the 39-year period applies.

If you have an office or other workplace you use solely for your business in your home, you are entitled to depreciate the business portion of the home. For example, if you use 10% of your home for your business, you may depreciate 10% of its cost (excluding the cost of the land). In the unlikely event your home has gone down in value since you bought it, you must use its fair market value on the date you began using your home office as your tax basis. You depreciate a home office over 39 years—the term used for nonresidential property. A home office is nonresidential property because you don't live in it.

Building Improvements

After a commercial building has been placed into service in a business, it is common to make improvements to it—for example, replacing the roof or remodeling the interior. The general rule is that building improvements must be separately depreciated. Improvements to a building or building component, such as a roof, must be depreciated over 39 years (nonresidential buildings) or 27.5 years (residential buildings). However, special rules allow many types of improvements to nonresidential buildings to be deducted in one year.

Section 179 Expensing for Roofs and Other Improvements

Owners of commercial buildings may use Section 179 to fully deduct in one year (subject to the annual $1,040,000 limit) any of the following improvements to their buildings made after they were first placed into service:

- roofs
- heating, ventilation, and air-conditioning property
- fire protection and alarm systems, and
- security systems.

In addition, IRS regulations permit building owners who replace building structural components, such as roofs or heating or cooling systems, to take a loss on the unrecovered basis (cost) of the old component. For example, if you replace an old roof with a new one, you'll be able to deduct the remaining unrecovered basis in the old roof.

Interior Building Improvements

The Tax Cuts and Jobs Act established a new category of depreciable real property starting in 2018: "qualified improvement property." This property consists of improvements to the interior of nonresidential real property after it has been placed into service in business. This includes interior improvements to restaurants, retail stores, and office buildings. However, it does not include improvements related to the enlargement of a building, an elevator or escalator, or the internal structural framework of a building.

When Congress wrote the Tax Cuts and Jobs Act, it intended to permit qualified improvement property to be fully deducted in one year using 100% bonus depreciation. If a taxpayer didn't want to use bonus depreciation, they could depreciate such property over 15 years using the straight-line method, instead of the usual 39 years. However, due to a drafting error, neither of these changes were included in the TCJA. Taxpayers were still able to deduct such improvements using Section 179 —but this deduction (1) can't result in a loss, and (2) is subject to an annual dollar limit.

Congress fixed these errors when it enacted the CARES Act in 2020. Thus, taxpayers who have qualified improvement property may deduct the cost in one of three ways:
- fully deduct the cost in one year with 100% bonus depreciation
- deduct the cost with Section 179 expensing, subject to a $1,050,000 annual limit for 2021, or
- depreciate the cost over 15 years using straight-line depreciation.

Using bonus depreciation can provide a substantial deduction that can result in a net operating loss (NOL) for the year, depending on the taxpayer's other income and expenses. NOLs for 2018 through 2020 may be carried back five years (deducted against income for those years) resulting in a tax refund for one or more of those years.

> **EXAMPLE:** Arthur leased a building for his restaurant business and placed it into service in 2015. In late 2020, he spends $100,000 to remodel the building to comply with government requirements that the space be made safer for diners in light of the coronavirus. He uses 100% bonus depreciation to fully deduct the cost in 2020. This results in a $50,000 NOL for 2020. He applies this NOL to his 2015 through 2019 taxes, resulting in a tax refund.

The 100% bonus depreciation and 15-year depreciation fixes are retroactive to 2018. Taxpayers who are depreciating qualified improvement property placed in service during 2018 or 2019 over 39 years, must correct their depreciation deductions for those years. This is not optional. They may now use bonus depreciation to fully deduct the cost of the improvements in one year. Alternatively, they may elect out of bonus depreciation and depreciate the improvements over 15 years instead of 39.

Taxpayers who have filed two or more annual returns depreciating 2018 or 2019 qualified improvement property over 39 years must file IRS Form 3115, *Application for Change in Accounting Method*, with their current-year tax return to correct the recovery period. Taxpayers who have only filed one annual return with the 39-year period may file an amended return for that prior year or may file Form 3115 with their current year return. The Form 3115 or amended return will show (1) the adjustments required if the taxpayer had claimed 100% bonus depreciation for the improvements, or (2) elect out of bonus depreciation and show the adjustments to depreciate the property over 15 years. It's wise to have a tax professional to prepare these forms.

Taxpayers who used Section 179 to fully deduct qualified improvement property for 2018 or 2019 don't have to do anything.

Intangible Assets

Tangible things like equipment and computers aren't the only business assets that wear out or get used up. Intangible assets can also get used up or become obsolete. Intangible assets are things you can't see or touch. They include intellectual property—patents, copyrights, trade secrets, and trademarks—and business goodwill.

The cost of intangible assets that get used up may be deducted over the useful life of the asset. This process is called "amortization," but it is the same as straight-line depreciation. You deduct an equal amount of the cost of the asset each year over its useful life.

If you buy an intangible asset from someone else, you may deduct its cost over its useful life. Except for trademarks, which are amortized over 15 years, the IRS has not established any set time periods for the useful lives of intangible assets. The taxpayer determines the useful life, subject to review by the IRS. The useful life of an invention or copyright for tax purposes can be complex to determine: It could be the entire legal duration of the copyright or patent (at least 70 years for copyrights, and up to 20 years for patents) or a shorter time if the asset will become valueless or obsolete more quickly.

However, patents and copyrights that you obtain through the purchase of another business or its assets are depreciated over 15 years using the straight-line method. (I.R.C. § 197.)

Generally, if you create an intangible asset yourself (such as an invention or copyrighted work of authorship like a book or film), you may currently deduct the cost. Any costs that you can't currently deduct may be amortized, as described above.

CAUTION

Amortization can be tricky. This is a complex area of taxation. Consult with a knowledgeable tax pro if you need to amortize an intangible asset.

Tax Reporting and Record Keeping

Bonus and regular depreciation and Section 179 deductions are reported on IRS Form 4562, *Depreciation and Amortization*. If you have more than one business for which you're claiming these deductions, you must use a separate Form 4562 for each business. If you're a sole proprietor, you carry over the amount of your bonus and regular depreciation and Section 179 deductions to your Schedule C and subtract them from your gross business income along with your other business expenses.

Form 4562 is one of the most complex and confusing IRS forms. If you want to complete it yourself, do yourself a favor and use a tax preparation program.

You need to keep accurate records for each asset you depreciate or expense under Section 179, showing:

- a description of the asset
- when and how you purchased the property
- the date it was placed in service
- its original cost
- the percentage of time you use it for business
- whether and how much you deducted under Section 179 and/or bonus depreciation
- the amount of depreciation you took for the asset in prior years, if any
- its depreciable basis
- the depreciation method used
- the length of the depreciation period, and
- the amount of depreciation you deducted for the year.

If you use tax preparation software, it should create a worksheet containing this information. Be sure to check worksheets carefully and save them. You can also use an accounting program such as *QuickBooks* to keep track of your depreciating assets. Simple checkbook programs like *Quicken* are not designed to keep track of depreciation. You may also use a spreadsheet program to create your own depreciation worksheet. Spreadsheet templates are available for this purpose. Of course, you can also do the job by hand.

For listed property, you'll also have to keep records showing how much of the time you use it for business and personal uses. You should also keep proof of the amount you paid for the asset: receipts, canceled checks, and purchase documents. You need not file these records with your tax return, but you must have them available to back up your deductions if you're audited.

Leasing Long-Term Assets

When you're acquiring a long-term asset for your business, you should consider whether it makes more sense to lease the item rather than purchase it. Almost everything a business needs can be leased—computers, office furniture, equipment. And leasing can be an attractive alternative to buying. However, it's important to understand the tax consequences of leasing when making your decision.

So which is better, leasing or buying? It depends. Leasing equipment and other long-term assets can be a better option for small business owners who have limited capital or who need equipment that must be upgraded every few years. Purchasing equipment can be a better option for businesses with ample capital or for equipment that has a long usable life. Each business's situation is unique and the decision to buy or lease must be made on a case-by-case basis. The following chart summarizes the major tax and nontax differences between leasing and buying equipment.

Before deciding whether to purchase or lease an expensive item, it's a good idea to determine the total actual costs of each option. This depends on many factors, including:

- the cost of the lease
- the purchase price for the item
- the item's useful life
- the interest rate on a loan to purchase the item
- the item's residual value—how much it would be worth at the end of the lease term
- whether you will purchase the item at the end of the lease and how much this would cost
- how much it would cost to dispose of the item
- your income tax bracket
- whether the item qualifies for one-year Section 179 expensing or must be depreciated, and
- if the item must be depreciated, the length of the depreciation period.

There are several lease-versus-buy calculators on the Internet that you can use to compare the costs of leasing versus buying.

Commercial software and computer spreadsheets can also be used for this purpose.

	Leasing	**Buying**

Tax Treatment	Lease payments are a currently deductible business operating expense.
	    No regular or bonus depreciation or Section 179 deductions.
		Up to $1,050,000 in equipment purchases can be deducted in one year under Section 179; 100% can be deducted through 2022 using bonus depreciation. Otherwise, cost is depreciated over several years (usually 5 to 7).
		    Interest on loans to buy equipment is currently deductible.

Initial Cash Outlay	Small. No down payment required. Deposit ordinarily required.	Large. At least a 20% down payment usually required. Bank loan may be required to finance the remaining cost.
Ownership	You own nothing at end of lease term.	You own the equipment.
Costs of Equipment Obsolescence	Borne by lessor because it owns equipment. Lessee may lease new equipment when lease expires.	Borne by buyer because buyer owns equipment, which may have little resale value.

Inventory

f your business makes or buys goods to sell to customers, you need to know about the tax rules for deducting inventory.

What Is Inventory?

Inventory (also called "merchandise") is the goods and products that a business owns to sell to customers in the ordinary course of business. It includes almost anything a business offers for sale, not including real estate. It makes no difference whether you manufacture the goods yourself or buy finished goods from others and resell them to customers. Inventory includes not only finished merchandise, but also unfinished work in progress, as well as the raw materials and supplies that will become part of the finished merchandise.

Only things you hold title to—that is, things you own—constitute inventory. Inventory includes items you haven't yet received or paid for, as long as you own them. For example, an item you buy with a credit card counts as inventory, even if you haven't paid the bill yet. However, if you buy merchandise that is sent C.O.D., you acquire ownership only after the goods are delivered and paid for. Similarly, goods that you hold on consignment are not part of your inventory because you don't own them.

Supplies Are Not Inventory

Materials and supplies that do not physically become part of the merchandise a business sells are not included in inventory.

These include:

- parts and other components acquired to maintain, repair, or improve business property
- fuel, lubricants, water, or similar items that are reasonably expected to be consumed in 12 months or less
- property that has an economic useful life of 12 months or less, and
- property with an acquisition or production cost of $200 or less. (IRS Reg. 1.162-3(c)(1).)

Unless they are incidental supplies as described below, the cost of these supplies must be deducted in the year in which they are used or consumed, which is not necessarily the year when you purchase them. This means that you must keep track of how many materials you use each year.

Incidental Supplies

There is an important exception to the rule that the cost of materials and supplies may be deducted only as they are used or consumed. The entire cost of supplies that are incidental to a taxpayer's business may be deducted in the year they are purchased. Supplies are incidental if all of the following are true:

- You do not keep a record of when you use the supplies.
- You do not take a physical inventory of the supplies at the beginning and end of the tax year.
- Deducting the cost of supplies in the year you purchase them does not distort your taxable income. (Treas. Reg. 1.162-3(a)(2).)

Merchandise to Include in Inventory	
Include the following merchandise in inventory:	**Do not include the following items in inventory:**
Purchased merchandise if title has passed to you, even if the merchandise is in transit or you do not have physical possession of it for some other reason	Goods you have sold, if title has passed to the buyer
	Goods consigned to you
Merchandise you've agreed to sell but have not separated from other similar merchandise you own to supply to the buyer	Goods ordered for future delivery, if you do not yet have title
	Assets such as land, buildings, and equipment used in your business
Goods you have placed with another person or business to sell on consignment	Supplies that do not physically become part of the item intended for sale
Goods held for sale in display rooms, merchandise mart rooms, or booths located away from your place of business	

Long-Term Assets

Long-term assets are things that last for more than one year—for example, equipment, tools, office furniture, vehicles, and buildings. Long-term assets that you purchase to use in your business are not a part of your inventory. They are deductible capital expenses that you may depreciate over several years or, in many cases, deduct in a single year using bonus depreciation or Section 179. (See Chapter 5 for more on deducting long-term assets.)

Deducting Inventory Costs

Before 2018, you were not allowed to deduct inventory costs in the same way you deduct other costs of doing business, such as your office rent or employee salaries. Instead you had to maintain inventory on your books and deduct it only in the year it was sold, which could be long after it was purchased. The Tax Cuts and Jobs Act changed this long-standing rule for smaller businesses. If the average annual gross receipts earned by your business over the past three years total less than $26 million, you now have two alternative ways to treat inventory. You can treat it:

- as nonincidental materials and supplies, or
- the same way it is treated in your financial statements or books and records. (I.R.C. § 471(c).)

Nonincidental Materials and Supplies Deduction

Businesses with less than $26 million in gross receipts may use the cash method of accounting and treat inventory as nonincidental materials and supplies. You deduct the cost of inventory treated as materials and supplies in the year in which it is first used or consumed in your business operations.

The impact of such treatment is greatest for businesses that manufacture products for sale. They may deduct the cost of purchased raw materials when the materials move out of storage into the work-in-process. For businesses that buy finished merchandise for resale, the impact is not so great. Their inventory is used or consumed when it is sold to customers. Thus, they get no deduction until the merchandise is sold, the same as under regular inventory rules.

However, there are other advantages to this method. The uniform capitalization rules, which require that a portion of overhead and other indirect costs be apportioned to inventory, do not apply. As a result, all the direct labor and overhead costs incurred in producing the goods should be deductible as incurred.

If your business previously used the accrual method of accounting, you must obtain IRS permission to change to the cash method and start deducting inventory as nonincidental materials and supplies. You do so filing IRS Form 3115, *Application for Change in Accounting Method*. The change is automatically accepted by the IRS, which has adopted simplified filing procedures. (See Rev. Proc. 2018-40.) Nevertheless, it is wise to have a tax pro help with this complex form. The form has to be filed by the due date of the business's tax return for the year (plus extensions).

Books and Records Deduction for Inventory

The second alternative method businesses with less than $26 million in gross receipts may use is to deduct inventory in accordance with their applicable financial statement. If a business doesn't have an applicable financial statement, then it can be done in conformance with its books and records prepared in accordance with its accounting procedures. (I.R.C. § 471(c)(1)(B).)

An "applicable financial statement" is something larger businesses have and includes audited financial statements and annual filings with the SEC and other government agencies by large businesses. Because smaller businesses don't have such statements, they may deduct inventory the same way it is treated in their books and records.

All businesses with less than $26 million in gross receipts are now allowed to use the cash method of accounting. Those that do so use this method in their financial statements and books and records.

With the cash method of accounting system, income is reported when cash is received and expenses are reported when cash is paid. Thus, inventory is expensed on a business's books when it is purchased. A sale (income) is shown on the books when purchased inventory is sold and cash received. There is no need to calculate cost of goods sold at the end of the year, and the uniform capitalization rules (requiring indirect costs be apportioned to inventory) do not apply.

Does this mean that smaller businesses that use the cash method can deduct all their inventory in the year it is purchased, instead of waiting until it is sold? New regulations issued by the IRS make clear that the answer is a qualified "yes." This revolutionary change in the tax treatment of inventory allows earlier deductions for smaller businesses that sell inventory.

The basic rule is that a cash basis taxpayer may currently deduct inventory the year it is purchased so long as it doesn't account for inventory in any of its books and records. The IRS takes an expansive view of what constitutes business "books and records." They include physical counts of inventory and electronic point-of-sale systems that track acquisition costs and inventory levels. If such physical or electronic records are used to allocate costs to inventory or make reports to banks or other creditors about the value of unsold inventory, the taxpayer may only deduct the cost of the goods sold during the year. (IRS Reg. 1.471-1(b)(6).)

EXAMPLE 1: Acme, Inc. is a retail seller of beer, wine, and liquor. It has no applicable financial statement and uses the cash method of accounting because its gross receipts are under $26 million. In its electronic bookkeeping software, Acme treats all costs paid during the year as currently deductible. However, Acme employees take a physical count of inventory on Acme's selling floor and warehouse on December 31 of each year. Acme uses this physical count as part of its books and records to capitalize and allocate costs to inventory. Acme also periodically lets its lender know the cost of inventory on hand for specific categories of products it sells. Acme may not currently deduct all of its costs paid during the year because its electronic records do not accurately reflect the inventory records used for nontax purposes. Instead, Acme may only deduct the cost of goods sold during the year in accordance with the physical inventory count taken on December 31, 2021. (IRS Reg. 1.471-1(b)(6)(iii)(A)(Example (1)).)

On the other hand, inventory may be currently deducted if physical counts or electronic records are only used for reordering purposes and not to capitalize and allocate costs to inventory.

EXAMPLE 2: Assume the same facts as in Example 1, except that Acme uses the electronic ledger and physical counts only for reordering purposes, not to allocate costs between ending inventory and cost of goods sold or make reports to creditors. Instead, in its records, it expenses the cost of the inventory in the year it is paid for. On December 20, 2021, Acme pays for $500,000 of beer, wine, and liquor. Acme may deduct the full amount in 2021. (IRS Reg. 1.471-1(b)(6)(iii)(A)(Example 6).)

If you need to switch from the accrual to the cash method of accounting, you'll need to file IRS Form 3115, *Application for Change in Accounting Method*. As discussed above, the change is automatically accepted by the IRS. In addition, to claim a deduction for unsold inventory from past years before you used the cash method, you'll need to make an I.R.C. Section 481(a) adjustment when you file Form 3115. This enables you to deduct the entire cost of unsold inventory from past years in a single year. Unfortunately, IRS Form 3115 is an extremely complex form. You'll likely need help from a tax professional to complete it properly.

RESOURCE

For more information on inventory, refer to:

- *The Accounting Game*, by Darrell Mullis and Judith Orloff (Sourcebooks, Inc.)
- *Small Time Operator*, by Bernard B. Kamoroff (Taylor Trade Publishing)
- IRS Publication 334, *Tax Guide for Small Business* (Chapter 7), and
- IRS Publication 538, *Accounting Periods and Methods*.

Maintaining an Inventory

If you don't deduct inventoriable items as nonincidental materials and supplies or use the cash method in accordance with your books and records, you must maintain an inventory. You then deduct the cost of inventory only as it is sold. You must carry unsold inventory items as an asset on your books. You can deduct the cost of these items only when they are sold or become worthless (as a business loss).

If you are required to maintain an inventory, each year you must calculate how much you spent on inventory and how much of it you sold to determine the cost of goods sold on your tax return. There is no single way to do this—standard methods for tracking inventory vary according to the type and size of business involved. As long as your inventory methods are consistent from year to year, the IRS doesn't care which method you use.

You must report the cost of goods sold on your tax return using the following formula:

	Inventory at beginning of year
Plus:	Purchases or additions during the year
Minus:	Goods withdrawn from sale for personal use
Equals:	Cost of goods available for sale
Minus:	Inventory at end of year
Equals:	Cost of goods sold

If you're a sole proprietor or the owner of a one-person LLC, the amount goes directly on your Schedule C, which tracks the formula above. Multimember LLCs and partnerships report their cost of goods sold on Schedule A of IRS Form 1065, *U.S. Return of Partnership Income*. S corporations report cost of goods sold on Schedule A of Form 1120-S, *U.S. Income Tax Return for an S Corporation*. C corporations report this information on Schedule A of Form 1120, *U.S. Corporation Income Tax Return*.

Office Expenses

E veryone who has a business needs to work someplace. A great many small business owners work from home, while others have an outside office. Either way, your office expenses are usually deductible. If you work from your home, you might be able to use the home office deduction. This deduction allows you to deduct many of the costs associated with running a business from your home. This chapter focuses on the home office deduction, because it is subject to many complex tax rules. If you have an outside office, your expenses will be deductible as well.

Qualifying for the Home Office Deduction

If you work from home, the federal government will help you out by letting you deduct your home office expenses from your taxable income. This is true whether you own your home or apartment or are a renter. Although this tax deduction is commonly called the "home office deduction," it is not only for space in your home devoted to office work. You can also use it for a workshop, lab, studio, or any other home workspace that you use for your business.

If you've heard stories about how difficult it is to qualify for the home office deduction, you can breathe more easily. Changes in the tax law have made it easier for businesspeople to qualify for the deduction.

Some people believe that taking the home office deduction invites an IRS audit. The IRS denies this. But even if taking the deduction increases your audit chances, the risk of an audit is still low. (See Chapter 16 for more on audits.) Moreover, you have nothing to fear from an audit if you're entitled to take the deduction and you keep good records to back it up. Unfortunately, because of these fears, only about one-third of all taxpayers who qualify for the home office deduction actually take it—as many as five million taxpayers who could take the deduction, don't. In an apparent effort to encourage small business owners to take the deduction, the IRS created a new simplified method of claiming the deduction. (See "Simplified Home Office Deduction Method," below.)

However, if you plan on taking the deduction, you need to learn how to do it properly. There are strict requirements you must follow to qualify for the home office deduction. You are entitled to the home office deduction if you:

- are in business
- use your home office exclusively for business (unless you store inventory or run a day care center), and
- use your home office for business on a regular basis.

These are the three threshold requirements that everyone must meet. If you get past this first hurdle, then you must also meet any one of the following requirements:

- Your home office is your principal place of business.
- You regularly and exclusively use your home office for administrative or management activities for your business and have no other fixed location where you perform such activities.
- You meet clients or customers at home.
- You use a separate structure on your property exclusively for business purposes.
- You store inventory or product samples at home.
- You run a day care center at home.

These rules apply whether you are a sole proprietor, a partner in a partnership, a limited liability company (LLC) owner, or an S corporation owner. If you have formed a regular C corporation that you own and operate and you work as its employee, then there are additional requirements you must meet. (See "Corporation Employees," below, for more on C corporations.)

Threshold Requirement: Regular and Exclusive Business Use

To take the home office deduction, you must have a home office—that is, an office or other workplace in your home that you use regularly and exclusively for business. Your home may be a house, apartment, condominium, or mobile home, or even a boat. You can also take the deduction for separate structures on your property that you use for business, such as an unattached garage, studio, barn, or greenhouse.

You Must Be in Business

You must be in business to take the home office deduction. You can't get the deduction for a hobby or another nonbusiness activity that you conduct out of your home. Nor can you take it if you perform investment activities at home—for example, researching the stock market. (See Chapter 2 for information on what constitutes a business for tax purposes.)

You don't have to work full time in a business to qualify for the home office deduction. If you satisfy the requirements, you can take the deduction for a side business that you run from a home office. However, you must use your home office regularly, and the total amount you deduct cannot exceed your profit from the business. (See "What Expenses Can You Deduct?" below, for more on the profit limitation.)

If you have more than one business, each business must qualify for the home office deduction. Depending on where you do your work, it's possible that one of your businesses will qualify while the other does not.

This rule can be important because of the profit limit on the amount of the home office deduction—that is, your deduction may not exceed the net profit you earn from your home office business or businesses. You'll want to make sure that your most profitable enterprises qualify for the deduction.

You Must Use Your Home Office Exclusively for Business

You can't take the home office deduction unless you use part of your home exclusively for your business. In other words, you must use your home office only for your business. The more space you devote exclusively to your business, the more your home office deduction will be worth. (See "Calculating the Home Office Deduction," below, for more on calculating your home office space.) This requirement doesn't apply if you store inventory at home or run a home day care center (discussed below).

If you use part of your home—such as a room or studio—as your business office, but you also use that space for personal purposes, you won't qualify for the home office deduction.

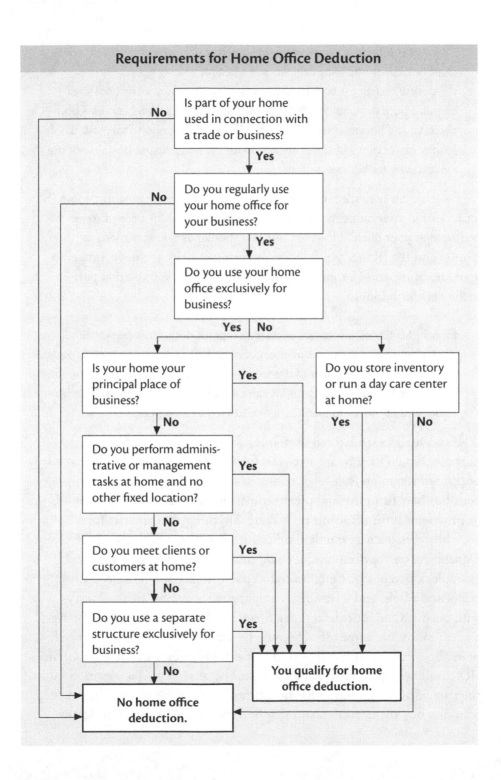

Requirements for Home Office Deduction

Is part of your home used in connection with a trade or business?
— **No**
— **Yes** → Do you regularly use your home office for your business?
— **No**
— **Yes** → Do you use your home office exclusively for business?
— **Yes** → Is your home your principal place of business?
— **No**
— Do you perform administrative or management tasks at home and no other fixed location?
— **No**
— Do you meet clients or customers at home?
— **No**
— Do you use a separate structure exclusively for business?
— **No**
— **Yes** (from several) → **You qualify for home office deduction.**
— **No** → Do you store inventory or run a day care center at home?
— **Yes** → **You qualify for home office deduction.**
— **No**

No home office deduction.

> **EXAMPLE:** Johnny, an accountant, has a den at home furnished with a desk, chair, bookshelf, and filing cabinet, and a bed for visiting guests. He uses the desk and chair for both business and personal reasons. The bookshelf contains both personal and business books, the filing cabinet contains both personal and business files, and the bed is used only for personal reasons. Johnny can't claim a business deduction for the den because he does not use it exclusively for business purposes.

The easiest way to meet the exclusive use test is to devote an entire room (or rooms) in your home to your business—for example, by using a spare bedroom as your office. However, not everybody has an extra room to spare—and the IRS recognizes this. You can still claim the deduction even if you use just part of a room as your office, as long as you use that part exclusively for business.

> **EXAMPLE:** Carlos, a software engineer, keeps his desk, chair, bookshelf, computer, and filing cabinet in one part of his den and uses them exclusively for business. The remainder of the room—one-third of the space—is used to store a bed for houseguests. Carlos can take a home office deduction for the two-thirds of the room that he uses exclusively as an office.

If you use the same room (or rooms) for your office and for other purposes, you'll have to arrange your furniture and belongings so that a portion of the room is devoted exclusively to your business. Place only your business furniture and other business items in the office portion of the room. Business furniture includes anything that you use for your business, such as standard office furniture like a desk and chair. Depending on your business, it could include other items as well—for example, a psychologist might need a couch, an artist might need work tables and easels, and a consultant might need a seating area to meet with clients. One court held that a financial planner was entitled to have a television in his home office because he used it to keep up on financial news. Be careful what you put in this space, however. In another case, the IRS disallowed the deduction for a doctor because he had a television in the part of his living room that he claimed as his home office. The court wouldn't buy the doctor's claim that he only watched medical programs.

The IRS does not require you to physically separate the space you use for business from the rest of the room. However, doing so will help you satisfy the exclusive use test. For example, if you use part of your living room as an office, you could separate it from the rest of the room with room dividers or bookcases.

As a practical matter, the IRS doesn't have spies checking to see whether you're using your home office just for business. However, complying with the rules from the beginning means you won't have to worry if you are audited.

The exclusive use requirement can easily trip you up if you don't think things through ahead of time. Use your common sense when you set up your home office. For example, if you live in a one-bedroom apartment and claim the entire bedroom as a home office, you'll have to be able to explain to the IRS where you sleep.

You Must Use Your Home Office Regularly

It's not enough to use a part of your home exclusively for business—you must also use it regularly. For example, you can't place a desk in a corner of a room and claim the home office deduction if you almost never use the desk for your business.

Unfortunately, the IRS doesn't offer a clear definition of regular use. The agency has stated only that you must use a portion of your home for business on a continuing basis—not just for occasional or incidental business. One court has held that 12 hours of use a week is sufficient. (*Green v. Commissioner*, 79 TC 428 (1982).) There is a good chance that you could also qualify with less use—for example, at least one hour a day—but no one knows for sure.

Additional Requirements

Using a home office exclusively and regularly for business is not enough by itself to qualify for the home office deduction: You also must satisfy at least one of the additional five tests described below.

Home as Principal Place of Business

The most common way to satisfy the additional home office deduction requirement is to show that you use your home as your principal place of business. How you accomplish this depends on where you do most of your work and what type of work you do at home.

If you only work at home: If, like many businesspeople, you do all or almost all of your work in your home office, your home is clearly your principal place of business and you'll have no trouble qualifying for the home office deduction. This would be the case, for example, for a writer who writes only at home or a salesperson who sells by phone and makes sales calls from home.

If you work in multiple locations: If you work in more than one location, your home office still qualifies as your principal place of business if you perform your most important business activities—those activities that most directly generate your income—at home.

> EXAMPLE: Charles is a self-employed author who uses a home office to write. He spends 30 to 35 hours per week in his home office writing and another ten to 15 hours a week at other locations conducting research, meeting with publishers, and attending promotional events. The essence of Charles's business is writing—this is how he generates his income. So, his home qualifies as his principal place of business, because it is where he writes.

If you perform equally important business activities in several locations, your principal place of business is where you spend more than half of your time. If there is no such location, you don't have a principal place of business.

> EXAMPLE: Sue sells costume jewelry on eBay from her home office and at crafts fairs and through consignments to craft shops. She spends 25 hours per week in her home office and 15 hours at fairs and crafts shops. Her home office qualifies as her principal place of business.

You Do Administrative Work at Home

Of course, many businesspeople spend the bulk of their time working away from home. This is the case, for example, for:

- building contractors who work primarily on building sites
- doctors who work primarily in hospitals
- traveling salespeople who visit clients at their places of business, and
- housepainters, gardeners, and home repair people who work primarily in their customers' homes.

Fortunately, legal changes that took effect in 1999 make it possible for these people to qualify for the home office deduction. Under the rules, your home office qualifies as your principal place of business, even if you work primarily outside your home, if both of the following are true:

- You use the office to conduct administrative or management activities for your business.
- There is no other fixed location where you conduct substantial administrative or management activities.

Administrative or management activities include, but are not limited to:

- billing clients or patients
- keeping books and records
- ordering supplies
- setting up appointments, and
- writing reports.

So, you can qualify for the home office deduction even if your home office is not where you generate most of your business income. It's sufficient that you regularly use it to administer or manage your business—for example, to keep your books, schedule appointments, do research, write reports, forward orders, or order supplies. As long as you have no other fixed location where you regularly do these things—for example, an outside office—you'll get the deduction.

> **EXAMPLE:** Sally, a handyperson, performs home repair work for clients in their homes. She has a home office that she uses regularly and exclusively to keep her books, arrange appointments, and order supplies. Sally is entitled to a home office deduction.

You don't have to perform all the administrative or management activities your business requires at home to qualify for the home office deduction. Your home office can qualify for the deduction even if you:

- have others conduct your administrative or management activities at locations other than your home—for example, another company does your billing from its place of business
- conduct administrative or management activities at places that are not fixed locations for your business, such as in a car or a hotel room, or
- occasionally conduct minimal administrative or management activities at a fixed location outside your home, such as your outside office.

EXAMPLE: Sandra is a solo practitioner attorney with a flourishing criminal defense practice. She has a small office she shares with several other attorneys but spends most of her work time in court, at local jails, and in her car. Sandra employs an outside firm to bill her clients and perform other bookkeeping for her business. She has a home office she uses to perform most of the administrative and management tasks she does herself, such as setting up appointments, writing briefs and memos, and ordering supplies. Sandra also performs some of these tasks, such as making appointments, while in court or in her car on the way to or from court. She rarely uses her outside office for these tasks.

Sandra's home office qualifies as her principal place of business for purposes of the home office deduction. She conducts administrative or management activities for her business there and has no other fixed location where she conducts substantial administrative or management activities. The fact that she occasionally performs some administrative tasks in her car or in court does not disqualify her for the deduction because they are not fixed locations for her law practice. Likewise, she doesn't lose the deduction because she has an outside company do her billing.

Moreover, you can qualify for the deduction even if you have suitable space to conduct administrative or management activities outside your home but choose to use your home office for those activities instead.

EXAMPLE: Ricardo is a self-employed anesthesiologist. He spends the majority of his time administering anesthesia and postoperative care in three local hospitals. One of the hospitals provides him with a small shared office where he could conduct administrative or management activities, but he rarely uses it. Instead, he uses a room in his home that he has converted to an office. He uses this room exclusively and regularly to contact patients, surgeons, and hospitals regarding scheduling; prepare for treatments and presentations; maintain billing records and patient logs; satisfy continuing medical education requirements; and read medical journals and books.

Ricardo's home office qualifies as his principal place of business for deducting expenses for its use. He conducts administrative or management activities for his business as an anesthesiologist there and has no other fixed location where he conducts substantial administrative or management activities for this business. His choice to use his home office instead of the one provided by the hospital does not disqualify it from being his principal place of business. The fact that he performs substantial nonadministrative or nonmanagement activities at fixed locations outside his home—that is, at hospitals—also does not disqualify his home office from being his principal place of business.

Meeting Clients or Customers at Home

Even if your home office is not your principal place of business, you may deduct your expenses for any part of your home that you use exclusively to meet with clients, customers, or patients. You must physically meet with others in this home location; phoning them from there is not sufficient. And the meetings must be a regular part of your business; occasional meetings don't qualify.

It's not entirely clear how often you must meet clients at home for those meetings to be considered regular. However, the IRS has indicated that meeting clients one or two days a week is sufficient. Exclusive use means you use the space where you meet clients only for business. You are free to use the space for business purposes other than meeting clients—for example, doing your business bookkeeping or other paperwork. But you cannot use the space for personal purposes, such as watching television.

> **EXAMPLE:** June, an attorney, works three days a week in her city office and two days in her home office, which she uses only for business. She meets clients at her home office at least once a week. Because she regularly meets clients at her home office, it qualifies for the home office deduction even though her city office is her principal place of business.

If you want to qualify under this part of the rule, encourage clients or customers to visit you at home, and keep a log or appointment book showing all of their visits.

Using a Separate Structure for Business

You can also deduct expenses for a separate freestanding structure, such as a studio, garage, or barn, if you use it exclusively and regularly for your business. The structure does not have to be your principal place of business or a place where you meet patients, clients, or customers.

Exclusive use means that you use the structure only for business—for example, you can't use it to store gardening equipment or as a guesthouse. Regular use is not precisely defined, but it's probably sufficient to use the structure ten or 15 hours a week.

> **EXAMPLE:** Deborah is a freelance graphic designer. She has her main office in a downtown office building but also works every weekend in a small studio in her backyard. Because she uses the studio regularly and exclusively for her design work, it qualifies for the home office deduction.

Storing Inventory or Product Samples at Home

You can also take the home office deduction if you're in the business of selling retail or wholesale products and you store inventory or product samples at home. To qualify, you can't have an office or other business location outside your home. And you must store your inventory in a particular place in your home—for example, a garage, closet, or bedroom. You can't move your inventory from one room to the other. You don't have to use the storage space exclusively to store your inventory to take the deduction—you just have to regularly use it for that purpose.

> **EXAMPLE:** Lisa sells costume jewelry door-to-door. She rents a home and regularly uses half of her attached garage to store her jewelry inventory and also park her Harley-Davidson motorcycle. Lisa can deduct the expenses for the storage space even though she does not use her entire garage exclusively to store inventory.

Operating a Day Care Center at Home

You're also entitled to a home office deduction if you operate a day care center at home. This is a place where you care for children, people who are at least 65 years old, or people who are physically or mentally unable to care for themselves. Your day care must be licensed by the appropriate licensing agency, unless it's exempt. You must regularly use part of your home for day care, but your day care use need not be exclusive—for example, you could use your living room for day care during the day and for personal uses at night.

Corporation Employees

If you form a corporation to own and operate your business, you'll probably work as its employee. Prior to 2018, employees could claim a home office deduction if they satisfied the requirements discussed above and maintained the home office for the convenience of the employer. In this event, they could claim the home office deduction as a personal miscellaneous itemized deduction on Schedule A. However, during 2018 through 2025, this deduction is no longer available for employees. This includes employees who were unable to work in their employer's office during the COVID-19 pandemic.

If you work as an employee of your own corporation (or a corporation owned by someone else), you should seek to have your home office expenses reimbursed by your employer. These expenses would include all the applicable amounts covered in "Calculating the Home Office Deduction," below. The corporation can then deduct this amount as an ordinary business expense for office space. If you satisfy the requirements discussed below, the reimbursement will not be taxable to you personally.

> **EXAMPLE:** Jill operates her consulting business as a corporation. She incurs $10,000 in home expenses during the year. She submits an expense report to her corporation for $10,000 in home office expenses. The corporation deducts the $10,000 as an office space expense. Jill, the employee-owner, has no taxable income for her employee expense reimbursement.

To avoid paying tax on your reimbursement, all of the following must be true:

- You satisfy all the requirements for the home office deduction discussed above in "Qualifying for the Home Office Deduction."
- You maintain the home office for the convenience of your employer.
- You keep careful track of your home office expenses and can prove them with receipts or other records.
- Your corporation formally approves reimbursement of your home office expenses and the approval is documented in its corporate minutes.
- You have an "accountable reimbursement plan"—a written agreement in which the corporation agrees to reimburse you if you provide proper substantiation for your expenses.
- You provide your corporation with a complete and accurate expense report. A good way to accomplish the reimbursement is to complete IRS Form 8829, *Expenses for Business Use of Your Home*, and attach it to your expense report.

The convenience of the employer requirement can be difficult to meet. An employee's home office is deemed to be for an employer's convenience only if it is:

- a condition of employment
- necessary for the employer's business to properly function, or
- needed to allow the employee to properly perform his or her duties.

When you own the business that employs you, you ordinarily won't be able to successfully claim that a home office is a condition of your employment—after all, as the owner of the business, you're the person who sets the conditions for employees, including yourself. But, if there is no other office where you do your work, you should be able to establish that your home office is necessary for your business to properly function and/or for you to perform your employee duties.

It will be more difficult to establish necessity if you have separate corporate offices. Nevertheless, business owners in this situation have successfully argued that their home offices were necessary—for example, because their corporate offices were not open or not usable during evenings, weekends, or other nonbusiness hours or were too far from home to use during off-hours. The necessity test would clearly be satisfied if you worked at home because your outside office was closed due to the COVID-19 pandemic.

Calculating the Home Office Deduction

This is the fun part—figuring out how much the home office deduction will save you in taxes. Whether you own or rent the space you're claiming, the home office deduction can result in substantial savings for you each year.

How Much of Your Home Is Used for Business?

To calculate your home office deduction, you need to determine what percentage of your home you use for business. The law says you can use "any reasonable method" to do this. Obviously, you want to use the method that will give you the largest home office deduction. To do this, you want to maximize the percentage of your home that you claim as your office. There is no single way to do this for every home office. Try both methods described below and use the one that gives you the larger deduction.

Square Footage Method

The most precise method of measuring your office space is to divide the square footage of your home office by the total square footage of your home. For example, if your home is 1,600 square feet and you use 400 square feet for your home office, 25% of the total area is used for business. Of course, you must know the square footage of your entire home and your office to make this calculation. Your home's total square footage might be listed on real estate documents or plans; you'll have to measure your office space yourself.

You are allowed to subtract the square footage of common areas—such as hallways, entries, stairs, and landings—from the total area that you are measuring. You can also exclude attics and garages from your total space if you don't use them for business purposes. You aren't required to measure this way, but doing so will give you a larger deduction because your overall percentage of business use will be higher.

Room Method

Another way to measure is the room method. You can use this method only if all of the rooms in your home are about the same size. With this method, you divide the number of rooms used for business by the total number of rooms in the home. Don't include bathrooms, closets, or other storage areas. You may also leave out garages and attics if you don't use them for business. For example, if you use one room in a five-room house for business, your office takes up 20% of your home.

TIP

The room method usually yields a larger deduction. Even though IRS Form 8829 (the form sole proprietors file to claim the home office deduction) seems to require you to use the square footage method, this isn't the case. As long as all of the rooms in your home are about the same size, you can use the room method. And unless you live in a rabbit warren, using the room method will almost always result in a larger deduction.

What Expenses Can You Deduct?

The home office deduction is not one deduction, but many. Most costs associated with maintaining and running your home office are deductible. However, because your office is in your home, some of the money you spend also benefits you personally. For example, your utility bill pays to heat your home office, but it also keeps the rest of your living space warm. The IRS deals with this issue by dividing home office expenses into two categories: direct expenses, which benefit only your home office, and indirect expenses, which benefit both your office and your home.

Direct Expenses

You have a direct home office expense when you pay for something just for the home office portion of your home. This includes, for example, painting your home office, carpeting it, or paying someone to clean it. The entire amount of a direct home office expense is deductible.

> **EXAMPLE:** Jean pays a housepainter $400 to paint her home office. She may deduct this entire amount as a home office deduction.

Virtually anything you buy for your office that wears out, becomes obsolete, or gets used up, is deductible. However, you may have to depreciate permanent improvements to your home over 39 years, rather than deduct them in the year that you pay for them. Permanent improvements are changes that go beyond simple repairs, such as adding a new room to your home to serve as your office. (See Chapter 5 for more on improvements versus repairs.)

Indirect Expenses

An indirect expense is a payment for something that benefits your entire home, including both the home office portion and your personal space. You may deduct only a portion of this expense—the home office percentage of the total.

> **EXAMPLE:** Instead of just painting her home office, Jean decides to paint her entire home, for $1,600. She uses 25% of her home as an office so she may deduct 25% of the cost, or $400.

Most of your home office expenses will be indirect expenses, including:
- **Rent.** If you rent your home or apartment, you can use the home office deduction to deduct part of your rent—a substantial expense that is ordinarily not deductible. Your tax savings will be particularly great if you live in a high-rent area.

EXAMPLE: Sam uses 20% of his one-bedroom Manhattan apartment as a home office for his consulting business. He pays $2,000 per month in rent and may therefore deduct $400 of his rent per month ($4,800 per year) as a home office expense. This saves him more than $2,000 in federal, state, and self-employment taxes.

• **Mortgage interest and property taxes.** Whether or not you have a home office, you might be able to deduct your monthly mortgage interest and property tax payments as a personal itemized income tax deduction on your Schedule A (the tax form where you list your personal income tax deductions). However, the Tax Cuts and Jobs Act has lessened the value of this deduction and made it impossible for many taxpayers to take it at all. You can take a personal deduction for mortgage interest and property tax only if you itemize your personal expenses on your return. You should do this only if your mortgage interest, property taxes, and other personal deductions exceed the standard deduction. The Tax Cuts and Jobs Act almost doubled the standard deduction. As a result, only about 10% of all taxpayers are able to itemize, compared with 30% in past years. In addition, starting in 2018 and continuing through 2025, the itemized deduction for property taxes is limited to $10,000 per year. Also, for homes purchased in 2018 through 2025, the deduction for home mortgage interest is limited to acquisition loans for a main and second home totaling a maximum of $750,000. The amount is $1 million for homes purchased before 2018.

If you have a home office, you have the option of deducting the home office percentage of your mortgage interest and property tax payments as part of your home office deduction. If you do this, you do not deduct this amount on your Schedule A (you can't deduct the same item twice). This means you can deduct this amount without itemizing. If you do itemize, these amounts don't count toward the limits on deducting property tax and home mortgage interest as a personal itemized deduction.

EXAMPLE: Ed pays $12,000 per year in property tax on his home. He uses 25% of the home as an office for his business. This enables him to deduct $3,000 of his property tax (25%) as part of his home office deduction. He deducts the remaining $9,000 as a personal itemized deduction on his Schedule A. Had he not had a home office, he could have deducted only $10,000 of his $12,000 in property tax as a personal itemized deduction.

Another advantage of deducting the home office percentage of your monthly mortgage interest and real estate tax payments as part of your home office deduction is that it is a business deduction, not a personal deduction; as such, it reduces the amount of your business income subject to self-employment taxes, as well as reducing your income taxes. The self-employment tax is 15.3%, so you save $153 in self-employment taxes for every $1,000 in mortgage interest and property taxes you deduct as part of your home office deduction.

EXAMPLE: Suzy, a sole proprietor medical record transcriber, uses 20% of her three-bedroom Tulsa home as a home office. She pays $10,000 per year in mortgage interest and property taxes. When she does her taxes for the year, she may deduct $2,000 of her interest and taxes as part of her home office deduction (20% of $10,000). She adds this amount to her other home office expenses and decreases her business income for both income tax and self-employment tax purposes. The extra $2,000 business deduction saves her $306 in self-employment tax (15.3% × $2,000). She may deduct the remaining $8,000 of mortgage interest and property tax as a personal deduction on her Schedule A.

- **Depreciation.** If you own your home, you're also entitled to a depreciation deduction for the office portion of your home. (See Chapter 5 for a detailed discussion of depreciation.)
- **Utilities.** You may deduct your home office percentage of your utility bills for your entire home, including electricity, gas, water, heating oil, and trash removal. If you use a disproportionately large amount of electricity for your home office, you might be able to deduct more.

EXAMPLE: Sheila, a pottery maker, works out of a home workshop that takes up 25% of the space in her home. Her pottery making requires that she use a substantial amount of electricity. About 50% of her monthly electricity bill is for her home workshop. She may deduct 50% of her electricity costs as a home office expense, instead of just 25%. However, to prove her deduction isn't too big, she should keep electricity bills for her home before she began using the workshop, or for periods when she doesn't use the workshop—for example, while she is on vacation—to show that her bills for these months are about 50% lower than the bills for her working months.

- **Insurance.** Both homeowners' and renters' insurance are partly deductible as indirect home office expenses. However, special insurance coverage you buy just for your home office—for example, insurance for your computer or other business equipment—is fully deductible as a direct expense.

- **Home maintenance.** You can deduct the home office percentage of home maintenance expenses that benefit your entire home, such as housecleaning of your entire house, roof and furnace repairs, and exterior painting. These costs are deductible whether you hire someone or do them yourself. If you do the work yourself, however, you can only deduct the cost of materials, not the cost of your own labor. Termite inspection, pest extermination fees, and snow removal costs are also deductible. However, the IRS won't let you deduct lawn care unless you regularly use your home to meet clients or customers. Home maintenance costs that don't benefit your home office—for example, painting your kitchen—are not deductible at all.

- **Casualty losses.** Casualty losses are damage to your home caused by such things as fire, floods, or theft. Casualty losses that affect your entire house—for example, a leak that floods your entire home— are deductible as a home office expense in the amount of your home office percentage. Casualty losses that affect only your home office—for example, a leak that floods only the home office area of the house—are fully deductible direct expenses. Casualty losses that don't affect your home office at all are not deductible as a home office expense—for example, if only your kitchen is flooded. There is a personal deduction for casualty losses to the nonoffice portions of a home, but during 2018 through 2025 it is limited to losses that occur in a presidentially declared disaster area. (See Chapter 14 for a detailed discussion of casualty losses.)

- **Condominium association fees.** These fees (often substantial) are partly deductible as an indirect expense if you have a home office.
- **Security system costs.** Security system costs are partly deductible as an indirect expense if your security system protects your entire home. If you have a security system that protects only your home office, the cost is a fully deductible direct expense.
- **Computer equipment.** Computers and peripheral equipment (such as printers) are deductible whether or not you qualify for the home office deduction. (See Chapter 4 for more on deducting business expenses.)
- **Supplies and materials.** Office supplies and materials you use for your business are deductible whether or not you qualify for the home office deduction.

Mileage Deductions for Leaving the House

If your home office is your principal place of business, you can deduct the cost of traveling from your home to other work locations for your business. For example, you can deduct the cost of driving to perform work at a client's or customer's office. The value of this deduction often exceeds the value of the home business deduction itself. If you don't have a tax deductible home office, these costs are not deductible. (See Chapter 8 for a detailed discussion of the business mileage deduction.)

Profit Limit for Deductions

Unfortunately, there is an important limitation on the home office deduction: You cannot deduct more than the net profit you earn from your home office. If you run a successful business out of your home office, this won't pose a problem. But if your business earns very little or is losing money, the limitation could prevent you from deducting part or even all of your home office expenses in the current year.

If your deductions exceed your profits, you can deduct the excess in the following year and in each succeeding year until you deduct the entire amount. There is no limit on how far into the future you can deduct these expenses; you can claim them even if you are no longer living in the home where they were incurred.

So, whether or not your business is making money, you should keep track of your home office expenses and claim the deduction on your tax return. You do this by filing IRS Form 8829, *Expenses for Business Use of Your Home*. (See "IRS Reporting Requirements," below, for more on tax reporting.) When you complete the form by plugging in the figures for your business income and home office expenses, it will show you how much you can deduct in the current year and how much you must carry over to the next year.

The profit limitation applies only to the home office deduction. It does not apply to business expenses that you can deduct under other provisions of the tax code. To figure out your home office deduction, you need to know what portion of your total income is from your home office work. Tax preparation software can perform the calculations for you.

If your business is organized as a partnership, an LLC, or a corporation, the income limit still applies to your home office deduction. Your income when computing your allowable deduction is based on the gross income from your business allocable to your home office, minus all other deductions of the LLC, partnership, or corporation. IRS Publication 587, *Business Use of Your Home*, contains a worksheet you can use to calculate this amount.

Special Concerns for Homeowners

If you've taken the home office deduction, are there any tax consequences if you sell your home for a profit? Yes, but they don't outweigh the benefit of the home office deduction.

If your home office was located within your home, you do not need to allocate the gain (profit) on the sale of the property between the business part of the property and the part used as a home. This means that your entire profit qualifies for the special home sale tax exclusion.

Under this exclusion, a substantial amount of the profit you make on the sale of your home is not taxable: up to $250,000 of the profit for single taxpayers and $500,000 for married taxpayers filing jointly. You qualify for the exclusion if you lived in your home for at least two out of five years before you sell it. (See IRS Publication 523, *Selling Your Home*.)

> **EXAMPLE:** Richard, a single taxpayer, lived in his home for ten years and had a home office in a bedroom, amounting to 20% of the home. He sells the home for $100,000 profit. Since the office was within the walls of his home, his entire profit qualifies for the $250,000 exclusion and Richard owes no tax on it.

On the other hand, if your home office was not located inside your home—for example, it was in an unattached garage, cottage, or guest house—you must allocate your profit between the living and office portions of the home and pay taxes on the profits that you allocate to your office.

> **EXAMPLE:** Assume that Richard from the above example has his home office in an unattached garage, amounting to 15% of his total home. Since his home office was not within the walls of his home, he must allocate his $100,000 profit between the main home and office. He owes tax on the $15,000 of capital gains attributable to his office (15% x $100,000 = $15,000).

To avoid this, you should eliminate the office outside the walls of your home and move it inside your home at least two years before you sell it.

However, you will have to pay a capital gains tax on the depreciation deductions you took after May 6, 1997 for your home office. This is the deduction you are allowed for the yearly decline in value due to wear and tear of the portion of the building that contains your home office. (See Chapter 5 for more on deducting a long-term asset.) These recaptured deductions are taxed at a 25% rate (unless your income tax bracket is lower than 25%).

> **EXAMPLE:** Carmin bought a $200,000 home six years ago and used one of her bedrooms as her home office. She sold her home this year for $300,000, realizing a $100,000 gain (profit). Her depreciation deductions for her home office for the last six years totaled $2,000. She must pay a tax of 25% of $2,000, or $500.

Having to pay a 25% tax on the depreciation deductions you took in the years before you sold your house is actually not a bad deal. This is probably no more—and is often less—tax than you would have to pay if you didn't take the deductions in the first place and instead paid tax on your additional taxable income at ordinary income tax rates.

You can avoid such depreciation recapture if you use the new simplified method of calculating the home office deduction (see "Simplified Home Office Deduction Method," below). When you use this method, you deduct $5 per square foot of your home office and your depreciation deduction for the home office is deemed to be zero for the year. Thus, you have no depreciation recapture when you sell your home. Also, the adjusted basis of your home does not change.

Simplified Home Office Deduction Method

Lots of people who qualify for the home office deduction don't take it because they don't think it's worth the trouble or they are afraid it will result in an IRS audit. In a rare move to simplify life for taxpayers, the IRS created a simplified optional home office deduction method. It's important to understand, however, that all the regular rules for qualifying for the home office deduction still apply if you use the optional simplified method—that is, you must use a portion of your home regularly and exclusively for business.

How the Simple Method Works

The simple method really is simple: You deduct $5 for every square foot of your home office. Thus, all you need to do is measure the square footage of your home office. For example, if your home office is 200 square feet, you'll get a $1,000 home office deduction. That's all there is to it.

You don't need to figure out what percentage of your home your office occupies. You also don't need to keep records of your direct or indirect home office expenses such as utilities, rent, mortgage payments, real estate taxes, or casualty losses. These expenses aren't deductible when you use the simplified method.

Another big plus: You don't have to complete Form 8829.

Homeowners using the new option cannot claim a depreciation deduction for their home office. However, they can claim allowable mortgage interest, real estate taxes, and deductible casualty losses on the home as itemized deductions on Schedule A. These deductions need not be allocated between personal and business use, as is required under the regular method. Business expenses unrelated to the home, such as advertising, supplies, and wages paid to employees are still fully deductible.

Comparison of Regular and Simplified Home Office Deduction Methods

Simplified Method	Regular Method
Deduction for home office use of a portion of a residence allowed only if that portion is exclusively used on a regular basis for business purposes	Same
Allowable square footage of home used for business (not to exceed 300 square feet)	Percentage of home used for business
Standard $5 per square foot used to determine home business deduction	Actual expenses determined and records maintained
Home-related itemized deductions claimed in full on Schedule A	Home-related itemized deductions apportioned between Schedule A and business schedule (Sch. C or Sch. F)
No depreciation deduction	Depreciation deduction for portion of home used for business
No recapture of depreciation upon sale of home	Recapture of depreciation on gain upon sale of home
Deduction cannot exceed gross income from business use of home less business expenses	Same
Amount in excess of gross income limitation may not be carried over	Amount in excess of gross income limitation may be carried over
Loss carryover from use of regular method in prior year may not be claimed	Loss carryover from use of regular method in prior year may be claimed if gross income test is met in current year

When you use the simplified method, your home office deduction is capped at $1,500 per year. You'll reach the cap if your home office is 300 square feet. Thus, for example, if your home office is 400 square feet, you'll still be limited to a $1,500 home office deduction if you use the simplified method. You can't carry over any part of the deduction to future years.

As with the regular home office deduction, your total annual deduction using the simplified method is limited to the gross income you earned from the business use of your home during the year. Moreover, if you use the simplified method, you can't carry over any excess to a future tax year—something you can do when you use the regular method. Nor can you deduct amounts carried over from past years that you couldn't deduct using the regular method. For this reason, you should never use the simplified method if the profit from your business for the year is less than the amount of your simplified home office deduction.

You may choose either the simplified method or the regular method for any year. You choose your method by using it on your timely filed, original federal income tax return for the year. Once you have chosen a method for a tax year, you cannot later change to the other method for that same year. If you use the simplified method for one year and use the regular method for any subsequent year, you must calculate the depreciation deduction for the subsequent year using the appropriate optional depreciation table. This is true regardless of whether you used an optional depreciation table for the first year the property was used in business.

Is the Simplified Method a Good Deal?

Is it a good idea to use the new simplified home office deduction? Only if the deduction you could obtain using the regular method isn't much more than $1,500. Many people with home offices, particularly those who rent their homes, can qualify for a home office deduction much larger than $1,500. For example, a person with a 100-square-foot home office in a 1,000-square-foot apartment who pays $2,000 per month in rent and utilities would qualify for a $500 deduction using the simplified method (100 sq. ft. x $5 = $500), and at least a $2,400 deduction using the regular method (10% x $24,000 = $2,400). On the other hand, the simplified method may work out better for homeowners because they have no rent to deduct using the home office deduction and can still deduct their mortgage interest and real estate taxes as an itemized personal deduction on Schedule A (but the personal deduction for property tax is limited to $10,000 per year during 2018 through 2025).

If you're thinking about using the simplified method, you should figure your deduction using both methods and use the one that gives you the larger deduction. The regular method does require more record keeping than the optional method, but you probably keep these types of records anyway. Doing the required calculations and filling out the form can be challenging but will be much easier if you use tax preparation software.

IRS Reporting Requirements

IRS reporting requirements for the home office deduction differ depending on how you've legally organized your business.

Sole Proprietors

If you are a sole proprietor or owner of a one-person LLC, you deduct your business operating expenses by listing them on IRS Schedule C, *Profit or Loss From Business (Sole Proprietorship)*. You also list your home office deduction on Schedule C, but, unlike for any other operating expense deduction, you must file a special tax form to show how you calculated the home office deduction. This form, Form 8829, *Expenses for Business Use of Your Home*, tells the IRS that you're taking the deduction and shows how you calculated it. You should file this form even if you can't currently deduct your home office expenses because your business has no profits. By filing, you can apply the deduction to a future year in which you earn a profit. For detailed guidance on how to fill out Form 8829, see IRS Publication 587, *Business Use of Your Home*.

LLCs and Partnerships

If you organize your business as a partnership or multimember LLC, you don't have to file Form 8829. Instead, you deduct your unreimbursed home office expenses (and any other unreimbursed business expenses) on

IRS Schedule E (Part II) and attach it to your personal tax return. You must attach a separate schedule to Schedule E listing the home office and other business expenses you're deducting.

Any home office expense for which your partnership or LLC reimbursed you must be listed on the partnership or LLC tax return, IRS Form 1065, *U.S. Return of Partnership Income.* These deductions pass through to you along with other partnership deductions.

Deducting an Outside Office or Workplace

If you have an outside office or other workplace, your tax life is simpler than if you use a home office. The expenses you can deduct depend on whether you rent or own your workspace.

Renting an Outside Workplace

Virtually all the expenses you incur for an outside office, lab, workshop, studio, or other workspace that you rent for your business are deductible, including:

- rent
- utilities
- insurance
- repairs
- improvements
- real estate broker fees and commissions to obtain the lease
- fees for option rights, such as an option to renew the lease
- burglar alarm expenses
- trash and waste removal
- security expenses
- parking expenses
- maintenance and janitorial expenses
- lease cancellation fees, and
- attorneys' fees to draft a lease.

If you sign a net lease, you'll have to pay part (or all) of the landlord's maintenance expenses, property taxes, insurance, and maybe even mortgage payments. These payments are treated the same as rent.

A rental deposit is not deductible in the year it is made if it is to be returned at the end of the lease. However, if the landlord applies the deposit to pay rent you owe, make repairs, or because you've breached the lease, you may deduct the amount in that year.

None of the rules applicable to the home office deduction covered above apply to outside offices. Thus, unlike the home office deduction, there is no profit limit on deductions for outside rental expenses—you get your entire deduction even if it exceeds the profits from your business. You report rental expenses for an outside office just like any other business expense. You don't have to file IRS Form 8829, which is required when sole proprietors take the home office deduction.

Because you will ordinarily be in your office for more than one year, some of the expenses you pay may benefit your business for more than a single tax year. In this event, you might have to deduct the expense over more than one year instead of currently deducting it all in a single year. (This discussion assumes that you, like most professionals, are a cash basis taxpayer and use the calendar year as your tax year.)

Current Versus Multiyear Deductions

You may currently deduct any expense you pay for use of your office during the current tax year.

> **EXAMPLE:** This year, Leona paid $800 rent each month for the outside office she uses for her import-export business. The $9,600 she paid is fully deductible on Leona's taxes for the year. The rental payments were a current expense because they only benefited Leona for a single tax year.

But if an expense you pay applies beyond the current tax year, the general rule is that you can deduct only the amount that applies to your use of the rented property during the current tax year. You can deduct the rest of your payment only during the future tax year to which it applies.

> **EXAMPLE:** Last January, Steve leased an outside office for three years for $6,000 a year. He paid the full lease amount up front: $18,000 (3 × $6,000). Each year, Steve can deduct only $6,000—the part of the rent that applies to that tax year.

Subject to the exceptions noted below, these rules apply to office expenses, not just rent you pay in advance. For example, they apply to all expenses you pay to get a lease.

> **EXAMPLE:** Maxine pays $2,000 in attorneys' fees to draft her office lease. The lease has a five-year term, so the payment was for a benefit that lasts beyond the end of the following tax year. Thus, Maxine may not currently deduct the entire $2,000 in one year. Instead, she must deduct the $2,000 in equal amounts over five years (60 months). This comes to $33.33 per month. Her lease began on March 1 so she can deduct $333.33 for the first year (10 months × $33.33).

12-Month Rule

There is an important exception to the general rule that you may be able to use. Under the "12-month rule," cash basis taxpayers may currently deduct any expense in the current year so long as it is for a right or benefit that extends no longer than the earlier of:

- 12 months, or
- until the end of the tax year after the tax year in which you made the payment.

To use the 12-month rule, you must apply it when you first start using the cash method for your business. You must get IRS approval if you haven't been using the rule and want to start doing so. Such IRS approval is granted automatically. (See "Accounting Methods," in Chapter 15.)

Determining Your Lease Term

How long a lease lasts is important because it can determine whether you can currently deduct an expense or have to deduct it over the entire lease term. If you have to deduct an expense over the entire lease term, the length of the lease will determine the amount of your deduction each year. It might seem simple to tell how long a lease lasts: just look at the lease term in the lease agreement. However, things are not so simple if your lease includes an option to renew.

The IRS says that the term of the lease for rental expense deductions includes all renewal options plus any other period for which you and the lessor reasonably expect the lease to be renewed. For example, a one-year lease with an option to renew for five years would be a six-year lease for deduction purposes.

However, this rule applies only if less than 75% of the cost of getting the lease is for the term remaining on the purchase date (not including any period for which you may choose to renew or extend the lease). Sound confusing? It is.

The crucial question is how you figure out how much of the cost of the lease was for the original lease term and how much was for the renewal term or terms. The IRS says only that the lease costs should be allocated between the original and renewal terms based on the facts and circumstances. The IRS also says that in some cases it may be appropriate to make the allocation using a present value computation. In such a computation, a present value—a value in today's dollars—is assigned to an amount of money in the future, based on an estimated rate of return over the long term. You'll probably want an accountant to do this for you.

Improvements and Repairs

It's very common for commercial tenants to make permanent improvements to their offices—for example, they might install new carpeting or new walls. Landlords often give these tenants an allowance to make improvements before they move in. You get no deduction in this event. The landlord, not you, gets to depreciate improvements he paid for.

However, if you pay for improvements with your own money, you may deduct the cost as a business expense. You can depreciate the improvements, or treat the money you spent for the improvements as rent.

If you treat your expenses for improvements as rent, you deduct the cost the same as any other rent. Rent is deductible in a single year (unless it is prepaid in advance). This means you'll get your deduction much more quickly than if you depreciated the improvements over several years. However, if the cost of the improvement is substantial, part of the cost may have to be treated as prepaid rent and deducted over the whole lease term as described above.

Whether an improvement must be depreciated or treated as rent depends on what you and your landlord intended. Your intent should be written into your lease agreement.

In contrast to improvements, repairs may be currently deducted. The key difference between a repair and an improvement is that a repair merely returns property to more or less the state it was in before it stopped working properly. The property is not substantially more valuable, long-lived, or useful than it was before the need for the repair arose. In contrast, an improvement makes property substantially more valuable and/or long-lived or useful than it was before the improvement. Good examples of repairs include repainting your property, fixing gutters or floors, fixing leaks, plastering, and replacing broken windows. Examples of improvements include installing a new heating system, or putting on a new roof.

Modifying or Canceling a Lease

You might have to pay an additional "rent" amount over part of the lease period to change certain provisions in your lease. You must ordinarily deduct these payments over the remaining lease period. You cannot deduct the payments as additional rent, even if they are described as rent in the agreement.

The only exception to this rule is where the 12-month rule can be used. The lease will have to have a short term for the rule to apply.

Unlike the cost of modifying a lease, you can ordinarily deduct as rent an amount you pay to cancel a business lease.

Buying an Outside Workplace

If you buy an outside workplace, you may currently deduct as ordinary and necessary business expenses your mortgage interest, real estate taxes, and expenses associated with the purchase. In addition, you may depreciate the value of the real estate (not including the land) over 39 years. The cost of repairs can be currently deducted, but permanent improvements to the property must be depreciated. (See Chapter 5 for more on depreciation.) As with rental expenses, there is no profit limit on these deductions. Purchasing your workplace can help you qualify for the pass-through tax deduction if your income exceeds certain levels. (See Chapter 10.)

Car and Local Travel Expenses

That expensive car parked in your garage not only looks great—it could also be a great tax deduction. This chapter shows you how to deduct expenses for local transportation—that is, business trips that don't require you to stay away from home overnight. These rules apply to local business trips using any means of transportation, but this chapter focuses primarily on car expenses, the most common type of deduction for local business travel.

Overnight trips (whether by car or other means) are covered in Chapter 9.

RESOURCE

Different rules apply for corporate employees. This chapter covers local transportation deductions by business owners—sole proprietors, partners in partnerships, or LLC members—not by corporate employees. Starting in 2018, if you have incorporated your business and work as its employee, you may not deduct your work-related local transportation expenses on your personal tax return. Instead, you should have your corporation reimburse you for your expenses. See Chapter 11.

CAUTION

Transportation expenses are a red flag for the IRS. Transportation expenses are the number one item that IRS auditors look at when they examine small businesses. These expenses can be substantial—and it is easy to overstate them—so the IRS will look very carefully to make sure that you're not bending the rules. Your first line of defense against an audit is to keep good records to back up your deductions. This is something no tax preparation program or accountant can do for you—you must develop good record-keeping habits and follow them faithfully to stay out of trouble with the IRS.

Deductible Local Transportation Expenses

Local transportation costs are deductible as business operating expenses if they are ordinary and necessary for your business, trade, or profession. The cost must be common, helpful, and appropriate for your business. (See Chapter 4 for a detailed discussion of the ordinary and necessary requirement.) It makes no difference what type of transportation you use to make the local trips—car, van, pickup, truck, motorcycle, taxi, bus, or train—or whether the vehicle you use is owned or leased. You can deduct these costs as long as they are ordinary and necessary and meet the other requirements discussed below.

Travel Must Be for Business

You can only deduct local trips that are for business—that is, travel to a business location. Personal trips—for example, to the supermarket or the gym—are not deductible as business travel expenses. A business location is any place where you perform business-related tasks, such as:

- the place where you have your principal place of business, including a home office
- other places where you work, including temporary job sites
- places where you meet with clients or customers
- the bank where you do business banking
- a local college where you take work-related classes
- the store where you buy business supplies, or
- the place where you keep business inventory.

Starting a New Business

The cost of local travel you do before you start your business, such as travel to investigate starting a new business, is not a currently deductible business operating expense. It is a start-up expense subject to special deduction rules. (See Chapter 3 for more on start-up expenses.)

You don't have to do all the driving yourself to get a car expense deduction. Any use of your car by another person qualifies as a deductible business expense if any of the following is true:

- The use is directly connected with your business.
- The use is properly reported by you as income to the other person (and, if you have to, you withhold tax on the income)—for example, when an employee uses your car (see Chapter 11).
- You are paid a fair market rental for the use of your car.

Thus, for example, you can count as business mileage a car trip your employee, spouse, or child takes to deliver an item for your business or for any other business purpose.

Commuting Is Not Deductible

Most business owners have an office, workshop, store, lab, or other principal place of business where they work on a regular basis. Unfortunately, you can't deduct the cost of traveling from your home to your regular place of business. These are commuting expenses, which are a nondeductible personal expense item.

> **EXAMPLE:** Sue lives in a Chicago suburb and drives 15 miles each day to her office in a downtown Chicago building. These trips are nondeductible commuting expenses.

Even if a trip from home has a business purpose—for example, to haul tools or supplies to your office or other work location—it is still considered commuting and is not deductible. (You may, however, deduct the cost of renting a trailer or any other extraordinary expenses you incur to haul the tools or supplies from your home.)

Nor can you deduct a commuting trip because you make business calls on your cellphone, listen to business-related tapes, or have a business discussion with an associate or employee during the commute. Also, placing an advertising display on your vehicle won't convert a commute to a business trip.

Because commuting is not deductible, where your business office or other principal workplace is located has a big effect on the amount you can deduct for business trips. You will get the fewest deductions if you work solely in an outside office—that is, your principal workplace is away from home in an office building, industrial park, or shopping mall. You lose out on many potential business miles this way because you can't deduct any trips between your home and your office.

EXAMPLE: Kim, a marketing consultant, runs her business from an office in a downtown office building. Every day, she drives 20 miles to and from her suburban home to her office. None of this commuting mileage is deductible. But she may deduct trips from her office to a client's office, or any other business-related trip that starts from her office.

As explained below, you can get the most deductions for local business trip expenses if you have a home office.

You Have a Home Office

If you have a home office that qualifies as your principal place of business, you can deduct the cost of any trips you make from home to another business location. You can get a lot of travel deductions this way. For example, you can deduct the cost of driving from home to a client's office or to attend a business-related seminar. The commuting rule doesn't apply if you work at home because, with a home office, you never commute to work (you're there already).

Your home office will qualify as your principal place of business if it is the place where you earn most of your income or perform most of your business administrative or management tasks. (See Chapter 7 for more on the home office deduction.) If your home office qualifies as your principal place of business, you can vastly increase your deductions for business trips.

EXAMPLE: Kim (from the above example) maintains a home office where she does the administrative work for her consulting business; she also has an outside office where she does her other work. She can deduct all her business trips from her home office, including the 20-mile daily trip to her outside office. Thanks to her home office, she can now deduct 100 miles per week as a business trip expense, all of which was a nondeductible commuting expense before she established her home office.

You Have No Regular Workplace

If you have no regular office—whether inside or outside your home—the location of your first business contact of the day is considered your office for tax purposes. Transportation expenses from your home to this first business contact are nondeductible commuting expenses. The same is true for your last business contact of the day—your trip home is nondeductible commute travel. You can deduct the cost of all your other trips during the day between clients or customers.

> **EXAMPLE:** Jim is a Bible salesman who works in the Houston metropolitan area. He works out of his car, with no office at home or anywhere else. One day, he makes ten sales calls by car. His trip from home to his first sales contact of the day is a nondeductible commuting expense. His next eight trips are deductible, and his trip home from his last sales contact is a nondeductible personal commuting expense.

There is an easy way to get around this rule about the first and last trip of the day: Open a home office. That way, all of your trips are deductible.

> **EXAMPLE:** Jim creates an office at home where he performs the administrative tasks for his sales business, such as bookkeeping. He may now deduct the cost of all of his business trips during the day, including driving from home to his first business contact and back home from his last contact of the day.

You Go to a Temporary Business Location

Commuting occurs when you go from home to a permanent work location that is either:
- your office or other principal place of business, or
- another place where you have worked or expect to work for more than one year.

If you have a regular place of business, travel between your home and a temporary work location is not considered commuting and is therefore deductible. A temporary work location is any place where you realistically expect to work less than one year.

> **EXAMPLE:** Sally is a computer trainer with a regular office in a downtown office building; she does not have a home office. She is hired by Acme Corporation to teach their employees how to use a new computer system. The job is expected to last three months. Sally may deduct the cost of driving from home to Acme Corporation's offices to conduct the training.

A temporary work location is any place where you perform services on an irregular basis with the reasonable expectation that the work there will last one year or less—for example:

- a restaurant where you meet a client for a business discussion
- a weekend-long continuing education seminar in your town that you attend each day and then go home each night, or
- a client's office.

Places like the bank and supply stores do not qualify as temporary work locations because you don't perform work there; you're a customer at these locations.

You can convert a nondeductible commute into a deductible local business trip by making a stop at a temporary work location on your way to your office. Stopping at a temporary work location converts the entire trip into a deductible travel expense.

> **EXAMPLE:** Eleanor's business office is in a downtown building. She has no home office. One morning, she leaves home, stops off at a client's office for a one hour meeting, and then goes to her office. The entire trip is deductible because she stopped at a temporary work location on her way to her office.

Keep in mind, though, that making such stops is necessary only if you don't have a home office. If Eleanor had a home office, the commuting rule wouldn't apply and the trip would be deductible with or without the stop.

If you don't have a regular office, the rules about travel to temporary work locations are more restrictive. Without a regular office, you can deduct the cost of going from home to a temporary work location only if the temporary work location is outside your metropolitan area.

EXAMPLE: Artie is a cosmetics salesman with no regular office. He lives in Boston and regularly visits customers in and around the Boston area. He can't deduct any expenses for his local travel around Boston. One day he travels from his Boston home to New Haven, Connecticut, to see a customer. He goes back home that same day. Artie can deduct this trip because he traveled outside of his metropolitan area.

What constitutes a metropolitan area is not defined in the tax law, which leads to confusion and uncertainty. The basic rule is that a metropolitan area includes the area within the taxpayer's city limits and the suburbs that are socially and economically integrated with it. (*Wheir v. Commissioner*, TC Summary Opinion 2004-117.)

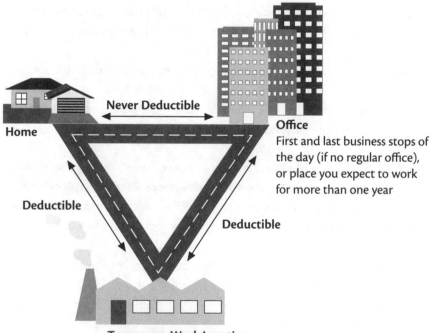

Never Deductible

Home

Deductible

Deductible

Office
First and last business stops of the day (if no regular office), or place you expect to work for more than one year

Temporary Work Location
If you have no regular outside or home office, trips to and from home are deductible only if temporary work location is outside metropolitan area of home.

Business Mileage Self-Test

See if you can figure out how many business miles were driven in each of the following examples.

1. John, a salesman with no home office, drives 25 miles to his downtown office in the morning, works all day, and then drives 25 miles back home. After dinner, he drives 30 miles to meet a client and then drives directly back home that night. Total business miles _____.

   Answer: 60. The trip to and from home to his office is nondeductible commuting, but the trip from home to the client and back is deductible because the client's office is a temporary work location for John.

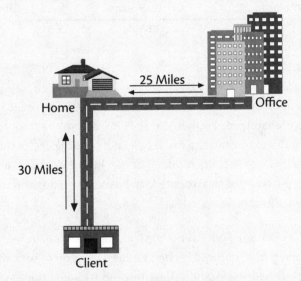

2. Sue is a freelance writer who works from home. She drives five miles to the grocery store and then heads off to the library five miles away to do research for an article. She then drives from the library back home, a distance of ten miles. Total business miles _____.

Business Mileage Self-Test (continued)

Answer: 20. This is a good example of how you can convert a personal trip into a business trip. Sue's trip to the grocery store isn't deductible, but her journey to the library is. Because the grocery store is en route to the library, she gets to deduct all ten miles (five to the grocery store; five to the library). It's ten miles back to her house from the library, so she gets a total of 20 business miles.

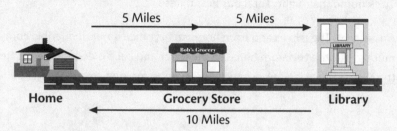

3. Nick is a bookie who works out of his car. One day he drives 20 miles from home to the racetrack. He then drives 15 miles from the track to the homes of three customers to make collections. At the end of the day, he drives ten miles to get back home. That evening, he drives 15 miles from home to the house of an associate for a business meeting and then drives back home. Total business miles _____.

Answer: 15. Because Nick has no fixed business location, he may not deduct travel from home to his first business location or back to home from his last business location. Thus, he cannot deduct the 20-mile trip to the track or the ten miles back home from the customer's house. Nor could he deduct the 30 miles round-trip later that night from home to the business meeting. He can only deduct the mileage for the two middle collection calls that he made.

Business Mileage Self-Test (continued)

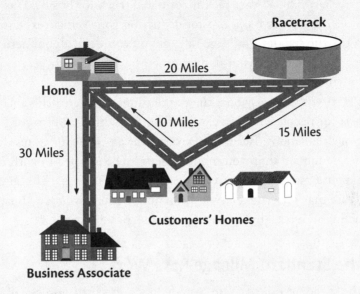

4. Gloria runs her home construction business from an outside office. She has no home office. One day she drives from home to a site 30 miles away where her company is building a house and then drives back home at the end of the day. The project is expected to last six months. Total business miles _____.

Answer: 60. Gloria is working at a temporary work location. Her travel from home to the building site is not considered commuting.

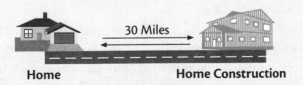

The Standard Mileage Rate

If you drive a car, SUV, van, pickup, or panel truck for business (as most people do), you have two options for deducting your vehicle expenses: You can use the standard mileage rate, or you can deduct your actual expenses. You can figure your deduction both ways the first year before deciding which method to use on your tax return.

Let's start with the easy one: the standard mileage rate. This method works best for people who don't want to bother with a lot of record keeping or calculations. But this ease comes at a price—it can result in a lower deduction than you might otherwise be entitled to with the actual expense method. However, this isn't always the case. The standard mileage rate may give you a larger deduction if you drive many business miles each year, especially if you drive an inexpensive car.

How the Standard Mileage Rate Works

Under the standard mileage rate, you deduct a specified number of cents for every business mile you drive. The IRS sets the standard mileage rate each year. For 2021, the standard mileage rate is 56 cents per mile.

To figure out your deduction, simply multiply your business miles by the standard mileage rate for the year. The rate is the same whether you own or lease your car.

> EXAMPLE: Ed, a self-employed salesperson, drove his car 10,000 miles for business during 2021. To determine his car expense deduction, he simply multiplies his business mileage by 56 cents. His deduction for 2021 is $5,600 (56 cents x 10,000 = $5,600).

The big advantage of the standard mileage rate is that it requires very little record keeping. You only need to keep track of how many business miles you drive, not the actual expenses for your car, such as gas, maintenance, or repairs.

If you choose the standard mileage rate, you cannot deduct actual car operating expenses—for example, maintenance and repairs, gasoline and its taxes, oil, insurance, and vehicle registration fees. All of these items are factored into the rate set by the IRS. And you can't deduct the cost of the car through regular or bonus depreciation or Section 179 expensing, because the car's depreciation is also factored into the standard mileage rate (as are lease payments for a leased car).

The only expenses you can deduct (because these costs aren't included in the standard mileage rate) are:

- interest on a car loan
- parking fees and tolls for business trips (but you can't deduct parking ticket fines or the cost of parking your car at your place of work), and
- personal property tax that you paid when you bought the vehicle, based on its value—this is often included as part of your auto registration fee.

Auto loan interest is usually the largest of these expenses. Unfortunately, many people fail to deduct it because of confusion about the tax law. Taxpayers are not allowed to deduct interest on a loan for a car that is for personal use, so many people believe they also can't deduct interest on a business car. This is not the case. You may deduct interest on a loan for a car you use in your business. This is a business interest expense deduction, not part of the mileage deduction.

If you use your car for both business and personal trips, you can deduct only the business use percentage of interest and taxes.

> **EXAMPLE:** Ralph uses his car 50% for his landscaping business and 50% for personal trips. He uses the standard mileage rate to deduct his car expenses. He pays $3,000 a year in interest on his car loan. He may deduct 50% of this amount, or $1,500, as a business operating expense in addition to his business mileage deduction.

Requirements to Use the Standard Mileage Rate

Not everyone can use the standard mileage rate. You won't be able to use it (and will have to use the actual expense method instead) if you can't meet the following requirements.

First-Year Rule

You must use the standard mileage rate in the first year you use a car for business, or you are forever foreclosed from using that method for that car. If you use the standard mileage rate the first year, you can switch to the actual expense method in a later year, and then switch back and forth between the two methods after that, provided the requirements listed below are met. For this reason, if you're not sure which method you want to use, it's a good idea to use the standard mileage rate the first year you use the car for business. This leaves all your options open for later years. However, this rule does not apply to leased cars. If you lease your car and you use the standard mileage rate for the first year, you must use it for the entire remainder of the lease period.

If you switch to the actual expense method after using the standard mileage rate, you'll have to reduce the tax basis of your car by a portion of the standard mileage rate deductions you already received. This will reduce your depreciation deduction. (See "Vehicle Depreciation Deductions," below.)

There are restrictions on switching back to the standard mileage rate after you have used the actual expense method. You can't switch back to the standard mileage rate after using the actual expense method if you took accelerated depreciation, a Section 179 deduction, or bonus depreciation on the car. You can switch back to the standard mileage rate only if you used the straight-line method of depreciation during the years you used the actual expense method. This depreciation method gives you equal depreciation deductions every year, rather than the larger deductions you get in the early years using accelerated depreciation methods. As a practical matter, once you switch from the standard rate to the actual expense method it's nearly impossible to switch back to the standard rate.

Five-Car Rule

You can't use the standard mileage rate if you have five or more cars that you use for business simultaneously. When the IRS says "simultaneously," it means simultaneously. You're barred from using the standard mileage rate only if you operate five or more cars for business *at the exact same time* (for example, in a fleet operation).

Corporation Employees

If you've incorporated your business and work as its employee, you can't use the standard mileage rate if:

- your corporation supplies you with a car, or
- you use your own car for business and your corporation reimburses you for your business mileage.

This rule applies to any employee who owns more than 10% of the company stock or is a close relative of a 10% or more owner—a brother, sister, parent, spouse, grandparent, or other lineal ancestor or descendent. In these instances, the employee must keep receipts for all business-related car expenses.

The Actual Expense Method

Instead of using the standard mileage rate, you can deduct the actual cost of using your car for business. This requires more record keeping, but it can result in a higher deduction. It all depends on the cost of your vehicle and how much you drive for business. As a general rule, the standard mileage rate results in a larger deduction if you drive many business miles, particularly if your car is cheap to operate. However, as a result of the Tax Cuts and Jobs Act, the actual expense method can result in much larger deductions than the standard mileage rate during the first several years you own a car.

Business Travel by Motorcycle

You must use the actual expense method if you ride a motorcycle or bicycle—the standard mileage rate is only for passenger vehicles. However, the limits on depreciation for passenger automobiles discussed in "Vehicle Depreciation Deductions," below, do not apply to bicycles or motorcycles. You may depreciate these items just like any other business property. Or, if you wish, you can deduct the cost of a motorcycle or bicycle in the year that you purchase it under Section 179 or the de minimis safe harbor deduction. (See Chapter 5 for more on Section 179.)

How the Actual Expense Method Works

As the name implies, under the actual expense method, you deduct the actual costs you incur each year to operate your car, plus depreciation. If you use this method, you must keep careful track of all the costs you incur for your car during the year, including:

- gas and oil
- repairs and maintenance
- depreciation of your original vehicle and improvements
- car repair tools
- license fees
- parking fees for business trips
- registration fees
- tires
- insurance
- garage rent
- tolls for business trips
- car washing
- lease payments
- interest on car loans
- towing charges, and
- auto club dues.

Watch Those Tickets

You may not deduct the cost of driving violations or parking tickets, even if you were on business when you got the ticket. Government fines and penalties are never deductible, as a matter of public policy.

When you do your taxes, add up the cost of all these items. For everything but parking fees and tolls, multiply the total cost of all items by your car's business use percentage. You determine your business use percentage by keeping track of all the miles you drive for business during the year and the total mileage driven. You divide the business mileage by your total mileage to figure your business use percentage. For parking fees and tolls that are business related, include (and deduct) the full cost. The total is your deductible transportation expense for the year.

> **EXAMPLE:** Laura, a salesperson, drove her car 8,000 miles for her business and a total of 16,000 miles. Her business use percentage is 50% (16,000 ÷ 8,000 = 50%). She can deduct 50% of the actual costs of operating her car, plus the full cost of any business-related tolls and parking fees. Her expenses amount to $10,000 for the year, so she gets a $5,000 deduction, plus $500 in tolls and parking for business.

If you have a car that you use only for business, you may deduct 100% of your actual car costs. Be careful, though. If you own just one car, it's usually hard to claim that you use it only for business. The IRS is not likely to believe that you walk or take public transportation everywhere except when you're on business. If you're a sole proprietor or owner of a one-person LLC, the IRS will know how many cars you own, because sole proprietors who claim transportation expenses must provide this information on their Schedule C.

Record-Keeping Requirements

When you deduct actual car expenses, you must keep records of all the costs of owning and operating your car. This includes not only the number of business miles and total miles you drive, but also gas, repairs, parking, insurance, tolls, and any other car expenses. Record keeping for car expenses is covered in Chapter 15.

Vehicle Depreciation Deductions

Using the actual expense method, you can deduct the cost of your vehicle. However, you can't deduct the entire cost in the year when you purchase your car. Instead, you must deduct the cost a portion at a time over several years, using a process called depreciation. (For more on depreciation generally, see Chapter 5.) Although the general concept of depreciation is the same for every type of property, special rules apply to depreciation deductions for cars. These rules give you a lower annual deduction for cars than you'd be entitled to using the normal depreciation rules.

The Tax Cuts and Jobs Act greatly increased the annual maximum depreciation deductions for vehicles starting in 2018. As a result, using the actual expense method may result in a much larger annual deduction for business mileage than the standard mileage rate (which doesn't allow a separate deduction for depreciation since it's included in the standard rate). This is especially likely if you purchase an expensive car and use it over 50% of the time for business.

> **EXAMPLE:** Jean purchases a $60,000 passenger automobile in 2021 that she uses 60% of the time for her real estate brokerage business. If Jean uses the actual expense method, she qualifies for a $10,860 depreciation deduction for 2021. She also gets to deduct 60% of what she spends to drive her car each year, including gas and repairs. She spent $2,000 on gas for her business driving, plus $1,000 for other business driving expenses so she adds this to her depreciation deduction for a total deduction of $13,860. If Jean uses the standard mileage rate instead, she can only deduct 56 cents for each business mile she drives that year. She would get no additional deduction for depreciation. If Jean drives 20,000 miles for business during year, her total deduction using the standard rate would be only $11,200.

Is Your Vehicle a Passenger Automobile?

First, you must figure out whether your vehicle is a passenger automobile as defined by the IRS. A passenger automobile is any four-wheeled vehicle made primarily for use on public streets and highways that has an unloaded gross weight of 6,000 pounds or less. The vehicle weight includes any part or other item physically attached to the automobile, or usually included in the purchase price of an automobile. This definition includes virtually all automobiles.

However, if your vehicle is classified as a truck or van by the manufacturer, it is a passenger automobile only if it has a gross loaded vehicle weight of 6,000 pounds or less. The truck or van classification can apply not only to traditional trucks or vans, but to other vehicles such as SUVs, minivans, and crossover vehicles. This is based on Department of Transportation rules that all car manufacturers must follow. The gross loaded weight is based on how much the manufacturer says the vehicle can carry and is different from unloaded weight—that is, the vehicle's weight without any passengers or cargo.

You can find out your vehicle's gross loaded and unloaded weight by looking at the metal plate in the driver's side doorjamb, looking at your owner's manual, checking the manufacturer's website or sales brochure, or asking an auto dealer. The gross loaded weight is usually called the Gross Vehicle Weight Rating (GVWR). The gross unloaded weight is often called the curb weight.

Vehicles that would otherwise come within the passenger automobile definition are excluded if they are not likely to be used more than a minimal amount for personal purposes—for example, moving vans, construction vehicles, ambulances, hearses, tractors, and taxis and other vehicles used in a transportation business. Also excluded are trucks and vans that have been specially modified so they are not likely to be used more than a minimal amount for personal purposes—for example, by installation of permanent shelving, or painting the vehicle to display advertising or a company's name. The restrictions on depreciation discussed in this section don't apply to these vehicles.

Passenger Automobiles Are Listed Property

All passenger automobiles are listed property: property that is often used for personal purposes. As explained in Chapter 5, the IRS imposes more stringent requirements on deductions for listed property to discourage fraudulent deduction claims. Because passenger automobiles are listed property, you must keep mileage records showing how much you use your car for business and personal purposes, and you must file IRS Form 4562, *Depreciation and Amortization*, with your annual tax return. (See "Records Required for Specific Expenses," in Chapter 15.)

Other Vehicles That Are Listed Property

Passenger automobiles are not the only vehicles that are listed property. Trucks, buses, boats, airplanes, motorcycles, and any other vehicles used to transport persons or goods are also listed property. The listed property rules apply to these vehicles even if they weigh more than 6,000 pounds and therefore don't qualify as passenger automobiles. However, some types of vehicles are not subject to the listed property rules, including vehicles not likely to be used more than a minimal amount for personal purposes (as described in "Is Your Vehicle a Passenger Automobile?," above) and any vehicle with a loaded gross vehicle weight of more than 14,000 pounds that is designed to carry cargo.

How Much You Can Depreciate

Your depreciation deductions are based on your total investment in a car (also called your "basis"). You multiply the basis amount by the percentage of business use of the car to determine the total amount you may depreciate. For example, if you use the car 100% for business, you may depreciate its entire basis. If you use it 50% for business, you may depreciate only 50% of its basis. You reduce the depreciable basis in the vehicle after each deduction is taken.

How you determine your car's basis depends on how you acquired it. If you buy a passenger automobile and use it for business that same year, your basis is its cost. You include the entire cost, even if you financed part of the purchase with a car loan. The cost also includes sales taxes, destination charges, and other fees the seller charges. It does not, however, include auto license and registration fees.

Before 2018, if you traded in an old car for a new one, you could elect to do a tax-free exchange in which the tax basis of the old car was subtracted from the cost of the new car. With such an exchange, there would be no tax due on the sale of the trade-in. However, the Tax Cuts and Jobs Act eliminated this type of treatment for cars and other personal property. Today, if you trade in an old car for a new one, you must treat the trade-in transaction as a taxable sale. You subtract the old car's tax basis (original cost minus depreciation deductions) from what the dealer pays you for it and pay tax on any gain (or deduct any loss).

> **EXAMPLE:** Phil owns a pickup truck he uses exclusively for his contracting business. He trades in the truck for a new model that cost $20,000. He paid the dealer $15,000 cash and received $5,000 from the dealer for trading in the old pickup. His old truck's adjusted basis was $4,000. Thus he earned a $1,000 profit on the trade-in on which he must pay tax at ordinary income rates. His starting basis in the new truck is $20,000.

If you convert a car that you previously owned for personal use to a business car, your basis in the car is the lower of what you paid for it (at the time you purchased it for personal use) or its fair market value at the time you convert it to business use. Your basis will usually be its fair market value, as this is usually the lower number. You can determine the fair market value by checking used car value guides, such as the *Kelley Blue Book*.

Annual Depreciation Limits for Passenger Vehicles

Depreciating a passenger automobile is unique in one very important way: The annual depreciation deduction for automobiles is subject to a maximum dollar limit. The Tax Cuts and Jobs Act greatly increased the annual limits for passenger vehicles. The amounts are shown in the following chart and they apply to all passenger vehicles, including automobiles, trucks, and vans that come within the definition. The chart shows that if you place a passenger vehicle into service and use it 100% for your business in 2021, you may take a maximum depreciation deduction of $10,100. The second year, you may deduct a whopping $16,100. That's $26,200 in depreciation deductions in the first two years—$34,200 if bonus depreciation is also claimed. These are by far the highest annual limits for passenger vehicle depreciation that have ever been allowed. In contrast, under prior law, only $3,160 could be deducted the first year and $5,100 the second year for passenger automobiles placed into service during 2017. The annual limits are now so high that only vehicles placed into service during 2021 that cost $50,000 or more are impacted.

Depreciation Limits for Passenger Vehicles Placed in Service in 2021 (must be reduced by percentage of personal use)	
1st tax year	$10,200 ($18,200 if $8,000 bonus depreciation claimed)
2nd tax year	$16,400
3rd tax year	$9,800
4th and later years	$5,860

This chart assumes 100% business use of the vehicle. If you use the vehicle for personal use as well as business use, the limits are reduced by the percentage of personal use. For example, if you use the vehicle 40% of the time for personal use, your annual deductions are reduced by 40%. Moreover, your actual depreciation deduction, up to the annual limit, depends on the cost of your car and how much you drive for business.

The depreciation limits are not reduced if a car is in service for less than a full year. This means that the limit is not reduced when the automobile is either placed in service or disposed of during the year.

Bonus Depreciation and Section 179 for Vehicles

Bonus depreciation may be used to deduct a substantial amount of an asset's cost the first year it is placed in service. For assets other than passenger vehicles, the bonus amount is 100% during 2018 through 2022. Bonus depreciation may be applied to passenger vehicles, but the bonus amount is fixed at a maximum of $8,000, no matter how much the vehicle costs. Thus, by using bonus depreciation, you can depreciate a maximum of $18,100 for a passenger vehicle first placed in service during 2021 instead of $10,100. However, you may use bonus depreciation only for new or used passenger vehicles you use more than 50% of the time for business purposes.

You may also use Section 179 expensing the first year up to the annual limit, but there is usually no point because you'll reach the limit using accelerated depreciation alone. Section 179 does not increase your deduction by one cent. In addition, due to a drafting error in the Tax Cuts and Jobs Act, if you use Section 179 the first year, you won't be allowed to take any additional depreciation deductions for the following five years. This error also affected car owners claiming the bonus depreciation deduction, but the IRS enacted a special safe harbor rule allowing them to take depreciation in years following the first year as described below. (Rev. Proc. 2019-13.)

When you claim bonus depreciation, Section 179 expensing, and/or accelerated depreciation for a vehicle, you must use the vehicle at least 50% of the time for business during the entire six-year recovery period. If your business use of a vehicle falls below 50% in the second through sixth years, you'll be subject to recapture. This requires you to recompute your depreciation deductions for the prior years using the straight-line method and add to your ordinary income the amount of depreciation you took in prior years that exceeded that amount. See Chapter 5 for more details on depreciation recapture.

Depreciation Methods for Vehicles

There are three regular depreciation methods that may be used for vehicles: two types of accelerated depreciation that provide larger deductions in the first two years, and straight-line depreciation. No matter which method you use, your deduction will be subject to the annual limits set forth above.

The following table shows how much of the cost of an automobile may be depreciated each year using the three regular depreciation methods and applying the half-year convention. (If more than 40% of all the depreciable property you placed in service during the year was placed in service during the last quarter of the year, you'll have to use the midquarter convention; see "Regular Depreciation," in Chapter 5.)

	Automobile Depreciation Table		
Year	200% Declining Balance Method (midyear convention)	150% Declining Balance Method (midyear convention)	Straight-Line Method (midyear convention)
1	20%	15%	10%
2	32%	25.5%	20%
3	19.2%	17.85%	20%
4	11.5%	16.66%	20%
5	11.5%	16.66%	20%
6	5.76%	8.33%	10%

If you use a business vehicle more than 50% of the time for business, you may use any of the three methods. Most people use accelerated depreciation wherever possible—preferably the 200% declining balance method. This way, you can deduct 71.2% of the tax basis (cost x business use percentage) of a passenger automobile costing $50,000 or less in the first three years.

If you use a vehicle less than 50% of the time for business, you can't take advantage of bonus depreciation, accelerated depreciation, or Section 179. Instead, you must depreciate the vehicle using the slowest method—straight-line depreciation—and you'll have to continue with this method even if your business use rises over 50% in later years.

> **EXAMPLE:** Jean purchases a $50,000 passenger automobile in 2021 that she uses 60% of the time for her real estate brokerage business. Her depreciable basis is $30,000 ($50,000 cost x 60% business use = $30,000 basis). Because she uses the vehicle more than 50% for business, she may use accelerated depreciation. Using the 200% declining balance method, her depreciation deduction for 2021 is 20% x $30,000 = $6,000, well within the $10,100 annual limit. Jean may also take bonus depreciation in 2021, which is an additional $4,000 deduction (50% of the $8,000 maximum bonus depreciation deduction). Her total 2021 depreciation deduction is $10,000. In 2022, she may deduct 32% x $30,000 = $9,600. In 2023, she may deduct 11.92% x $30,000 = $3,576. Thus, in the first three years she deducts $23,176 of her $30,000 basis.

How Long Do You Depreciate an Auto?

Because of the annual limits on depreciation and Section 179 deductions for passenger automobiles, you might not be able to deduct the entire cost of a car over the six-year recovery period. Don't worry: As long as you continue to use your car for business, you can keep taking annual deductions after the six-year recovery period ends, until you recover your full basis in the car. The maximum amount you can deduct each year is determined by the date you placed the car in service and your business use percentage.

If you sell an automobile before it's fully depreciated to a third party unrelated to you, you subtract its adjusted basis from the sales price to determine if you realize a gain (profit) or incur a loss. The adjusted basis is the car's original basis (cost + sales tax + improvements) minus each year's depreciation deductions. This means that, in effect, you must give back all the depreciation deductions you took on the car. If you realize a gain on the sale, the amount is taxed at ordinary income rates. If you incur a loss, the loss is deductible as a business expense.

Heavy Deductions for Heavy Metal: Bonus Depreciation for SUVs and Other Weighty Vehicles

The depreciation limits discussed above apply only to passenger automobiles—that is, passenger vehicles with a gross unloaded weight (curb weight) of less than 6,000 pounds. However, in the case of trucks and vans, the 6,000-pound weight limit is based on gross loaded weight. (See "Is Your Vehicle a Passenger Automobile?" above.) Vehicles that weigh more than this are not subject to the limits. Using bonus depreciation and/or Section 179, you may be able to deduct all or most of the cost of such a vehicle in a single year—a potentially enormous deduction for businesspeople who purchase heavy SUVs and similar vehicles for their business.

Bonus Depreciation

If a more than 6,000-pound vehicle is placed in service during 2018 through 2022, it will qualify for 100% first-year bonus depreciation. This means you can deduct 100% of the cost in one year if you use the vehicle 100% for business.

> **EXAMPLE:** Arthur purchases a $100,000 truck in 2019 that he uses 100% of the time for his hauling business. He may deduct the entire $100,000 cost in 2021 using 100% bonus depreciation.

If you use the vehicle less than 100% for business, you must reduce your deduction accordingly. However, you must use the vehicle at least 51% of time for business to use bonus depreciation.

> **EXAMPLE:** Bill purchases a 6,500-pound SUV for $50,000 in 2021. He uses the vehicle 60% of the time for his nursery business, thus his depreciable basis is $30,000 (60% x $50,000 = $30,000). He may deduct his entire $30,000 basis in 2021 with 100% bonus depreciation.

Section 179

The Section 179 deduction for SUVs placed in service during 2021 is limited to $25,900. For these purposes, an SUV is any four-wheeled vehicle primarily designed or used to carry passengers over public streets, roads, or highways that has a gross vehicle weight of 6,000 to 14,000 pounds. However, with bonus depreciation set at 100% during 2018 through 2022, there would appear to be little reason to use Section 179 for this purpose.

Auto Repairs and Improvements

Auto repairs and maintenance costs are fully deductible in the year they are incurred. You add these costs to your other annual expenses when you use the actual expense method. (You get no extra deduction for repairs when you use the standard mileage rate.) If you fix your car yourself, you may deduct the cost of parts and depreciate or deduct tools, but you get no deduction for your time or labor.

Unlike repairs, improvements to your car must be depreciated over several years, not all deducted in the year when you pay for them. What's the difference between a repair and an improvement? Good question. Unlike a repair, an improvement:

- makes the vehicle much better than it was before

- restores the vehicle to operating condition after it has fallen into disrepair, or
- adapts the vehicle to a new use.

EXAMPLE 1: Doug spends $100 to flush the carburetor on his business car. This expense simply keeps the vehicle in good running order. It does not make the car substantially better, restore it, or adapt it to a new use. So, the expense is a repair.

EXAMPLE 2: Doug spends $2,500 for a brand-new engine for his car. This is an improvement because it makes the vehicle much better than it was before.

Improvements to vehicles can often be fully deducted in a single year through bonus depreciation or Section 179 expensing (but only if a passenger vehicle is used more than 50% for business). The de minimis safe harbor deduction may be used for personal property expenses up to $2,500. The routine maintenance safe harbor allows you to fully deduct in one year the cost of any car parts (including installation) that could reasonably be expected to have to be replaced at least twice over the first five years the car is owned.

Improvements that must be depreciated over several years are depreciated separately from the vehicle itself—that is, they are treated as a separate item of depreciable property. The same rules apply to depreciating improvements as for regular auto depreciation. Depreciation of the original automobile and the later improvements are combined for purposes of the annual depreciation limits. The recovery period begins when the improvement is placed in service.

Leasing a Car

If you lease a car that you use in your business, you can use the actual expense method to deduct the portion of each lease payment that reflects the business percentage use of the car. You cannot deduct any part of a lease payment that is for commuting or personal use of the car.

> **EXAMPLE:** John pays $400 a month to lease a Lexus. He uses it 50% for his dental tool sales business and 50% for personal purposes. He may deduct half of his lease payments ($200 a month) as a local transportation expense for his sales business.

Leasing companies typically require you to make an advance or down payment to lease a car. You can deduct the business use percentage of this cost, but you must spread out the deduction equally over the entire lease period.

You get no depreciation deduction when you lease a vehicle, since you don't own the property. The lessor who owns the vehicle gets to claim depreciation, not the lessee. If you buy a vehicle you leased, you may claim regular and bonus depreciation. However, Section 179 expensing is not available on the purchase of a vehicle you leased because you used the property before you purchased it.

You always have the option of using the standard mileage rate instead of the actual expense method to deduct your business use of a leased car. If you choose the standard mileage method, you deduct a set amount per business mile. You don't get to deduct your lease payments. Whichever method you choose, you must stick with it for the entire term of your lease plus any extensions. You cannot switch.

When you lease a car for more than 30 days and use the actual expense method, you are required to reduce your deduction by a relatively small amount—called the inclusion amount—if the car exceeds a certain value. For vehicles placed into service in 2021, the inclusion amount will only apply to vehicles that cost over $50,000. The inclusion amount is calculated to make the lease deduction about the same as the depreciation deduction that would have been available if the automobile had been purchased. The IRS recalculates it each year. You can find the inclusion amount for the current year in the tables published in IRS Publication 463, *Travel, Gift, and Car Expenses.*

Other Local Transportation Expenses

You don't have to drive a car or other vehicle to get a tax deduction for local business trips. You can deduct the cost of travel by bus or other public transit, taxi, train, ferry, motorcycle, bicycle, or any other means. However, all the rules limiting deductions for travel by car discussed in "Commuting Is Not Deductible," above, also apply to other transportation methods. This means, for example, that you can't deduct the cost of commuting from your home to your office or other permanent work location. The same record-keeping requirements apply as well.

When Clients or Customers Reimburse You

Some small business owners have their local travel expenses reimbursed by their clients or customers. This is especially common for professionals, such as lawyers. You need not include such reimbursements in your income if you provide an adequate accounting of the expenses to your client and comply with the accountable plan rules. Basically, this requires that you submit all your documentation to the client in a timely manner and return any excess payments. Accountable plans are covered in detail in Chapter 11. Record-keeping rules for business driving are covered in Chapter 15.

> EXAMPLE: Erica, a sole proprietor accountant, is hired by Acme Corp. to handle an audit. She keeps a complete mileage log showing that she drove 500 miles while working on the audit. Acme reimburses Erica $267 for the business mileage. Erica need not include this amount in her income for the year. Acme may deduct it as a business expense.

If you do not adequately account to your client for these expenses, you must include any reimbursements or allowances in your income. They should also be included in any 1099 form the client provides to the IRS reporting how much you were paid. The client can still deduct the reimbursement as compensation paid to you. You may deduct the expenses on your own return, but you'll need documentation to back them up in the event of an audit.

EXAMPLE: Assume that Erica doesn't keep proper track of her mileage. At the end of the year, she estimates that she drove 500 miles on Acme's behalf. Acme reimburses Erica $267, but concludes she didn't adequately account for her expenses under the IRS rules. It deducts the $267 on its tax return as compensation paid to Erica, and includes the $267 on the 1099 form it sends the IRS the following February reporting how much it paid her. Erica deducts the $267 on her return as a business expense. Two years later, Erica is audited by the IRS. When the auditor asks her for her records showing how many miles she drove while representing Acme, Erica tells him she doesn't have any. The auditor disallows the deduction.

Reporting Transportation Expenses on Schedule C

If you're a sole proprietor or owner of a one-person LLC, you list your car expenses on Schedule C, *Profit or Loss From Business (Sole Proprietorship)*. Schedule C asks more questions about this deduction than almost any other deduction (reflecting the IRS's general suspicion about auto deductions).

Part IV of Schedule C is reproduced below. If you answer "Yes" to Question 45, you cannot claim to use your single car 100% for business. If you answer "No" to Questions 47a or 47b, you do not qualify for the deduction.

Part IV **Information on Your Vehicle.** Complete this part **only** if you are claiming car or truck expenses on line 9 and are not required to file Form 4562 for this business. See the instructions for line 13 on page C-5 to find out if you must file Form 4562.

43 When did you place your vehicle in service for business purposes? (month, day, year) ▶ ..../......../........

44 Of the total number of miles you drove your vehicle during 2009, enter the number of miles you used your vehicle for:

a Business .... **b** Commuting (see instructions) .... **c** Other ....

45 Was your vehicle available for personal use during off-duty hours? . . . . ☐ Yes ☐ No

46 Do you (or your spouse) have another vehicle available for personal use?. . . . . ☐ Yes ☐ No

47a Do you have evidence to support your deduction? . . . . ☐ Yes ☐ No

b If "Yes," is the evidence written? . . . . ☐ Yes ☐ No

How to Reduce Your Schedule C Auto Deduction

If you deduct the interest you pay on a car loan, you have the option of reporting the amount in two different places on your Schedule C: You can lump it in with all your other car expenses on Line 9 of the schedule, titled "Car and truck expenses," or you can list it separately on Line 16b as an "other interest" cost. Reporting your interest expense separately from your other car expenses reduces the total car expense shown on your Schedule C. This can help avoid an IRS audit.

You must also file IRS Form 4562, *Depreciation and Amortization.* This form is used to report your Section 179 and depreciation deductions for the vehicle.

Corporations, LLCs, and Partnerships

If your business is legally organized as a corporation, multimember LLC, or partnership, there are special complications when it comes to deducting car expenses. Moreover, you have the option of having your business own (or lease) the car you use, instead of using your personal car for business driving.

Using Your Own Car

If you use your own car for business driving, how your expenses may be deducted depends on whether your business is a corporation, an LLC, or a partnership.

LLCs and Partnerships

If you have organized your business as an LLC (with more than one member), you'll usually seek reimbursement for your deductible car and other local travel expenses from your business entity. You can use either the standard mileage rate or actual expense method to calculate your expenses.

As long as you comply with the record-keeping rules for car expenses and your reimbursement is made under an accountable plan, any reimbursement you receive will not be taxable income. Basically, you must submit all your documentation to the business in a timely manner and return any excess payments. Accountable plans are covered in detail in Chapter 11.

The business can deduct the amount of the reimbursed car expenses on its tax return (Form 1065) and reduce its taxable profit for the year. Or, in many cases, the business will obtain reimbursement from the client on whose behalf you did your local business travel.

> **EXAMPLE:** Rick, a partner in a CPA firm organized as an LLC, uses his personal car for local business driving. He uses the standard mileage rate and keeps careful track of all of his business mileage. He submits a request for reimbursement to the firm, along with his mileage records. He was entitled to a $4,050 reimbursement from his firm. This money is not taxable income to Rick, and the firm may list it on its tax return as a business expense or seek reimbursement from Rick's clients.

Instead of seeking reimbursement, you can deduct car expenses on your personal tax return, provided either of the following is true:

- You have a written partnership agreement or LLC operating agreement that provides that the expense will *not* be reimbursed by the partnership or LLC.
- Your business has an established routine of not reimbursing the expense.

Absent such a written agreement or established routine, *no personal deduction may be taken*. You must seek reimbursement from the partnership or LLC instead. If you take a personal deduction for your car expenses, your business does not list them on its tax return and they do not reduce your business's profits. But they will reduce your taxable income. (See Chapter 11 for a detailed discussion.)

You deduct your unreimbursed car expenses (and any other unreimbursed business expenses) on IRS Schedule E (Part II) and attach it to your personal tax return. You must attach a separate schedule to Schedule E listing the car and other business expenses you're deducting.

EXAMPLE: Assume that Rick's CPA firm has a written policy that all the partners must personally pay for their own car expenses. Instead of seeking reimbursement, Rick lists his $4,050 car expense on his own tax return, Schedule E, reducing his taxable income by that amount. The accounting firm does not list the expense on its return, and it does not reduce the firm's income.

Corporations

If your business is legally organized as a corporation (whether C or S corporation), you are probably working as its employee. Special rules govern all business expense deductions by employees. Your best option is to have your corporation reimburse you for your car expenses. You get reimbursement in the same way as described above for LLCs and partnerships. You must comply with all the documentation rules for car expenses and the accountable plan requirements. If you do, your corporation gets to deduct the expense and you don't have to count the reimbursement as taxable income. If you fail to follow the rules, any reimbursements must be treated as employee income subject to tax. (See Chapter 11.) If you are not reimbursed, you may not deduct your business mileage as a personal itemized deduction. The Tax Cuts and Jobs Act eliminated the deduction for all unreimbursed employee expenses, including mileage, for 2018 through 2025.

Using a Company Car

If your business entity buys a car that you use (that is, your business, not you, holds the title to the car), the dollar value of your business driving is a tax-free working condition fringe benefit provided to you by your business. In addition, the business gets to deduct all of its actual car expenses on its tax return—for example, depreciation, interest on a car loan, maintenance, fuel it pays for, and insurance costs.

You get no personal deduction for these expenses; but, of course, if your business is a pass-through entity, the deduction on its return will reduce the amount of taxable profit passed on to your tax return.

However, you can personally deduct the actual cost of fuel or maintenance you pay for yourself, and the cost of anything else you buy for the car. You can't use the standard mileage rate to figure your costs. You must keep track of your mileage using one of the methods described above; and, if you personally buy fuel or other items for the car, you must comply with all the documentation rules for car expenses, covered in Chapter 15.

> **EXAMPLE:** John, a veterinarian, is a one-third owner of a group business organized as an LLC. The LLC buys a $20,000 car this year that John uses 100% for business driving. He drove the car 6,000 miles. The LLC may deduct on its tax return all the expenses it incurs from owning the car:

Interest on car loan	$ 1,100
Depreciation	11,160
Fuel	1,200
Maintenance	1,000
Insurance	1,000
Total	$ 15,460

> John's LLC lists the $15,460 as a deduction on its tax return. As a result, instead of reporting a $300,000 annual profit, it has a $284,540 profit. John pays income and self-employment tax on his distributive share of this amount, which is one-third. John gets no personal deduction for these expenses, but he may personally deduct as a business expense the cost of fuel he paid for using his own money. This gives him a $400 deduction. John need not pay any tax on the value of having the car because it is a tax-free working condition fringe benefit provided to him by the LLC.

Things get more complicated if, as is often the case, you use a company car for both business and personal driving. The dollar value of your personal use of the car is treated as a taxable fringe benefit. The amount must be added to your annual compensation, and income, Social Security, and Medicare taxes must be paid on it.

EXAMPLE: Assume that John from the above example uses his company car 60% for business driving and 40% for personal driving. His LLC still gets the $15,460 deduction for its car expenses. However, the dollar value of John's personal driving is a taxable fringe benefit that must be added to his annual compensation. If the value of his personal driving was $5,000, he has to pay income and self-employment tax on this amount. He still gets to deduct the cost of fuel he paid for when he drove the car for business.

Here's a key question: How do you place a dollar value on your personal use of a company car? (This determines how much money must be added to your income for such use.) You may be able to use any of three different methods to figure this out, and they may yield very different results. The easiest way is to use the IRS Annual Lease Value Table, contained in IRS Publication 15-B, *Employer's Tax Guide to Fringe Benefits*.

If your company leases a car it provides you, all the rules above still apply. But with a lease, it's much easier to figure out the value of your personal use of the car—simply multiply the annual lease payments by the percentage of personal use.

CHAPTER

9

Business Travel

I f you travel overnight for business, you can deduct your airfare, hotel bills, and other expenses. If you plan your trip right, you can even mix business with pleasure and still get a deduction. However, IRS auditors closely scrutinize these deductions. Many taxpayers claim them without complying with the copious rules the IRS imposes. To avoid unwanted attention, you need to understand the limitations on this deduction and keep proper records.

What Is Business Travel?

For tax purposes, business travel occurs when you travel away from your tax home overnight for your business. You don't have to travel any set distance to get a travel expense deduction. However, you can't take this deduction if you just spend the night in a motel across town. You must travel outside your city limits. If you don't live in a city, you must go outside the general area where your business is located.

You must stay away overnight or at least long enough to require a stop for sleep or rest. You cannot satisfy the rest requirement by merely napping in your car.

If you don't stay overnight, your trip will not qualify as business travel and your expenses will not be deductible as business travel expenses subject to one exception for lodging expenses—see "IRS Rule on Deducting Lodging Expenses," below. However, this does not necessarily mean that you can't take a tax deduction. Local business trips, other than commuting, are deductible. However, you may only deduct your transportation expenses—the cost of driving or using some other means of transportation. You may not deduct meals or other expenses as when you travel for business and stay overnight.

RELATED TOPIC

For a detailed discussion of tax deductions for local business travel, see Chapter 8.

IRS Rule on Deducting Lodging Expenses

For decades, the rule has been that you can deduct business travel expenses, such as hotel or other lodging expenses, only when you travel away from your tax home overnight for your business. However, the IRS has created an exception to this rule. It now allows local lodging expenses—that is, hotel or other lodging expenses while an individual is not away from his or her tax home—to be deducted if all of the following apply:

- The lodging is necessary for the person to participate fully in, or be available for, a bona fide business meeting, conference, training activity, or other business function.
- The lodging lasts for no more than five calendar days and does not recur more than once per calendar quarter.
- In the case of an employee, the employer requires the person to remain at the activity or function overnight.
- The lodging is not lavish or extravagant and does not provide any significant element of personal pleasure, recreation, or benefit. (IRS Reg. § 1.162-32(a).)

EXAMPLE: Acme, Inc., conducts a three-day training session for its freelance salespeople at a hotel near its main office. Some salespeople attending the training are not traveling away from home. Acme requires all attendees to remain at the hotel overnight, at their own expense, for the bona fide purpose of facilitating the training. The salespeople may deduct the cost as a business expense.

Where Is Your Tax Home?

Your tax home is the entire city or general area where your principal place of business is located. This is not necessarily the place where you live.

EXAMPLE: Tim is a political lobbyist who maintains his office in Washington, DC. However, his family lives in New York City. He spends weekends with his family in New York and stays in a hotel during the week when he works in Washington. Tim's tax home is in Washington, DC. This means that when he travels back and forth between his Washington office and his New York home, his trips are nondeductible commuting. In addition, he gets no travel expense deductions while staying in Washington—for example, he can't deduct his hotel room or meals as a business travel expense. Because Washington, DC, is his tax home, he's not traveling while staying there.

The IRS doesn't care how far you travel for business. You'll get a deduction as long as you travel outside your tax home's city limits and stay overnight. Thus, even if you're just traveling across town, you'll qualify for a deduction if you manage to stay outside your city limits (or if you fall within the IRS exemption—see "IRS Rule on Deducting Lodging Expenses," above).

> EXAMPLE: Pete, a tax adviser, has his office in San Francisco. He travels to Oakland for an all-day meeting with a client. At the end of the meeting, he decides to spend the night in an Oakland hotel rather than brave the traffic back to San Francisco. Pete's stay qualifies as a business trip even though the distance between his San Francisco office and the Oakland business meeting is only eight miles. Pete can deduct his hotel and meal expenses.

If you don't live in a city, your tax home covers the general area where your business is located. This general area is anywhere within about 40 miles of your principal place of business.

Multiple Work Locations

If you work in more than one location, your tax home is your main place of business. To determine this, consider:

- the total time you spend in each place
- the level of your business activity in each place, and
- the amount of income you earn from each place.

> EXAMPLE: Lee, a dentist, has his own dental office in Houston, Texas. In addition, he works in his father's dental office in Dallas, Texas. He spends three weeks a month in Houston and one week in Dallas. He makes $150,000

per year from his Houston practice and $50,000 per year from his work in Dallas. Houston—where he spends more time and makes more money— is his tax home.

No Main Place of Business

Some people have no main place of business—for example, a salesperson who is always on the road, traveling from sales contact to sales contact. In this event, your home (main residence) can qualify as your tax home, as long as you:

- perform part of your business there and live at home while doing business in that area
- have living expenses at your home that you must duplicate because your business requires you to travel away from home, and
- satisfy one of the following three requirements:
  - You have not abandoned the area where your home is located— that is, you work in the area or have other contacts there.
  - You have family living at the home.
  - You often live in the home yourself.

EXAMPLE: Ruth is a liquor salesperson whose territory includes the entire southern United States. She has a home in Miami, Florida, where her mother lives. Ruth's sales territory includes Florida. She uses her home for her business when making sales in the Miami area and lives in it when making sales calls in the area. She spends about 12 weeks a year at home and is on the road the rest of the time. Ruth's Miami home is her tax home because she satisfies all three factors listed above: (1) She does business in the Miami area and stays in her Miami home when doing so; (2) she has duplicate living expenses; and (3) she has family living at the home.

Even if you satisfy only two of the three factors, your home may still qualify as your tax home, depending on all the facts and circumstances.

EXAMPLE: Assume that Ruth in the above example has the Northeast as her sales territory and does no work in the Miami area where her home is located. She fails the first factor but still satisfies the other two. Her Miami home would probably qualify as her tax home.

If you can satisfy none or only one of the three factors, you have no tax home. You are a transient for tax purposes. If you're a transient, you may not deduct any travel expenses, because you are never considered to be traveling away from home. Obviously, this is not a good situation to find yourself in, tax wise.

EXAMPLE: James Henderson was a stagehand for a traveling ice skating show. He spent most of his time on the road, but spent two to three months a year living rent free in his parents' home in Boise, Idaho. Both the IRS and the courts found that he was a transient for tax purposes because he failed to satisfy the first two of the three criteria listed above. Namely, he did no work in Boise and he had no home living expenses that he had to duplicate while on the road because he didn't pay rent to his parents. Thus, Henderson was not entitled to a tax deduction for his travel expenses. (*Henderson v. Commissioner*, 143 F.3d 497 (9th Cir. 1998).)

If you travel a lot for business, you should do everything you can to avoid being considered a transient. This means you must take steps to satisfy at least two of the three factors listed above. For example, James could avoid his transient status if he performed work in the Boise area, paid his parents for his room (thereby resulting in duplicate expenses), and spent more time at his parents' home.

Temporary Work Locations

You may regularly work at your tax home and also work at another location. It may not always be practical to return from this other location to your tax home at the end of each workday. Your overnight stays at these temporary work locations qualify as business travel as long as your work there is truly temporary—that is, it is reasonably expected to last no more than one year. If that is the case, your tax home does not change and you are considered to be away from home for the entire period you spend at the temporary work location.

EXAMPLE: Betty is a self-employed sexual harassment educator. She works out of her home office in Chicago, Illinois. She is hired to conduct sexual harassment training and counseling for a large company in Indianapolis, Indiana. The job is expected to last three months. Betty's assignment is temporary, and Chicago remains her tax home. She may deduct the expenses she incurs traveling to and staying in Indianapolis.

Even if the job ends up lasting more than one year, the job location will be treated as temporary and you can still take your travel deductions, if you reasonably expected the job to last less than one year when you took it. However, if at some later point, the job is expected to exceed one year, then the job location will be treated as temporary only until the earlier of: (1) when your expectations changed, or (2) 12 months.

EXAMPLE: Dominic, a self-employed computer expert who lived in Louisiana, took on a project as an independent contractor for a company located in Houston, about 320 miles away from his home. The project was expected to last nine to ten months, although Dominic was hired on a month-to-month basis. However, due to technological delays, the project ended up taking 13 months. The tax court held that Houston was a temporary work location for Dominic because he reasonably expected the project to last less than one year when he took it. Thus, the court held he was entitled to deduct his travel expenses from Louisiana to Houston for the first 12 months. (*Senulis v. Commissioner*, T.C. Summ. Op. 2009-97 (2009).)

On the other hand, if you reasonably expect your work at the other location to last more than one year, that location becomes your new tax home and you cannot deduct your travel expenses while there.

EXAMPLE: Carl is a plumbing contractor whose place of business is Seattle, Washington. He is hired to install the plumbing in a new subdivision in Boise, Idaho, and the job is expected to take 18 months. Boise is now Carl's tax home, and he may not deduct his travel expenses while staying there.

If you go back to your tax home from a temporary work location on your days off, you are not considered away from home while you are in your hometown. You cannot deduct the cost of meals and lodging there. However, you can deduct your expenses, including meals and lodging, while traveling between your temporary work location and your tax home. You can claim these expenses up to the amount it would have cost you to stay at your temporary work location. In addition, if you keep your hotel room during your visit home, you can deduct that cost.

Your Trip Must Be for Business

Your trip must be primarily for business to be deductible, and you must have a business intent and purpose before leaving on the trip. You have a business purpose if the trip benefits your business in some way. Examples of business purposes include:

- finding new customers or markets for your products or services
- dealing with existing customers or clients
- learning new skills to help in your business
- contacting people who could help your business, such as potential investors, or
- checking out what the competition is doing.

For example, a taxpayer who manufactured and sold weight-lifting equipment was entitled to deduct the cost of attending the summer Olympics in Rome because the purpose of the trip was to find new customers for his product line. (*Hoffman v. Commissioner*, 798 F.2d 784 (3d Cir. 1962).)

It's not sufficient merely to claim that you had a business purpose for your trip. You must be able to prove this by showing that you spent at least part of the time engaged in business activities while at your destination. Acceptable business activities include:

- visiting or working with existing or potential clients or customers
- attending trade shows or conventions, or
- attending professional seminars or business conventions where the agenda is clearly connected to your business.

On the other hand, business activities do not include:

- sightseeing
- recreational activities that you attend by yourself or with family or friends, or

- attending personal investment seminars or political events.

Use common sense when deciding whether to claim that a trip is for business. If you're audited, the IRS will likely question any trip that doesn't have some logical connection to your existing business.

Travel for a New Business or Location

You must actually be in business to have deductible business trips. Trips you make to investigate a potential new business or to actually start or acquire a new business are not currently deductible business travel expenses. However, they might be deductible as business start-up expenses, which means you can deduct up to $5,000 of these expenses the first year you're in business if your total start-up expenses are less than $50,000. (See Chapter 3 for more on start-up expenses.)

Travel as an Education Expense

You may deduct the cost of traveling to an educational activity directly related to your business. For example, a French translator can deduct the cost of traveling to France to attend formal French language classes. However, you can't take a trip and claim that the travel itself constitutes a form of education and is therefore deductible. For example, a French translator who travels to France may not take a business travel deduction if the purpose of the trip is to see the sights and become familiar with French language and culture. (See Chapter 14 for more on education expenses.)

Visiting Business Colleagues

Visiting business colleagues or competitors may be a legitimate business purpose for a trip. But you can't just socialize with them. You must use your visit to learn new skills, check out what your competitors are doing, seek investors, or attempt to get new customers or clients.

What Travel Expenses Are Deductible

Subject to the limits covered in "How Much You Can Deduct," below, virtually all of your business travel expenses are deductible. These fall into two broad categories: your transportation expenses and the expenses you incur at your destination.

Transportation expenses are the costs of getting to and from your destination—for example:

- fares for airplanes, trains, or buses
- driving expenses, including car rentals, and
- shipping costs for your personal luggage or samples, displays, or other things you need for your business.

If you drive your personal car to your destination, you may deduct your costs by using either the standard mileage rate or your actual expenses. You may also deduct your mileage while at your destination. (See Chapter 8 for more on deducting car expenses.)

You may also deduct the expenses you incur to stay alive (food and lodging) and do business while at your destination. Destination expenses include:

- hotel or other lodging expenses for business days
- taxi, Uber/Lyft, public transportation, and car rental expenses at your destination
- telephone and Internet expenses
- computer rental fees
- laundry and dry cleaning expenses, and
- tips you pay on any of the other costs.

You may deduct meals you eat alone while traveling on business or meals with business associates while traveling. Business associates include current or potential customers, consultants, clients, or similar business contacts. You (the business owner) or an employee must be present at the meal, but you don't have to eat anything if a business associate does. Ordinarily, meals are only 50% deductible; but restaurant meals are 100% deductible for 2021-2022 (see "Limits on Meal Expense Deduction" below).

You may not deduct entertainment expenses when you travel, even if you incur them for business purposes. So, you can't deduct the cost of a nightclub, concert, or ball game while on the road, even if you take a client or business associate along. The Tax Cuts and Jobs Act eliminated all such entertainment deductions starting in 2018. However, you can deduct the cost of a meal at an event like a ball game if you're separately billed for it.

Traveling First Class or Steerage

To be deductible, business travel expenses must be ordinary and necessary. This means that the trip and the expenses you incur must be helpful and appropriate for your business, not necessarily indispensable. You may not deduct lavish or extravagant expenses, but the IRS gives you a great deal of leeway here. You may, if you wish, travel first class, stay at four-star hotels, and eat at expensive restaurants. On the other hand, you're also entitled to be a cheapskate—for example, you could stay with a friend or relative at your destination to save on hotel expenses and still deduct meals and other expenses.

Taking People With You

You may deduct the expenses you pay for a person who travels with you only if that person:
- is your employee
- has a genuine business reason for going on the trip with you, and
- would otherwise be allowed to deduct the travel expenses.

These rules apply to your family as well as to nonfamily members. So, you can deduct the expense of taking your spouse, child, or other relative only if the person is your employee and has a genuine business reason for going on a trip with you. Typing notes or assisting in entertaining customers is not enough to warrant a deduction; the work must be essential to your business. For example, if you hire your son as a salesperson for your product or service and he calls on prospective customers during the trip, both your expenses and his are deductible.

So, this doesn't mean that you can't take any deductions at all when you travel with your family. You may still deduct your business expenses as if you were traveling alone—and you don't have to reduce your deductions, even if others get a free ride with you. For example, if you drive to your destination, you can deduct the entire cost of the drive, even if your family rides along with you. Similarly, you can deduct the full cost of a single hotel room even if you obtain a larger, more expensive room for your whole family.

EXAMPLE: Yamiko travels from New Orleans to Sydney, Australia, for her landscape design business. She takes her husband and young son with her. The total airfare expense for her and her family is $2,500. She may deduct the cost of a single ticket: $1,000. She spends $500 per night for a two-bedroom hotel suite in Sydney. She may deduct the cost of a single room for one person: $250 per night.

How Much You Can Deduct

If you spend all of your time at your destination on business, you may deduct 100% of your expenses (except meal expenses, which can be either 50% or 100% deductible—see "Limits on Meal Expense Deduction," below). However, things are more complicated if you mix business and pleasure. Different rules apply to your transportation expenses and the expenses you incur while at your destination ("destination expenses").

Travel Within the United States

Business travel within the United States is subject to an all-or-nothing rule: You may deduct 100% of your transportation expenses only if you spend more than half of your time on business activities while at your destination. If you spend more time on personal activities than on business, you get no transportation deduction. In other words, your business days must outnumber your personal days. You may also deduct the destination expenses you incur on the days you do business. Expenses incurred on personal days at your destination are nondeductible personal expenses. (See "Calculating Time Spent on Business," below, for the rules used to determine what constitutes a business day.)

EXAMPLE: Tom works in Atlanta. He takes the train for a business trip to New Orleans. He spends six days in New Orleans, where he spends all his time on business and spends $400 for his hotel, meals, and other living expenses. On the way home, he stops in Mobile for three days to visit his parents and spends $100 for lodging and meals there. His round-trip train fare is $250. Tom's trip consisted of six business days and three personal days, so he spent more than half of the trip on business. He can deduct 100% of his train fare and the entire $400 he spent while on business in New Orleans. He may not, however, deduct the $100 he spent while visiting his parents. His total deduction for the trip is $650.

Reimbursement for Business Travel Expenses

If a client or customer reimburses you for all or part of your business travel expenses, you get no deduction for the amount of the reimbursement—the client gets the deduction. However, you don't have to count the amounts you're paid as business income.

EXAMPLE: Clarence, a lawyer, travels from Philadelphia to Nashville, Tennessee, to try a case for his client, Acme Corporation. He stays two weeks and incurs $5,000 in travel expenses. He bills Acme for this amount and receives the reimbursement. Clarence may not deduct the cost of the trip. Acme may deduct the $5,000 as a business expense. Clarence need not report the $5,000 reimbursement from Acme as business income.

If your trip is primarily a vacation—that is, you spend more than half of your time on personal activities—the entire cost of the trip is a non-deductible personal expense. However, you may deduct any expenses you have while at your destination that are directly related to your business. This includes such things as phone calls or faxes to your office or the cost of renting a computer for business work. It doesn't include transportation, lodging, or food.

EXAMPLE: Tom (from the above example) spends two days in New Orleans on business and seven days visiting his parents in Mobile. His entire trip is a nondeductible personal expense. However, while in New Orleans he spends $50 on long distance phone calls to his office—this expense is deductible.

As long as your trip is primarily for business, you can add a vacation to the end of the trip, make a side trip purely for fun, or go to the theater and still deduct your entire airfare. What you spend while having fun is not deductible, but you can deduct all of your business and transportation expenses.

> **EXAMPLE:** Bill flies to Miami for a four-day business meeting. He spends three extra days in Miami swimming and enjoying the sights. Because he spent more than half his time on business—four days out of seven—the cost of his flight is entirely deductible, as are his hotel and meal costs during the business meeting. He may not deduct his hotel, meal, or other expenses during his vacation days.

Travel Outside the United States

Travel outside the United States is subject to more flexible rules than travel within the country. The rules for deducting your transportation expenses depend on how long you stay at your destination.

Trips of Up to Seven Days

If you travel outside the United States for no more than seven days, you can deduct 100% of your airfare or other transportation expenses, as long as you spend part of the time on business. You can spend a majority of your time on personal activities, as long as you spend at least some time on business. Seven days means seven consecutive days, not counting the day you leave but counting the day you return to the United States. You may also deduct the destination expenses you incur on the days you do business. (See "Calculating Time Spent on Business," below, for the rules used to determine what constitutes a business day.)

> **EXAMPLE:** Billie flies from Portland, Oregon, to Vancouver, Canada. She spends four days sightseeing in Vancouver and one day visiting suppliers for her import-export business. She may deduct 100% of her airfare, but she can deduct her lodging, meal, and other expenses from her stay in Vancouver only for the one day she did business.

Trips for More Than Seven Days

The IRS does not want to subsidize foreign vacations, so more stringent rules apply if your foreign trip lasts more than one week. For these longer trips, the magic number is 75%. If you spend more than 75% of your time on business at your foreign destination, you can deduct what it would have cost to make the trip if you had not engaged in any personal activities. This means you may deduct 100% of your airfare or other transportation expense, plus your living expenses while you were on business and any other business-related expenses.

> EXAMPLE: Sean flies from Boston to Dublin, Ireland. He spends one day sightseeing and nine days in business meetings. He has spent 90% of his time on business, so he may deduct 100% of his airfare to Dublin and all of the living and other expenses he incurred during the nine days he was in Dublin on business. He may not deduct any of his expenses (including hotel) for the day he spent sightseeing.

If you spend more than 50%—but less than 75%—of your time on business, you can deduct only the business percentage of your transportation and other costs. You figure out this percentage by counting the number of business days and the number of personal days to come up with a fraction. The number of business days is the numerator (top number), and the total number of days away from home is the denominator (bottom number). For ease in determining the dollar amount of your deduction, you can convert this fraction into a percentage.

> EXAMPLE: Sam flies from Las Vegas to London, where he spends six days on business and four days sightseeing. He spends six-tenths (or 60%) of his total time away from home on business. Therefore, he can deduct 60% of his travel costs—that is, 60% of his round-trip airfare, hotel, and other expenses. The trip costs him $3,000, so he gets an $1,800 deduction.

If you spend less than 51% of your time on business during foreign travel that lasts more than seven days, you cannot deduct any of your costs.

Side Trips

Expenses you incur if you stop at a nonbusiness (personal) destination en route to, or returning from, your business destination are not deductible. For example, if you stop for three vacation days in Paris on your way to a weeklong business meeting in Bangladesh, you may not deduct your expenses from your Paris stay.

Determining how much of your airfare or other transportation costs are deductible when you make side trips is a three-step process:

1. You must determine the percentage of the time you spent on vacation.
2. You multiply this vacation percentage by what it would have cost you to fly round-trip from your vacation destination to the United States.
3. You subtract this amount from your total airfare expense to arrive at your deductible airfare expense.

EXAMPLE: Jason lives in New York. On May 5, he flew to Paris to attend a business conference that began that same day. The conference ended on May 14. That evening, he flew from Paris to Dublin to visit friends until May 21, when he flew directly home to New York. The entire trip lasted 18 days, 11 of which were business days (the nine days in Paris and the two travel days) and seven of which were vacation days. He spent 39% of his time on vacation (7 ÷ 18 = 39%). His total airfare was $2,000. Round-trip airfare from New York to Dublin would have been $1,000. To determine his deductible airfare, he multiplies $1,000 by 39% and then subtracts this amount from his $2,000 airfare expense: $1,000 × 39% = $390; $2,000 − $390 = $1,610. His deductible airfare expense is $1,610.

Conventions

Your travel to, and stay at, a convention is deductible in the same manner as any other business trip, as long as you satisfy the following rules.

Conventions Within North America

You may deduct the expense of attending a convention in North America if your attendance benefits your business. You may not, however, deduct any expenses for your family.

How do you know if a convention benefits your business? Look at the convention agenda or program (and be sure to save a copy). The agenda does not have to specifically address what you do in your business, but it must be sufficiently related to show that your attendance was for business purposes. Examples of conventions that don't benefit your business include those for investment, political, or social purposes.

You probably learned in school that North America consists of the United States, Canada, and Mexico. However, for convention expense purposes, North America includes much of the Caribbean and many other great vacation destinations.

Foreign Conventions

More stringent rules apply if you attend a convention outside of North America (as defined above). You can take a deduction for a foreign convention only if both of the following are true:

- The convention is directly related to your business (rather than merely benefiting it).
- It's as reasonable for the convention to be held outside of North America as it is inside North America.

To determine if it's reasonable to hold the convention outside of North America, the IRS looks at the purposes of the meeting and the sponsoring group, the activities at the convention, where the sponsors live, and where other meetings have been or will be held.

As a general rule, if you want a tax deduction, avoid attending a convention outside of North America unless there is a darn good reason for holding it there. For example, it would be hard to justify holding a convention for New York plumbing contractors in Tahiti. On the other hand, it would probably be okay for a meeting of European and American brain surgeons to be held in Paris.

Travel by Ship

You can deduct travel by ship if a convention or other business event is conducted on board a ship, or if you use a ship as a means of transportation to a business destination. The following additional rules apply to travel by sea.

Shipboard Conventions and Seminars

Forget about getting a tax deduction for a pure pleasure cruise. You may, however, be able to deduct part of the cost of a cruise if you attend a business convention, seminars, or similar meetings directly related to your business while on board. Personal investment or financial planning seminars don't qualify.

But there is a major restriction: You must travel on a U.S.-registered ship that stops only in ports in the United States or its possessions, such as Puerto Rico or the U.S. Virgin Islands. If a cruise sponsor promises you'll be able to deduct your trip, investigate carefully to make sure it meets these requirements.

If you go on a cruise that is deductible, you must file with your tax return a signed note from the meeting or seminar sponsor listing the business meetings scheduled each day aboard the ship and certifying how many hours you spent in attendance. Make sure to get this statement from the meeting sponsor. Your annual deduction for attending conventions, seminars, or similar meetings on ships is limited to $2,000.

Calculating Time Spent on Business

To calculate how much time you spend on business while on a business trip, you must compare the number of days you spend on business with the days you spend on personal activities. All of the following are considered business days:

- any day in which you work for more than four hours
- any day when you must be at a particular place for your business—for example, to attend a business meeting—even if you spend most of the day on personal activities
- any day in which you spend more than four hours on business travel; travel time begins when you leave home and ends when you reach your hotel, or vice versa.
- any day in which you drive 300 miles for business (you can average your mileage). For example, if you drive 1,500 miles to your destination in five days, you may claim five 300-mile days, even if you drove 500 miles on one of the days and 100 miles on another.

- any day in which your travel and work time together exceed four hours
- any day you are prevented from working because of circumstances beyond your control—for example, a transit strike or terrorist act, and
- any day sandwiched between two workdays if it would have cost more to go home than to stay where you are. This rule can let you count weekends as business days.

EXAMPLE: Mike, a self-employed inventor who hates flying, travels by car from his home in Reno, Nevada, to Cleveland, Ohio, for a meeting with a potential investor concerning his latest invention: diapers for pet birds. He makes the 2,100-mile drive in six days, arriving in Cleveland on Saturday night. He has his meeting with the investor for one hour on Monday. The investor is intrigued with Mike's idea but wants him to flesh out his business plan. Mike works on this for five hours on Tuesday and three hours on Wednesday, spending the rest of his time resting and sightseeing. He has his second investor meeting, which lasts two hours, on Thursday. He sightsees the rest of the day and then drives straight home on Friday. Mike's trip consisted of 15 business days: 11 travel days, one sandwiched day (the Sunday before his first meeting), two meeting days, and one day when he worked more than four hours. He had one personal day: the day when he spent only three hours working.

Be sure to keep track of your time while you're away. You can do this by making simple notes on your calendar or travel diary. (See Chapter 15 for a detailed discussion of record keeping while traveling.)

Limits on Meal Expense Deduction

There are two ways to calculate your meal expense deduction: You can keep track of your actual expenses or use a daily rate set by the federal government. During 2021–2022, the actual expense method can give you a much larger deduction.

Deducting Actual Meal Expenses

If you use the actual expense method, you must keep track of what you spend on meals (including tips and tax) en route to and at your business destination. When you do your taxes, you add these amounts together to determine your total deduction.

> **EXAMPLE:** Frank goes on a business trip from Santa Fe, New Mexico, to Reno, Nevada. He gets there by car. On the way, he spends $200 for meals. While in Reno, he spends another $200. His total meal expense for the trip is $400.

If you combine a business trip with a vacation, you may deduct only those meals you eat while on business—for example, meals you eat while attending business meetings or doing other business-related work. Meals that are part of business entertainment are subject to the rules on entertainment expenses, covered in Chapter 10.

Ordinarily, you may only deduct 50% of the total cost of a business meal. So, for example, if a meal costs $100, you may deduct $50. However, in the wake of the economic devastation the COVID-19 pandemic caused to restaurants, Congress enacted a special rule for 2021 and 2022. During these years, you may deduct 100% of the cost of business meals and beverages purchased from restaurants. (IRC 274(n)(2)(D).) This special rule is intended to help restaurants get back on their feet.

For these purposes, a "restaurant" is a business that prepares and sells food or beverages to retail customers for immediate consumption, which includes everything from high-end French restaurants to McDonald's and Starbucks.

However, you don't have to eat the food at the restaurant to get the 100% deduction. You can order restaurant take-out while traveling and deduct the full cost. Likewise, you can deduct 100% of the cost of business meals ordered from restaurants through delivery services like Grubhub or Uber Eats.

"Restaurants" do not include businesses that predominantly sell prepackaged food or beverages for later consumption—for example, grocery stores, liquor stores, drug stores, specialty food stores, and vending machines. So, food or beverages purchased from these places while traveling is still subject to the 50% limitation. Hotel room service should qualify for the 100% deduction. But food or beverages you grab from a hotel minibar should be subject to the 50% limit.

> **EXAMPLE:** Frank from the above example spent $375 on food from restaurants and $25 for prepackaged sandwiches from grocery stores. He may deduct the entire $375 for restaurant meals, but only 50% ($12.50) of the cost of the grocery store food.

You do not necessarily have to keep all your receipts for your business meals, but you need to keep careful track of what you spend, and you should be able to prove that the meal was for business. Also, during 2021–2022, you should separately track your total costs for meals and beverages purchased from restaurants and those for meals from other places like grocery stores and liquor stores. See Chapter 15 for a detailed discussion of record keeping for meal expenses.

Using the Standard Meal Allowance

When you use the actual expense method, you must keep track of what you spend for each meal, which can be a lot of work. So the IRS provides an alternative method of deducting meals: Instead of deducting your actual expenses, you can deduct a set amount for each day of your business trip. This amount is called the "standard meal allowance." It covers your expenses for business meals, beverages, tax, and tips. The amount of the allowance varies depending on where and when you travel.

There is one good thing and two bad things about the standard meal allowance.

The good thing is that you don't need to keep track of how much you spend for meals and tips. You only need to keep records to prove the time, place, and business purpose of your travel. (See Chapter 14 for more on meal and entertainment expenses.)

One bad thing about the standard meal allowance is that it is based on what federal workers are allowed to charge for meals while traveling and is therefore relatively modest. In 2021, the daily rates for domestic travel ranged from $56 per day for travel in the least expensive areas to up to $76 for high-cost areas, which include most major cities.

Standard Meal Allowance Can't Be Used by Some Employees

The standard meal allowance may not be used by an employer to reimburse an employee for travel expenses if the employee:

- owns more than 10% of the stock in an incorporated business, or
- is a close relative of a 10% or more owner—a brother, sister, parent, spouse, grandparent, or other lineal ancestor or descendent.

In these instances, the employee must deduct actual meal expenses for business-related travel to be reimbursed by the employer. Thus, if you've incorporated your business and work as its employee, you must keep track of what you spend on meals when you travel for business and are reimbursed for your expenses by your corporation. (See "Reimbursing Employees for Business-Related Expenditures," in Chapter 11, for a detailed discussion.)

But the worst thing about the standard meal allowance is that your deduction is always limited to one-half of the allowance amount. You may not deduct 100% of the amount for meals purchased from restaurants during 2021–2022. In contrast, you can deduct 100% of the cost of restaurant meals with the actual expense method during 2021–2022.

EXAMPLE: Art travels from Los Angeles to San Francisco on business during 2021 and stays overnight. While in San Francisco, he spends $20 for breakfast, $25 for lunch, $40 for dinner at restaurants, and $5 for coffee from Starbucks. If he uses the standard allowance method, he may deduct 50% of the $76 actual expense allowance for San Francisco, which results in a $38 deduction. If he uses the actual expense method, he may deduct 100% of his actual costs for a $90 deduction.

If you use the standard meal allowance, you must use it for all of the business trips you take during the year. You can't use it for some trips and then use the actual expense method for others. For example, you can't use the standard allowance when you go to an inexpensive destination and the actual expense method when you go to a pricey one. If you travel to more than one location in one day, you must use the rate in effect for the area where you spend the night.

Because the standard meal allowance is so small, it's better to use it only if you travel exclusively to low-cost areas or if you are simply unable or unwilling to keep track of what you actually spend for meals.

Standard Meal Allowance Amount

The standard meal allowance is revised each year. You can find the current rates for travel within the United States on the Internet at www.gsa.gov. (Look for the link to "Per Diem Rates.") The U.S. Department of State sets the rates for foreign travel, which can be found at www.state.gov. When you look at these rate listings, you'll see several categories of numbers. You want the "M & IE Rate," short for "meals and incidental expenses," such as tips. Rates are also provided for lodging, but these don't apply to nongovernmental travelers.

Maximizing Your Business Travel Deductions

Here are some simple strategies you can use to maximize your business travel deductions.

Plan Ahead

Plan your itinerary carefully before you leave to make sure your trip qualifies as a business trip. For example, if you're traveling within the United States, you must spend more than half of your time on business for your transportation to be deductible. If you know you're going to spend three days on business, arrange to spend no more than two days on personal activities so this rule is satisfied. If you're traveling overseas for more than 14 days, you'll have to spend at least 75% of your time on business to deduct your transportation; you might be able to do this by using strategies to maximize your business days. (See "Maximize Your Business Days," below.)

Make a Paper Trail

If you are audited by the IRS, there is a good chance you will be questioned about business travel deductions. Of course, you'll need to have records showing what you spent for your trips. (See Chapter 15 for a detailed discussion on record keeping.) However, you'll also need documents proving that your trip was for your existing business. You can do this by:

- making a note in your calendar or daily planner of every business meeting you attend or other business-related work you do—being sure to note the time you spend on each business activity
- obtaining and saving business cards from anyone you meet while on business
- noting in your calendar or daily planner the names of all the people you meet for business on your trip
- keeping the program or agenda from a convention or training seminar you attend, as well as any notes you made
- after you return, sending thank-you notes or emails to the business contacts you met on your trips—being sure to keep copies, and
- keeping copies of business-related correspondence or emails you sent or received before the trip.

Maximize Your Business Days

If you mix business with pleasure on your trip, you have to make sure that you have enough business days to deduct your transportation costs. You'll need to spend more than 50% of your days on business for domestic trips and more than 75% for foreign trips of more than 14 days.

You don't have to work all day for that day to count as a business day: Any day in which you work at least four hours is a business day, even if you goof off the rest of the time. The day will count as a business day for purposes of determining whether your transportation expenses are deductible, and you can deduct your lodging, meal, and other expenses during the day, even though you worked only four hours.

You can easily maximize your business days by taking advantage of this rule. For example, you can:

- work no more than four hours in any one day whenever possible

- spread your business over several days—for example, if you need to be present at three meetings, try to spread them over two or three days instead of one, and
- avoid using the fastest form of transportation to your business destination—travel days count as business days, so you'll add business days to your trip if you drive instead of fly. Remember, there's no law that says you have to take the quickest means of transportation to your destination.

Take Advantage of the Sandwich Day Rule

IRS rules provide that days when you do no business-related work count as business days when they are sandwiched between workdays, as long as it's cheaper to spend the off days away than to go back home for them. If you work on Friday and Monday, this rule allows you to count the weekend as business days, even though you did no work.

> EXAMPLE: Kim flies from Houston to Honolulu, Hawaii, for a business convention. She arrives on Wednesday and returns the following Wednesday. She does not attend any convention activities during the weekend and goes to the beach instead. Nevertheless, because it was cheaper for her to stay in Hawaii than to fly back to Houston just for the weekend and fly back to Hawaii, she may count Saturday and Sunday as business days. This means she can deduct her lodging and meal expenses for those days (but not the cost of renting a surfboard).

How to Deduct Travel Expenses

How you deduct your travel expenses depends on how your business is legally organized. If you're a sole proprietor, you deduct your expenses on your personal tax return. However, if your business is an LLC or a partnership, your expenses may have to be deducted on the LLC or partnership return, not your personal tax return. If your business is a corporation, any personal deduction will be limited.

Sole Proprietors

If you're a sole proprietor or owner of a one-person LLC, you will list your travel expenses on Schedule C, *Profit or Loss From Business (Sole Proprietorship)*. Travel expenses other than meals are listed on Line 24a. Meals are listed on Lines 24b–d. You list the full amount of meal expenses, but only deduct 50% of the total.

Partnerships and LLCs

If your business is organized as a multimember LLC or partnership, it will ordinarily be taxed as a partnership. Your business can reimburse you for your travel expenses and then deduct them on its tax return; or, in some cases, you can deduct them on your own return.

You're Reimbursed for Your Expenses

Unless one very important exception, noted below, applies, you'll have to seek reimbursement for your deductible travel expenses from your business. The amount of the reimbursement is not taxable income to you, provided you comply with all required record-keeping rules for car expenses, and the reimbursement is made under an accountable plan. Basically, this requires that you submit all your documentation to the business in a timely manner and return any excess payments. Accountable plans are covered in detail in Chapter 11. The amount of the reimbursed travel expenses is listed on the partnership's tax return (Form 1065) and reduces its taxable profit for the year.

> EXAMPLE: Rick, co-owner of a construction business organized as an LLC, flies from Chicago to St. Paul to attend a two-day seminar on marketing for construction contractors. He incurs $1,500 in travel expenses. He keeps careful track of all of his expenses. After he gets back, he submits a request for reimbursement from the LLC, along with an expense report and all required receipts. The LLC pays him the $1,500. This money is not taxable income to Rick and the LLC may list it on its tax return as a business expense.

You Take a Personal Deduction for Your Expenses

The exception to the reimbursement rule permits you to deduct your car expenses on your personal tax return. But this is allowed only if: (1) A written partnership agreement or LLC operating agreement provides that the expense will *not* be reimbursed by the partnership or LLC, or (2) your business has an established routine of not reimbursing the expense. Absent such a written statement or routine, *no personal deduction may be taken*. Reimbursement from the partnership or LLC must be sought instead. If you take a personal deduction for your car expenses, your business does not list them on its tax return and they do not reduce your business's profits. But they will reduce your taxable income. (See Chapter 11.)

You deduct your unreimbursed car expenses (and any other unreimbursed business expenses) on IRS Schedule E (Part II) and attach it to your personal tax return. Don't use Schedule C. You must attach a separate schedule to Schedule E listing the car and other business expenses you're deducting.

> EXAMPLE: Assume that Rick's LLC has a written policy that all the company's owners must personally pay for their own travel expenses. Instead of seeking reimbursement, Rick lists his $1,500 travel expense on his own tax return, Schedule E, reducing his taxable income by that amount. The LLC does not list the expense on its return, thus it does not reduce the business's income.

Corporations

If your business is legally organized as a corporation (whether C or S corporation), you will ordinarily be its employee. The Tax Cuts and Jobs Act eliminated all deductions for unreimbursed job expenses by employees starting in 2018. Thus, your best option is to have your corporation reimburse you for your travel expenses. This process is the same as for LLCs and partnerships, described above. If you comply with all the documentation rules for car expenses and accountable plan requirements, your corporation gets to deduct the expense on its tax return and you don't have to count the reimbursement as income. If you fail to follow the rules, any reimbursements must be treated as employee income subject to tax (and you won't be able to deduct your expenses on your personal tax return).

Travel Expenses Reimbursed by Clients or Customers

Business owners who travel while performing services for a client or customer often have their expenses reimbursed by the client. You need not include such reimbursements in your income if you provide an adequate accounting of the expenses to your client and comply with the accountable plan rules. Basically, this requires that you submit all your documentation to the client in a timely manner, and return any excess payments. Accountable plans are covered in detail in Chapter 11. Record-keeping rules for long distance travel are covered in Chapter 15.

> **EXAMPLE:** Farley, an architect, incurs $5,000 in travel expenses while working on a new shopping center for a client. He keeps complete and accurate records of his expenses and provides it to his client, who reimburses him the $5,000. Farley need not include the $5,000 in his income for the year. Farley's client may deduct the reimbursement as a business expense.

If you do not adequately account to your client for these expenses, you must include any reimbursements or allowances in your income, and they should also be included in any 1099 form the client is required to provide to the IRS reporting how much you were paid (see Chapter 11). The client can still deduct the reimbursement as compensation paid to you. You may deduct the expenses on your own return, but you'll need documentation to back them up in the event of an audit.

The Pass-Through Tax Deduction

The Tax Cuts and Jobs Act established a new income tax deduction for owners of pass-through businesses. This is commonly referred to as the pass-through deduction or qualified business income (QBI) deduction. Pass-through owners who qualify can deduct up to 20% of their net business income from their income taxes, reducing their effective income tax rate by 20%. The deduction was intended to avoid placing pass-through owners at a disadvantage compared with regular C corporations, whose tax rate was lowered to a flat rate of 21% by the Tax Cuts and Jobs Act.

This deduction began in 2018 and is scheduled to last through 2025, unless it is extended (or earlier terminated) by Congress. Here are the basic requirements you must satisfy to qualify for this complex deduction.

You Must Have a Pass-Through Business

You have to have a pass-through business to qualify for this deduction. A pass-through business is any business that is owned and operated through a pass-through business entity. This includes any business that is:

- a sole proprietorship (a one-owner business in which the owner personally owns all the business assets; technically, a proprietorship is not a "pass-through entity" but it still qualifies for the deduction)
- a partnership
- an S corporation
- a limited liability company (LLC), or
- a limited liability partnership (LLP).

For tax purposes, what distinguishes these type of businesses is that they pay no taxes themselves. Instead, the profits (or losses) from these businesses are passed through the business and the owners pay tax on the money on their individual tax returns at their individual tax rates. The vast majority of smaller businesses are pass-through entities. Indeed, over 86% of all businesses without employees are sole proprietorships.

Regular C corporations do not qualify for this deduction; however, starting in 2018, they do qualify for a flat 21% corporate tax rate.

Employees may not take this deduction from their employment income. However, if you've formed an S corporation for your business and work as its employee, you may take the deduction from your corporate distributions.

Should Employees Become Independent Contractors?

Some employees may be tempted to have their employers reclassify them as independent contractors because independent contractors who are sole proprietors can qualify for the pass-through deduction. This is highly problematic. IRS regulations make it clear that employees cannot get the deduction simply by having their employers reclassify them as independent contractors. The regulations provide that if a worker is reclassified as a contractor but continues to perform the same work directly or indirectly for the hiring firm, the IRS will presume that worker doesn't qualify for the pass-through deduction for the next three years. This presumption can be overcome only by convincing the IRS that the worker really qualifies as an independent contractor.

As discussed in detail in Chapter 11, to qualify as an independent contractor, you must be operating your own independent business. You should market your services to the public, have multiple clients, incur business expenses, and have a risk of losing money. The hiring firm can't control you on the job the way it does employees. You also can't receive employee benefits like health insurance and paid vacations.

You can't "quit" your job and continue to do the same work full time for the same hiring firm in the same way year after year and qualify as an independent contractor. Your employer would be crazy to reclassify you as an independent contractor under such circumstances because it could be subject to severe fines and penalties for worker misclassification. If you quit your job and start a real independent business, you can qualify for the pass-through deduction. You can continue to do some work for your old employer, but you should have other clients as well. The new pass-through deduction makes the rewards of starting your own independent business greater than ever—presumably, the intended purpose of the deduction.

You Must Have Qualified Business Income

Individuals who earn income through pass-through businesses may qualify to deduct from their income tax up to 20% of their "qualified business income" ("QBI") from each pass-through business they own—however, your actual deduction may be less depending on your taxable income and occupation. (I.R.C. § 199A.) QBI is the net income (profit) your pass-through business earns during the year. You determine this by subtracting all your regular business deductions from your total business income.

QBI does not include:

- short-term or long-term capital gain or loss—for example, the capital gain (or loss) earned from selling business property
- dividend income
- interest income
- wages paid to S corporation shareholders
- guaranteed payments to partners in partnerships or LLC members, or
- business income earned outside the United States.

If you're a member of a multimember LLC, a partnership, an LLP, or an S corporation, your QBI is determined at the shareholder-partner level. This means each shareholder, partner or other owner takes into account his or her pro rata share of the pass-through business's income, deductions, gains, and losses.

Ordinarily, QBI is determined separately for each separate business you own (but nonservice business owners have the option of combining multiple businesses; see below). If you have a qualified business loss—that is, your net QBI is zero or less—you get no pass-through deduction for the year. Any loss is carried forward to the next year and the pass-through deduction for that next year (or the next future year with positive QBI) is reduced (but not below zero) by 20% of the loss.

> **EXAMPLE:** During 2021, George earned $20,000 in QBI from his bitcoin mining business and had a $50,000 loss from his bakery business. He has a $30,000 qualified business loss, so he gets no pass-through deduction for 2021 and his loss must be carried forward to 2022. His pass-through deduction for 2022 must be reduced by 20% of his $30,000 loss, or $6,000.

You Must Have Taxable Income

To determine your pass-through deduction, you must first figure your total taxable income for the year (not counting the pass-through deduction). This is your total taxable income from all sources (business, investment, and job income) minus deductions, including the standard deduction ($12,550 for singles; $25,100 for marrieds filing jointly in 2021). However, you do not include net capital gains for the year in your taxable income (such amounts already receive preferential tax treatment). If you're married and file jointly, include your spouse's income in your taxable income.

Your pass-through deduction can never exceed 20% of your taxable income. This limitation will apply (and reduce your pass-through deduction to less than 20% of QBI) if you don't have enough nonbusiness income to offset your personal deductions that reduce your taxable income below the amount of your qualified business income.

> **EXAMPLE:** Larry earned $100,000 in profit from his consulting business in 2021. He had no other income and took the standard deduction. His taxable income is $87,450 ($100,000 − $12,550 standard deduction = $87,450). Even though Larry had $100,000 in QBI, his pass-through deduction cannot exceed 20% of $87,450, or $17,490. If Larry had $12,550 in additional nonbusiness income, he would have had $100,000 in taxable income and qualified for the full 20% of QBI deduction, or $20,000.

Deduction for Taxable Income Up to $164,900 ($329,800 if Married)

If your 2021 taxable income is at or below $164,900 if single, or $329,800 if married filing jointly, your pass-through deduction is equal to 20% of your qualified business income (QBI). However, as discussed above, the deduction may not exceed 20% of your taxable income.

EXAMPLE: Tom is single and operates his public relations business as a sole proprietorship. His business earns $100,000 in qualified business income during 2021. He also earned $32,550 in investment income and took the $12,550 standard deduction. His total taxable income for the year is $120,000 (($100,000 + $32,550) − $12,550 = $120,000). His pass-through deduction is 20% x $100,000 = $20,000. He may deduct $20,000 from his income taxes.

If your taxable income is at or below the $164,900/$329,800 thresholds, that's all there is to the pass-through deduction. You're effectively taxed on only 80% of your business income.

Deduction for Income Above $164,900 ($329,800 if Married)

If your 2021 taxable income exceeds $164,900 if single, or $329,800 if married, calculating your deduction is much more complicated and depends on your total income, the type of work you do, and whether you have employees or business property.

Are You a Specified Service Business?

First of all, you need to determine whether your business is a "specified service trade or business" or SSTB. SSTBs are not favored under the pass-through deduction. Indeed, they lose the deduction entirely at certain income levels. There are no such limitations on pass-through owners who are not specified service businesses.

There are several specific types of business activities that are SSTBs, and one "catch-all" category. These are shown in the following chart.

There is a final catchall category that includes any business where the *principal* asset is the reputation or skill of one or more of its owners or employees. IRS regulations very narrowly define the catch-all category to include only cases where a person:

- receives fees or other income for endorsing products or services
- licenses that person's image, likeness, name, signature, voice, or trademark, or
- receives fees or other income for appearing at an event or on radio, television, or another media format.

Specified Service Trades or Businesses ("SSTB")		
Business Activity	**SSTB**	**Not SSTB**
Health	Doctors, pharmacists, nurses, dentists, veterinarians, physical therapists, psychologists, and similar healthcare professionals (it is not necessary to provide medical services directly to patients)	People who provide services not directly related to medicine, even though they might improve health, such as the operators of health clubs or spas, or people engaged in research, testing, and sale of pharmaceuticals or medical devices
Law	Lawyers, paralegals, legal arbitrators, and mediators	People who provide nonlegal services such as printing, delivery, or stenography
Accounting	Accountants, enrolled agents, return preparers, financial auditors, bookkeepers, and similar professionals	Payment processing and billing analysis
Actuarial Science	Actuaries and similar professionals	Analysts, economists, mathematicians, and statisticians not engaged in analyzing or assessing the financial costs of risk or uncertainty of events
Performing Arts	Actors, singers, musicians, entertainers, directors, and other professionals who participate in creation of performing art, including songwriters and screenplay writers	People who broadcast or disseminate video or audio to the public, or maintain or operate equipment or facilities used for performing arts
Consulting	People who provide professional advice and counsel to clients to assist in achieving goals and solving problems, including government lobbyists	Salespeople and those who provide training or educational courses
Athletics	Athletes, coaches, team managers in sports such as baseball, basketball, football, soccer, hockey, martial arts, boxing, bowling, tennis, golf, skiing, snowboarding, track and field, billiards, and racing	Broadcasters and people who maintain or operate equipment used in athletic events

Specified Service Trades or Businesses ("SSTB") (continued)		
Business Activity	SSTB	Not SSTB
Financial Services	People providing financial services to clients, including managing wealth, developing retirement or transition plans, merger and acquisition advice, and valuation work—for example, financial advisers, investment bankers, wealth planners, and retirement advisers.	Bankers
Brokerage Services	Stockbrokers	Real estate brokers, insurance brokers
Investment Management	People who receive fees for providing investing, asset management, or investment management services	Real property managers
Trading	Traders in securities, commodities, or partnership interests	Farmers or manufacturers who engage in hedging transactions as part of their trade or business

This eliminates most people from falling within the catch-all category.

Architecture and engineering services are expressly not included in the list of personal services.

If the same business sells products or merchandise and also provides services that fall within one of the SSTB categories, the business will not be treated as an SSTB so long as less than 10% of the gross receipts of the business come from providing the service. For example, if a business earns $1 million selling computers, and $90,000 providing computer consulting services, it will not be treated as an SSTB. If the business has gross receipts over $25 million, the 10% limit is reduced to 5%. If the 10%/5% thresholds are exceeded, the entire business is treated as an SSTB.

Deduction for Nonservice Businesses (Income Above $164,900/$329,800)

If your business is not included in the list of specified service businesses, and your 2021 taxable income exceeds the $164,900/$329,800 thresholds, how you figure your pass-through deduction depends on your taxable income.

Taxable Income Above $214,900 ($429,800 if Married)

If your 2021 taxable income exceeds $214,900 (single) or $429,800 (married filing jointly), your maximum possible pass-through deduction is 20% of your QBI, just like at the lower income levels. However, when your income is this high, a W-2 wage/business property limitation takes full effect. Your deduction is limited to the greater of:

- 50% of your pro rata share of W-2 employee wages paid by the business, or
- 25% of W-2 wages *plus* 2.5% of your pro rata share of the acquisition cost of your depreciable business property.

Thus, if you have neither employees nor depreciable property, you get no deduction. This is intended to encourage pass-through owners to hire employees and/or buy property for their business.

W-2 wages means the total wages and benefits reported by the employer to the Social Security Administration. The business property must be depreciable long-term property used in the production of income—for example, the real property or equipment used in the business (not inventory). The cost is its unadjusted basis—the original acquisition cost, minus cost of land, if any. It makes no difference whether you deduct the full cost the first year with bonus depreciation or Section 179. The 2.5% deduction can be taken during the entire depreciation period for the property; however, it can be no shorter than ten years. Thus, property with a depreciation period of five or seven years still counts for a full ten years after purchase. You can't count any property you sell during the year.

EXAMPLE: Hal and Wanda are married and file jointly. Their taxable income this year is $500,000, including $400,000 in QBI they earned from the bar business they own through an LLC. They employed four bartenders during the year to whom they paid $150,000 in W-2 wages. They own their bar building. They bought it four years ago for $600,000 and the land is worth $100,000, so its unadjusted acquisition basis is $500,000. Their maximum possible pass-through deduction is 20% of their $400,000 QBI, which equals $80,000. However, because their taxable income was over $429,800, their pass-through deduction is limited to the greater of (1) 50% of the W-2 wages they paid their employees, or (2) 25% of W-2 wages plus 2.5% of their bar building's $500,000 basis. Alternative (1) is $75,000 (50% x $150,000 = $75,000); (2) is $50,000 (2.5% x $500,000) + (25% x $150,000) = $50,000. The first calculation is greater so their pass-through deduction is $75,000.

Taxable Income $164,901 to $214,900 ($329,801 to $429,800 if Married)

If your 2021 taxable income is $164,901 to $214,900 (single) or $329,801 to $429,800 (married filing jointly), the W-2 wages/property limitation is phased in—that is, only part of your deduction is subject to the limit and the rest is based on 20% of your QBI. The phase-in range is $100,000 for marrieds filing jointly, and $50,000 for singles. For example, the limit would be 50% phased in for married taxpayers with taxable income of $379,800 ($50,000 over $329,800, which equals 50% of the $100,000 phase-in range). At the top of the income range ($214,900 for singles, $429,800 for marrieds), your entire deduction is subject to the W-2 wages/business property limit. Thus, if you have no W-2 wages or business property, you get no deduction.

To calculate the phase-in, first determine what the amount of your deduction would be if the W-2 wages/property limit didn't apply at all (20% x your QBI). Next, calculate your deduction as if the W-2 wages/property limit applied in full. Your phase-in amount is based on the difference between these two calculations multiplied by your phase-in percentage.

EXAMPLE: Sid and Nancy are married and operate an equipment rental business as an LLC. Their QBI this year is $359,800, and the business pays $100,000 in W-2 wages and owns no property. Their phase-in percentage is 30% because their $359,800 QBI is $30,000 over the $329,800 limit ($30,000 ÷ $100,000 phase-in range = 30%). Their deduction if the W-2 wages/property limit didn't apply would be 20% of their $359,800 QBI, which equals $71,960. Their fully limited deduction based on W-2 wages is $50,000 (50% of $100,000 W-2 wages = $50,000). They should lose 30% of the difference between the full deduction of $71,960 and the fully limited deduction of $50,000. The difference amounts to $6,588 (30% x ($71,960 − $50,000) = $6,588). Thus, they should lose $6,588 from the full $71,960 deduction. Sid and Nancy can take a $65,372 pass-through deduction on their return. Had their QBI been $429,800, their phase-in percentage would have been 100% and their total deduction limited to 50% of their W-2 wages, or $50,000.

Deduction for Specified Service Business Owners (Income Above $164,900/$329,800)

If your business is a specified service business, and your 2021 taxable income exceeds $164,900 (single) or $329,800 (married), your pass-through deduction is gradually phased out up to $214,900/$429,800 of QBI. At the top of the income range, you get no deduction at all. That is, if your total 2021 taxable income exceeds $214,900 (single) or $429,800 (married), you get no deduction. This was intended to prevent highly compensated employees who provide personal services—lawyers, for example—from having their employers reclassify them as independent contractors so they could benefit from the pass-through deduction. There is no such phase-out of the entire deduction for nonservice providers.

To calculate your deduction, you start by using the same formula as for nonservice providers discussed above. Your maximum possible deduction is 20% of your QBI. However, your deduction may not exceed the greater of:

- 50% of your share W-2 employee wages paid by the business, or
- 25% of W-2 wages plus 2.5% of the acquisition cost of depreciable property used in the business.

Thus, if you have no employees or depreciable business property, you get no deduction.

Next, you calculate the phase-out of the deduction. If you're married and you have employees or property, your deduction is phased-out by 1% for every $1,000 your income exceeds the $329,800 threshold. When your income reaches $429,800 you get no deduction. If you're single, your deduction is reduced by 2% for every $1,000 your income exceeds the $164,900 threshold and you get no deduction if your income reaches $214,901 or more.

> **EXAMPLE:** Mark is married and files jointly. He earned $359,800 in taxable income this year. His sole proprietorship consulting business earned $359,800 and paid $100,000 to employees. Consulting is one of the specified service businesses, so his pass-through deduction is subject to the phase-out. His $359,800 taxable income is $30,000, or 30%, over the $329,800 threshold. Before the phase-out, his deduction is limited to 50% of the W-2 wages he paid, which was $50,000 (50% x $100,000 W-2 wages = $50,000). Because his phase-out percentage is 30%, he gets 70% of the full deduction, or $35,000 (70% x $50,000 = $35,000).

Pass-Through Deduction Thresholds, Limits, and Phase-Ins (2021)

	Taxable Income: Single: Up to $164,900 Married: Up to $329,800	Taxable Income: Single: $164,901–$214,900 Married: $329,801–$429,800	Taxable Income: Single: $214,901 or more Married: $429,801 or more
Specified Service Business	Full 20% deduction No W-2/property limit	20% deduction subject to phase-out; W-2/property limit applied	No deduction
Nonspecified Service Business	Full 20% deduction No W-2/property limit	20% deduction subject to phase-in of W-2/property limit	20% deduction permitted but fully subject to W-2/property limit

Taking the Pass-Through Deduction

The pass-through deduction is a personal deduction you may take on your Form 1040 whether or not you itemize. To compute and claim the deduction, you must complete IRS Form 8995, *Qualified Business Income Deduction Simplified Computation*. But if your taxable income exceeds the applicable threshold amount, you should file Form 8995-A, *Qualified Business Income Deduction*. You then transfer the amount of the deduction to your Form 1040.

The pass-through deduction is not an "above the line" deduction on the first page of Form 1040 that reduces your adjusted gross income (AGI). Thus, for example, it does not reduce your income for purposes of qualifying for Obamacare health insurance credits. Moreover, the deduction only reduces income taxes, not Social Security or Medicare taxes, or Net Investment Income taxes (a 3.8% tax paid by higher income people on rental and investment income over certain levels).

Strategies to Maximize the Pass-Through Deduction

There are many planning strategies high-income pass-through owners can take to preserve and maximize the pass-through deduction.

Keep Service Business Income Below the $214,900/$429,800 Threshold

Be sure to keep track of your taxable income during the year. If your business is a specified service business, it's absolutely vital to keep your taxable income for the year at or below the cut-off amount: For 2021, this is $214,900 for singles and $429,800 for marrieds filing jointly. If you earn one dollar more than this you get no deduction.

Ideally, your taxable income should be at or below $164,900 (single) or $329,800 (married) so you can avoid the phase-in of the W-2 employee/property limitation and qualify for the full 20% of QBI deduction (the only exception would be if you have employees). Your taxable income is your total income (not including capital gains) minus your deductions.

If you don't itemize, this would include your standard deduction ($12,550 for singles; $25,100 for marrieds in 2021). So, if you take the standard deduction, you could have $177,450 (single) or $354,900 (married) in income and come within the income limits to qualify for the full 20% of QBI deduction.

If your income is at or near these limits, there are lots of things you can do to reduce your taxable income for the year. For example, you can:

- Contribute to retirement accounts such as IRAs and 401(k)s— your contributions are deducted from your taxable income subject to annual limits (in 2021, business owners can contribute up to $58,000 to retirement plans).
- Give money to charity if you're so inclined (make sure you're able to itemize your personal deductions).
- Avoid billing clients or collecting amounts due your business near the end of the year.
- Increase your business deductions to reduce your taxable income— for example, buy equipment or other property for your business (all the long-term personal property you buy for your business is 100% deductible in one year using 100% bonus deprecation or Section 179 expensing).

Separating Out Nonservice Income?

We've seen that specified service trade or business owners with taxable income that exceeds $214,900 (single) or $429,800 (married filing jointly) get no pass-through deduction. These service business owners could attempt to separate out business functions that don't involve providing services and establish them as separate pass-through businesses— a process called "cracking."

> **EXAMPLE:** Portia, a married chiropractor, earns $750,000 per year from her practice, far over the $429,800 cutoff for the pass-through deduction for SSTBs. She owns the building where her practice is located. She forms a limited liability company with herself as owner and contributes the building to it. Her chiropractic practice pays the building LLC $200,000 per year in rent. After expenses, the LLC earns $150,000 in profit. Is the $150,000 eligible for the 20% pass-through deduction?

Unfortunately, IRS regulations largely prohibit this strategy. They provide that a separate business entity created by the owners of an SSTB will also be treated as an SSTB if:

- the owners of the SSTB that created the separate entity own at least 50% of the separate entity, and
- the separate entity provides 80% or more of its property or services to the SSTB.

Thus, Portia in the above example could not apply the pass-through deduction to the rental income received by her LLC. The only exception would be if she owned less than a 50% interest in the LLC, or the building was at least 80% rented to other tenants. But, even if the separate business provides less than 80% of its property or services to an SSTB, the portion provided to the commonly owned SSTB is treated as part of the SSTB. Thus, if Portia rented 20% of the building, 20% of the rental income would be SSTB income.

Form an S Corporation

If your business is not a service business and your taxable income exceeds $164,900 (single) or $329,800 (married, filing jointly), your pass-through deduction will be fully or partly subject to the W-2 wage/property limitation. If you don't pay W-2 wages and/or have depreciable property, you could form an S corporation to operate your business and work as its employee. Your employee income would constitute W-2 wages on which you can base all or part of your pass-through deduction. Tax experts have calculated that 28.57% of S corporation income should be paid as W-2 wages to maximize the pass-through deduction. Why not pay even more as wages? Paying more actually results in a smaller deduction because the total pass-through deduction may not exceed 20% of your qualified business income: The wages an S corporation pays its owners don't count as qualified business income. However, wages S corporations pay owners/employees must be reasonable; depending on the circumstances, paying 28.57% of income as shareholder wages may be too much or too little.

EXAMPLE: Mary, a married taxpayer, buys and sells goods online. She operates the business from rented premises and has no employees. She earned $415,000 in profit from the business and earned $35,100 in other income. Her taxable income is $425,000 ($450,100 − $25,100 standard deduction = $425,000). At this income level, the W-2/property limitation is completely phased in. That is, her pass-through deduction is limited to 50% of W-2 wages or 25% of W-2 wages plus 2.5% of depreciable property. If her business is a sole proprietorship or an LLC, she would get no pass-through deduction since she has no employees or depreciable property. However, she has formed an S corporation, of which she is the sole shareholder and employee. The corporation pays her $121,428 in W-2 wages, leaving $303,572 in qualified business income for the corporation. She is entitled to a pass-through deduction of 50% x her W-2 wages, which is $60,714 (which is also 20% of her corporation's QBI).

If you have a service business, the S corporation strategy only works if your taxable income is in the phase-out range: $164,901 to $214,900 for single taxpayers and $329,801 to $429,800 for marrieds filing jointly. If your income is higher than this, you get no pass-through deduction. If it's lower than the phase-out threshold amount, the deduction is equal to 20% of your QBI, with no W-2 wage/property limit so paying W-2 wages will not increase your deduction.

Sole proprietors, owners of LLCs taxed as partnerships, or partners in partnerships cannot pay themselves W-2 wages. Thus, S corporations (or LLCs taxed as S corporations) can be far more advantageous than these other business forms at higher income levels where the W-2 wage limitation applies.

Combine Multiple Nonservice Businesses

If you own multiple nonservice businesses, you have the option of combining (aggregating) them for purposes of the pass-through deduction. There is no benefit in doing this if your taxable income is no more than $164,900 for singles and $329,800 for married joint filers. But, if your income is higher than this, the pass-through deduction is based wholly or partly on how much you pay your employees and how much business property you own.

So, combining multiple businesses at these income levels can result in a larger pass-through deduction than computing the deduction separately for each business. For example, if one business has lots of profit and few employees and/or property, and another has little profit and many employees and/or property, combining them can result in a larger deduction.

You can combine (aggregate) multiple businesses only if the same person or group of people owns 50% or more of each business for a majority of the year, which must include the last day of the year. None of the businesses may be specified service businesses (see the list above) and they must share the same tax year. In addition, at least two of the following requirements must be satisfied:

- The businesses provide products, property, or services that are the same or customarily offered together.
- The businesses share facilities or significant centralized business elements, such as personnel, accounting, legal, manufacturing, purchasing, human resources, or information technology resources.
- The businesses are operated in coordination with, or reliance upon, one or more of the businesses in the combined group (for example, supply chain interdependencies).

The same people do not need to own an interest in each business that is being combined.

> **EXAMPLE:** Andrea, a single taxpayer, owns a catering business and restaurant that share the same kitchen and other facilities. She treats each business as a separately owned sole proprietorship. The catering business has QBI of $400,000, but no W-2 wages because all the work is done by independent contractors. The restaurant business has QBI of only $25,000, but it has regular employees with $190,000 of W-2 wages. If Andrea keeps the two businesses separate, her deduction from the catering business is $0 (50% × zero W-2 wages = $0), and her deduction from the restaurant is $5,000 (20% × QBI of $25,000), for a total deduction of only $5,000. If Rebecca combines the two businesses, her deduction is $85,000—the lesser of $85,000 (20% × aggregated QBI of $425,000) or $95,000 (50% × aggregated W-2 wages of $190,000). Thus, her QBI deduction would be $80,000 higher by combining the businesses.

You must file an election with your tax return each year listing the businesses being aggregated. Despite the annual election requirement, the election is irrevocable. This means it can't be changed from year to year unless there is a material change in circumstances. However, new businesses can be added to the existing group if they meet the above requirements. For this reason, you must think carefully before using this strategy. It might be beneficial one year, but result in smaller pass-through deductions in future years if your circumstances change.

File a Separate Return

The vast majority of married people file joint returns in which their income and deductions are combined. However, married couples have the option of filing separate tax returns. When they do this, each spouse reports and pays tax on their income, credits, and deductions on their own return. In some cases, a married person could qualify for the pass-through deduction by filing a separate return rather than filing jointly with his or her spouse.

> EXAMPLE: Jack and Jill are a married couple who live in New York. Jack earns $100,000 per year form his consulting business. His wife Jill earns $300,000 from her medical practice. They also earned $100,000 from investments. They both have service businesses and their combined income of $500,000 is well over the $429,800 cut off for the pass-through deduction for service businesses. Thus, if they file a joint return, they get no pass-through deduction. However, if they each file separately, Jack will have only $100,000 of business income on his return, plus $50,000 in investment income. His $150,000 in taxable income puts him well under the $164,900 threshold for married taxpayers filing separately. Thus, he will be entitled to a 20% pass-through deduction on his $100,000 consulting income, a $20,000 deduction.

This strategy won't work if you live in one of the nine community property states: Arizona, California, Idaho, Louisiana, Nevada, New Mexico, Texas, Washington, and Wisconsin. Reason: In a community property state, the income spouses earn is split evenly between them when they file separately, as are expenses (unless they are paid by one spouse with his or her separate noncommunity funds—for example, money earned or inherited before marriage). Thus, if Jack and Jill from the above example lived in California, they would have to evenly split their $500,000 total income, leaving them each with $250,000, well over the $214,900 limit to qualify for the pass-through deduction for a service business for single filers.

Also, there are several tax disadvantages when a married couple files separately. So creating a pass-through deduction, where none was available when filing jointly, may not lower a couple's taxes. You need to compare your total tax liability when filing jointly and separately to see which filing status is best.

Hiring Workers

This chapter is about the host of tax rules that apply to businesses that hire people to help them, whether as employees or as independent contractors. These rules apply when you hire strangers or family members, or when your incorporated business hires you.

Employees Versus Independent Contractors

As far as the IRS is concerned, the only two types of people you can hire to help in your business are employees and independent contractors (ICs). It's very important to understand the difference between the two, because the tax rules are very different for each. If you hire an employee, you become subject to a wide array of state and federal tax requirements.

You must withhold taxes from your employee's pay, and you must pay other taxes yourself. You must also comply with complex and burdensome bookkeeping and reporting requirements. If you hire an independent contractor, none of these requirements apply. Tax deductions for businesses that hire employees and independent contractors differ as well.

ICs go by a variety of names: self-employed, freelancers, free agents, consultants, entrepreneurs, or business owners. What they all have in common is that they are people who are in business for themselves. Employees work for someone else's business.

Initially, it's up to you to determine whether any person you hire is an employee or an IC. However, your decision about how to classify a worker is subject to review by various government agencies, including:

- the IRS
- your state's tax department
- your state's unemployment compensation insurance agency, and
- your state's workers' compensation insurance agency.

These agencies are mostly interested in whether you have classified workers as independent contractors when you should have classified them as employees. The reason is that you must pay money to each of these agencies for employees, but not for independent contractors. The more workers are classified as employees, the more money flows into the agencies' coffers. In the case of taxing agencies, employers must withhold tax from employees' paychecks and hand it over to the government; ICs pay their own taxes, which means the government must wait longer to get its money and faces the possibility that ICs won't declare their income or will otherwise cheat on their taxes. An agency that determines that you misclassified an employee as an IC may impose back taxes, fines, and penalties.

Scrutinizing agencies use various tests to determine whether a worker is an IC or an employee. The determining factor is usually whether you have the right to control the worker. If you have the right to direct and control the way a worker performs—both as to the final results and the details of when, where, and how the work is done—then the worker is your employee. On the other hand, if your control is limited to accepting or rejecting the final results the worker achieves, then that person is an IC.

An employer may not always exercise its right of control. For example, if an employee is experienced and well trained, the employer may not feel the need to closely supervise him or her. But the employer still maintains the right to do so at any time.

> **EXAMPLE:** Mary takes a job as a hamburger cook at the local AcmeBurger. AcmeBurger personnel carefully train her in how to make an AcmeBurger hamburger—including the type and amount of ingredients to use, the temperature at which the hamburger should be cooked, and so forth.
>
> Once Mary starts work, AcmeBurger managers closely supervise how she does her job. Virtually every aspect of Mary's behavior on the job is under AcmeBurger control, including what time she arrives at and leaves work, when she takes her lunch break, what she wears, and the sequence of tasks she must perform. If Mary proves to be an able and conscientious worker, her supervisors may choose not to look over her shoulder very often. But they have the right to do so at any time. Mary is AcmeBurger's employee.

In contrast, a worker is an independent contractor if the hiring firm does not have the right to control the person on the job. Because the worker is an independent businessperson not solely dependent on you (the hiring party) for a living, your control is limited to accepting or rejecting the final results the IC achieves.

EXAMPLE: AcmeBurger develops a serious plumbing problem. AcmeBurger does not have any plumbers on its staff, so it hires Plumbing by Jake, an independent plumbing repair business owned by Jake. Jake looks at the problem and gives an estimate of how much it will cost to fix it. The manager agrees to hire him, and Jake and his assistant commence work. Jake is an independent contractor.

In a relationship of this kind where Jake is clearly running his own business, it's virtually certain that AcmeBurger does not have the right to control the way Jake performs his plumbing services. Its control is limited to accepting or rejecting the final result. If AcmeBurger doesn't like the work Jake has done, it can refuse to pay him.

The difficulty in applying the right of control test is that control isn't always easy to determine. Government auditors can't look into your mind to see if you are controlling a worker. They rely instead on indirect or circumstantial evidence indicating control or lack of it—for example, whether you provide a worker with tools and equipment, where the work is performed, how the worker is paid, and whether you can fire the worker. The following chart shows the primary factors used by the IRS and most other government agencies to determine if you have the right to control a worker.

Part-Timers and Temps Can Be Employees

Don't think that a person you hire to work part time or for a short period must be an IC. People who work for you only temporarily or part time are your employees if you have the right to control the way they work.

RESOURCE

For a detailed discussion of the practical and legal issues hiring firms face when hiring ICs, see *Working With Independent Contractors*, by Stephen Fishman (Nolo).

IRS Test for Worker Status		
	Workers will more likely be considered ICs if:	**Workers will more likely be considered employees if:**
Behavioral Control	• you do not give them instructions • you do not provide them with training	• you give them instructions they must follow about how to do the work • you give them detailed training
Financial Control	• they have a significant investment in equipment and facilities • they pay business or travel expenses themselves • they make their services available to the public • they are paid by the job • they have opportunity for profit or loss	• you provide them with equipment and facilities free of charge • you reimburse their business or travel expenses • they make no effort to market their services to the public • you pay them by the hour or other unit of time • they have no opportunity for profit or loss—for example, because they're paid by the hour and have all expenses reimbursed
Relationship Between You and the Worker	• they don't receive employee benefits such as health insurance • they sign a client agreement with the hiring firm • they can't quit or be fired at will • they perform services that are not part of your regular business activities	• they receive employee benefits • they have no written client agreement • they can quit at any time without incurring any liability to you • they can be fired at any time • they perform services that are part of your core business

Tax Deductions and Credits for Employee Pay and Benefits

Hiring employees costs you money, but you may deduct most or all of what you pay them as a business expense. Thus, for example, if you pay an employee $50,000 per year in salary and benefits, you'll ordinarily get a $50,000 tax deduction. In some cases, you can also get an additional pass-through deduction equal to 50% of what you pay your employees (see Chapter 10). You should factor this into your calculations whenever you're thinking about hiring an employee or deciding how much to pay that employee.

You can also get valuable tax credits when you hire employees, including special temporary credits during the COVID-19 pandemic.

Employee Pay

Employee pay may be in the form of salaries, sales commissions, bonuses, vacation allowances, sick pay (as long as it's not covered by insurance), or fringe benefits. For tax deduction purposes, it doesn't really matter how you measure or make the payments. The amounts you pay an employee may fall into any of the four basic categories of deductible business expenses:

- business operating expenses
- business start-up expenses
- long-term asset purchase expenses, or
- inventory costs.

The general rules for each of these types of expenses are discussed in other chapters. Let's see how employee pay can fall into each category.

Operating Expenses

Most of the time, amounts you pay employees to work in your business will be business operating expenses. These expenses are currently deductible as long as they are:

- ordinary and necessary
- reasonable in amount
- paid for services actually performed, and
- actually paid or incurred in the year the deduction is claimed (as shown by your payroll records).

An employee's services are ordinary and necessary if they are common, accepted, helpful, and appropriate for your business; they don't have to be indispensable. An employee's pay is reasonable if the amount is in the range of what other businesses would pay for similar services. These requirements usually won't pose a problem when you hire an employee to perform any legitimate business function.

> **EXAMPLE:** Ken, the owner of a coffee bar, hires Kim to work as a barista and pays her $2,000 per month—what baristas are typically paid in the area. Ken can deduct Kim's $2,000 monthly salary as a business operating expense. If Kim works a full year, Ken will get a $24,000 deduction.

Payments to employees for personal services are not deductible as business expenses.

> **EXAMPLE:** Ken hires Samantha to work as a live-in nanny for his three children. Samantha is Ken's employee, but her services are personal, not related to his business. Thus, Ken may not deduct her pay as a business expense.

Special rules apply if you hire family members to work in your business or if you hire yourself. (See "Employing Your Family or Yourself," below.)

Start-Up Expenses

Employee compensation for services performed during the start-up phase of your business is a business start-up expense. It is not currently deductible, but you may deduct up to $5,000 in start-up expenses the first year you're in business, provided your expenses don't exceed $50,000. Any excess can be deducted over 180 months. (See Chapter 3 for more on deducting start-up expenses.)

> **EXAMPLE:** Michelle, a famous chef, hires Benjamin to work as her full-time personal assistant while she works to start up a new restaurant. Benjamin helps Michelle find and rent a space for the restaurant, hire and train employees, and deal with myriad other details involved in starting such a complex business. Benjamin works for Michelle for four months before the restaurant opens for business. His salary during this start-up phase—$10,000—is a business start-up expense from which Michelle may deduct $5,000 the first year she's in business and the remaining $5,000 over 180 months ($333 per calendar year).

Long-Term Asset Expenses

If you pay an employee to help purchase, transport, install, or improve a long-term asset, the payments are not business operating expenses. Instead, they are added to the basis (cost) of the asset. As such, you may either depreciate them over several years or (in most situations) currently deduct them using the de minimis safe harbor, bonus depreciation, or Section 179. (See Chapter 5 for more on deducting long-term assets.)

> EXAMPLE: John owns a fleet of 50 used delivery trucks. He employs Martha, a mechanic, to install new $3,000 engines in the trucks. The engines are long-term asset purchases. What John pays Martha to install the engines is added to their purchase price to arrive at their value for tax purposes (their taxable basis). John can depreciate this amount over five years or deduct the entire amount in one year with 100% bonus depreciation or Section 179 (in most situations).

Inventory Costs

Larger businesses—those with more than $26 million in annual gross receipts—are required to maintain inventories. If such a business hires an employee to help manufacture products for sale to customers, the employee's compensation is not a regular business expense. Instead, it is considered part of the cost of the products. These products are inventory, the cost of which may be deducted only as each item is sold. (See Chapter 6 for more on inventory.)

> EXAMPLE: Richard owns a factory that manufactures clothes hangers for sale to clothing companies. He pays his ten employees a total of $25,000 each month. He adds this cost to the other costs he incurs to produce the hangers (rent, materials, equipment, electricity, and so forth) to figure his total cost of goods sold. He deducts this amount from his gross income to determine his business's gross profit.

Payroll Taxes

Whenever you hire an employee, you become an unpaid tax collector for the government. You are required to withhold and pay both federal and state taxes for the worker. These taxes are called payroll taxes or employment taxes. Federal payroll taxes consist of:

- Social Security and Medicare taxes—also known as "FICA"
- unemployment taxes—also known as "FUTA," and
- federal income taxes—also known as "FITW."

You must periodically pay FICA, FUTA, and FITW to the IRS electronically. You are entitled to deduct as a business expense payroll taxes that you pay yourself. You get no deductions for taxes you withhold from employees' pay.

Every year, employers must file IRS Form W-2, *Wage and Tax Statement*, for each of their workers. The form shows the IRS how much the worker was paid and how much tax was withheld.

RESOURCE

IRS Publication 15, Circular E, *Employer's Tax Guide*, provides detailed information on these requirements. You can get a free copy by downloading it from the IRS website, at www.irs.gov.

Employer's FICA Contributions

FICA is an acronym for "Federal Income Contributions Act," the law requiring employers and employees to pay Social Security and Medicare taxes. FICA taxes consist of a 12.4% Social Security tax on income up to an annual ceiling; in 2021, the annual Social Security ceiling was $142,800. Medicare taxes are levied at a 2.9% rate, up to an annual ceiling—$200,000 for single taxpayers and $250,000 for married couples filing jointly. Income above the ceiling is taxed at a 3.8% rate. This combines to a total 15.3% tax on employment income up to the Social Security tax ceiling.

Employers and employees split the cost of FICA taxes—the employer pays half and withholds the other half from the employee's pay. This means that the employer and employee each pay 7.65% up to the Social Security tax ceiling. You are entitled to deduct as a business expense the portion of the tax that you pay yourself.

The ceiling for the Social Security tax changes annually. You can find out what the Social Security tax ceiling is for the current year from IRS Publication 15, Circular E, *Employer's Tax Guide*; the amount is printed right on the first page.

Payment of Deferred 2020 Employer FICA Contributions

Due to the coronavirus (COVID-19) pandemic, employers had the option of deferring their 2020 FICA payments. All such payments due beginning on March 27, 2020 (the date the CARES Act was signed into law) and ending on December 31, 2020, could be deferred. Half of the deferred payroll taxes are due on December 31, 2021, with the remainder due on December 31, 2022. The deferral applies only to the employer portion of FICA taxes.

FUTA

FUTA is an acronym for the "Federal Unemployment Tax Act," the law that establishes federal unemployment taxes. Most employers must pay both state and federal unemployment taxes. Even if you're exempt from the state tax, you may still have to pay the federal tax. Employers alone are responsible for FUTA—you may not collect or deduct it from employees' wages.

You must pay FUTA taxes if either of the following is true:
- You pay $1,500 or more to employees during any calendar quarter— that is, any three-month period beginning with January, April, July, or October.
- You had one or more employees for at least some part of a day in any 20 or more different weeks during the year. The weeks don't have to be consecutive, nor does it have to be the same employee each week.

The FUTA tax rate is 6%. However, in practice you rarely pay this much. You are given a credit of 5.4% if you pay the applicable state unemployment tax in full and on time. This means that the actual FUTA tax rate is usually 0.6%. In 2021, the FUTA tax was assessed on the first $7,000 of an employee's annual wages. The FUTA tax, then, is usually $42 per year per employee in 2021. This amount is a deductible business expense.

FITW

FITW is an acronym for "federal income tax withholding." You must calculate and withhold federal income taxes from your employees' paychecks. Employees are solely responsible for paying federal income taxes. Your only responsibility is to withhold the funds and remit them to the government. You get no deductions for FITW.

State Payroll Taxes

Employers in every state are required to pay and withhold state payroll taxes. These taxes include:

- state unemployment compensation taxes in all states
- state income tax withholding in most states, and
- state disability taxes in a few states.

Employers in every state are required to contribute to a state unemployment insurance fund. Employees make no contributions, except in Alaska, New Jersey, Pennsylvania, and Rhode Island, where employers must withhold small employee contributions from employees' paychecks. The employer contributions are a deductible business expense.

If your payroll is very small—below $1,500 per calendar quarter—you probably won't have to pay unemployment compensation taxes. In most states, you must pay state unemployment taxes for employees if you're paying federal FUTA taxes. However, some states have more strict requirements. Contact your state labor department for the exact rules and payroll amounts.

All states except Alaska, Florida, Nevada, South Dakota, Tennessee, Texas, Washington, and Wyoming have income taxation. If your state has income taxes, you must withhold the applicable tax from your employees' paychecks and pay it to the state taxing authority. Each state has its own income tax withholding forms and procedures. Contact your state tax department for information. Of course, employers get no deductions for withholding their employees' state income taxes.

California, Hawaii, New Jersey, New York, and Rhode Island have state disability insurance that provides employees with coverage for injuries or illnesses that are not related to work. Employers in these states must withhold their employees' disability insurance contributions from their pay. Employers must also make their own contributions in Hawaii, New Jersey, and New York—these employer contributions are deductible.

Bookkeeping Expenses Are Deductible

Figuring out how much to withhold, doing the necessary record keeping, and filling out the required forms can be complicated. If you have a computer, accounting programs such as *QuickBooks* or *QuickPay* can help with all the calculations and print out your employees' checks and IRS forms. You can also hire a bookkeeper or payroll tax service to do the work. Amounts you pay a bookkeeper or payroll tax service are deductible business operating expenses. You can find these services on the Internet under payroll tax services. You can also find a list of payroll service providers on the IRS website, at www.irs.gov.

CAUTION

Be aware, however, that even if you hire a payroll service, you remain personally liable if your payroll taxes are not paid on time. The IRS recommends that employers: (1) keep their company address on file with the IRS, rather than the address of the payroll service provider, so that the company will be contacted by the IRS if there are any problems; (2) require the payroll service provider to post a fiduciary bond to pay any penalties and interest due to IRS deficiency notices in case it defaults on its obligation; and (3) ask the service provider to enroll in and use the Electronic Federal Tax Payment System (EFTPS) so the employer can confirm payments made on its behalf. (See www.eftps.gov for more information.)

In addition, subject to some important exceptions, employers in all states must provide their employees with workers' compensation insurance to cover work-related injuries. Workers' compensation is not a payroll tax. Employers must purchase a workers' compensation policy from a private insurer or state workers' compensation fund. Your worker's compensation insurance premiums are deductible as a business insurance expense. (See Chapter 14 for more on deducting business insurance.)

> CAUTION
> **Employers in California must withhold for parental leave.** Employers in California are also required to withhold (as part of their disability program) a certain amount for parental leave. For more information on the program, go to www.edd.ca.gov.

Employee Fringe Benefits

No law that says you must provide your employees with any fringe benefits —not even health insurance (except in Hawaii and Massachusetts), sick pay, or vacation. But large employers (those with at least 50 or more full-time equivalent employees) are required to provide health insurance to their full-time employees or pay a penalty to the IRS. In addition, the tax law encourages you to provide employee benefits by allowing you to deduct the cost as a business expense. (These expenses should be deducted as employee benefit expenses, not employee compensation.) Moreover, your employees do not have to treat the value of their fringe benefits as income on which they need pay tax. So you get a deduction, and your employees get tax-free goodies.

In contrast, if you're a business owner (a sole proprietor, partner in a partnership, 2% or more owner of an S corporation, or LLC member), you must include in your income and pay tax on the value of any fringe benefits your company provides to you—the only exception is for de minimis fringes.

Tax-free employee fringe benefits include:
- health insurance
- accident insurance
- Health Savings Accounts (see Chapter 13)
- dependent care assistance (ordinarily, this tax-free benefit is limited to $5,000 per year; but it is $10,500 for 2021 only)
- educational assistance
- group term life insurance coverage—limits apply based on the policy value
- qualified employee benefits plans, including profit-sharing plans, stock bonus plans, and money purchase plans
- employee stock options
- lodging on your business premises
- achievement awards
- commuting benefits (not deductible by the employer; see below)
- employee discounts on the goods or services you sell
- supplemental unemployment benefits
- de minimis (low-cost) fringe benefits such as low-value birthday or holiday gifts, event tickets, traditional awards (such as a retirement gift), other special occasion gifts, and coffee and soft drinks, and
- cafeteria plans that allow employees to choose among two or more benefits consisting of cash and qualified benefits.

Small employers (those with 100 or fewer employees) can offer their employees a simple cafeteria plan—a plan not subject to the nondiscrimination requirements of traditional cafeteria plans.

Health insurance is by far the most important tax-free employee fringe benefit; it is discussed in detail in Chapter 13. (See IRS Publication 15-B, *Employer's Tax Guide to Fringe Benefits*, for more information on the other types of benefits.)

Employees may also be supplied with working condition fringe benefits. These are property and services you provide to employees so that they can perform their jobs. A working condition fringe benefit is tax free to an employee to the extent the employee would be able to deduct the cost of the property or services as a business or depreciation expense if he or she had paid for it. If the employee uses the benefit 100% for work, it is tax free. But the value of any personal use of a working condition fringe benefit must be included in compensation, and an employee must pay tax on it. The employee must meet any documentation requirements that apply to the deduction.

> EXAMPLE: Sam, the owner of a small architecture firm, leases a computer and gives it to his employee Paul so that he can perform design work at home. If Paul uses the computer 100% for his work, it is tax free to him. But if he uses it only 50% of the time for work and 50% of the time for personal purposes, he would have to pay income tax on 50% of its value.

The value of the personal use is determined according to the benefit's fair market value.

> EXAMPLE: It cost Sam $200 a month to rent the computer he gave Paul. If Paul uses the computer 50% of the time for work and 50% of the time for nondeductible personal uses, he would have to add $100 per month to his taxable compensation.

Transportation fringe benefits are among the most popular. These include employer-paid parking, mass transit passes, and vanpool transportation. For 2021, an employer may pay up to $270 per month for any of these benefits for each employee, and the amount is tax free to the employee. However, as a result of the Tax Cuts and Jobs Act, the employer may not deduct the cost of transportation benefits. The only exception is if the employer treats the benefit as additional compensation on the employee's W-2. In this event, it is not tax free to the employee.

Another common working condition fringe benefits is a company car. If an employee uses a company car part of the time for personal driving, the value of the personal use must be included in the employee's income. The employer determines how to value the use of a car, and there are several methods that may be used. The most common is for the employer to report a percentage of the car's annual lease value as determined by IRS tables. For a detailed discussion of these valuation rules, refer to IRS Publication 15-B.

Employee Retention Credit

In 2020, Congress created a new temporary employee retention credit (ERC) to encourage employers to keep their employees on the payroll during the COVID-19 pandemic. In 2021, Congress expanded the ERC and extended it through December 31, 2021. The ERC can be incredibly valuable: up to $28,000 per employee for 2021 alone. Moreover, the ERC is refundable, meaning you get the full amount even if it exceeds your tax liability for the year; the IRS pays the excess amount to you as a refund.

ERC Only for Employees Unrelated to Employer

A business may collect the ERC for wages paid to both full and part-time employees. But the ERC is not available for wages paid to employees who are related to the employer. In the case of an individually owned business, this means an employee who is a relative or dependent of the owner, including children and their descendants, siblings, parents, stepparents, nieces, nephews, aunts, uncles, and in-laws.

> EXAMPLE: Jill individually owns her own consulting business. She has two employees: her son, Bob, and Sue, who is not related to Jill. Jill may collect the ERC for wages she pays to Sue but not for wages paid to Bob.

An incorporated business can't collect the ERC for employees related to 51% or more owners of the corporate stock. A noncorporate entity, such as an LLC, can't collect the ERC for employees related to owners of a 51% or more interest in the entity's capital assets or profits. If you're self-employed, you can't collect the ERC on what you pay yourself. You also can't collect the ERC for wages paid to household employees, such as a nanny.

What about employee wages paid to owners of corporations or their spouses? It is unclear whether they qualify. The IRS will have to provide further guidance.

The ERC and Paycheck Protection Program (PPP) Loans

Originally, you couldn't obtain both a Paycheck Protection Program (PPP) loan from the Small Business Administration (SBA) and an ERC, which caused many businesses to avoid the ERC. They preferred PPP loans that the SBA could forgive—that is, the loans didn't have to be paid back.

However, Congress changed this rule. You can obtain both a PPP loan and the ERC retroactive back to 2020. But employee wages used to obtain PPP loan forgiveness can't be used to determine the ERC amount. (The same rule applies to wages taken into account as payroll costs for SBA restaurant revitalization grants and shuttered venue assistance.)

To obtain PPP loan forgiveness, you must spend at least 60% of the loan on employee payroll during the 24 or eight-week period after you obtained the loan. You cannot count these same wages for the ERC. You are free to pick and choose which wages are claimed for the ERC and PPP loan forgiveness. Wages paid to employees related to you can count toward PPP forgiveness. Complex calculations might be required to maximize your ERC and PPP loan forgiveness. A tax pro can help.

The 2021 ERC

Starting January 1, 2021, a business or nonprofit was eligible for a 2021 ERC if it:

- fully or partially suspended operations during 2021 due to a government order limiting commerce, travel, or group meetings (for commercial, social, religious, or other purposes) due to COVID-19, or
- experienced a 20% or more decline in gross receipts during a calendar quarter in 2021 compared with the same quarter in 2019.

The 2021 ERC is equal to 70% of wages paid to each employee, including health benefits, during an eligible quarter in 2021. The maximum credit is $7,000 per employee per quarter. So, the maximum credit for 2021 is $28,000 per employee.

> **EXAMPLE:** Jill, the self-employed consultant from the above example, had a 30% decline in receipts for the first and second quarters of 2021 compared with 2019. During the third and fourth quarters of 2021, her gross receipts were only 10% less than in 2019. Jill qualifies for an ERC for the first and second quarters of 2021, but not the third or fourth. Jill paid her employee Sue $10,000 in wages during the first and second quarters of 2021. Jill qualifies for an ERC of $14,000 (70% of the $20,000 Sue was paid).

The 2020 ERC

The 2020 ERC began March 13, 2020 and expired December 31, 2020. It was available to all private employers:

- whose operations were fully or partly suspended during any calendar quarter in 2020 due to a government COVID-19 related order, or
- who experienced a 50% or greater decline in gross receipts during any 2020 calendar quarter compared with the same quarter in 2019—the decline need not have been due to the pandemic.

The 2020 ERC was equal to 50% of up to $10,000 in qualified wages paid to full-time employees during all eligible calendar quarters beginning March 13, 2020 and ending December 31, 2020. An "eligible calendar quarter" is one in which the employer experienced economic hardship as defined above. "Qualified wages" included the cost of employer-provided health care. The maximum credit was $5,000 per employee per quarter. So, the maximum credit for 2020 was $20,000 per employee.

The ERC for Recovery Startup Businesses

What if your business began after 2019? It doesn't qualify for the regular 2020 or 2021 ERCs. But there is a special ERC for "recovery startup businesses." These are businesses that:

- began after February 15, 2020
- earn no more than $1 million in annual gross receipts
- did not have operations fully or partially suspended due to COVID-19, and
- did not have gross receipts 20% less than for the same calendar quarter in 2019 or 2020.

A recovery startup business may claim a 2021 ERC of up to $50,000 per quarter after applying the $10,000 wage limit per employee.

Employees Who Work and Don't Work

The ERC was designed to encourage employers to keep employees on the payroll even if they are not working due to the coronavirus pandemic. Larger employers are denied the credit for employees who are still actively working in the business. The rules differ for 2020 and 2021.

For employers who averaged more than 100 full-time employees in 2019, the 2020 ERC could only be claimed for wages paid to employees for time they did *not* work. However, if a business had 100 or fewer full-time employees on average in 2019, the credit is based on wages paid to all employees, regardless of whether they worked or not. This made the credit much more attractive for smaller employers with fewer than 100 full-time employees.

For the 2021 ERC, employers with fewer than 500 full-time employees may claim the credit for all their employees, even those who are still working. Only businesses with more than 500 employees are denied the credit for employees still providing services. But even these larger businesses can count all their employees, including those working, if they suffered a 90% or more decline in gross receipts compared to the same quarter in 2019.

How to Claim the ERC

Employers could immediately claim the ERC by reducing by the amount of their employer share of payroll taxes on employee wages. Ordinarily, employers must pay these taxes every quarter. For March 13, 2020 through June 30, 2021, employers could immediately claim the ERC by reducing the amount of their employer share of Social Security taxes—a 7.65% tax on employee wages up to an annual ceiling. For July 1, 2021 through December 31, 2021, the ERC could only be deducted from the employer portion of the Medicare tax paid for each employee—a 1.45% tax on all employee wages.

If an employer did not owe enough payroll taxes to cover the amount of the credit, it could request an advance payment of the credit from the IRS by faxing IRS Form 7200, *Advance Payment of Employer Credits Due to COVID-19*. However, in 2021, advances are not available for employers with more than 500 employees. Alternatively, an employer can claim the ERC on its quarterly payroll tax return (IRS Form 941) and receive a refund of previously paid tax deposits.

The employee retention credit is a refundable credit; so, the employer may collect the full amount from the IRS even if it reduces its tax liability below zero. And, if your business qualified for the 2020 ERC but didn't claim it, you may still do so by amending your payroll tax returns using IRS Form 941-X. You have until April 15, 2024, to do this.

No Deduction for Employee Wages Used for ERC

Ordinarily, employee wages (and health benefits) are a deductible business expense for the employer. However, an employer cannot deduct wages equal to the amount of the ERC it received in 2020 or 2021. Employers still come out ahead, though, because the ERC is a dollar-for-dollar reduction in taxes, while the deduction for wages only reduces taxable income.

> **EXAMPLE:** Jill, from the above examples, pays 30% in federal income taxes. She received a $14,000 ERC in 2021. So, she can't deduct $14,000 of the wages she paid her employee. Jill must pay a 30% tax on this $14,000, which increases her total tax by $4,200. She still comes out ahead by $9,800 ($14,000 − $4,200 = $9,800).

Payroll Tax Credits for COVID-19 Sick and Family Leave

During April 2020 through December 31, 2020, employers with fewer than 500 full-time employees were required to provide ten days of paid sick leave and 12 weeks of family leave to employees impacted by the COVID-19 pandemic (but businesses with fewer than 50 employees could get an exemption). Employers could claim a tax credit to cover the cost of such leave, plus the cost to maintain employee health insurance coverage during the leave period. These credits were refundable, meaning the IRS pays the employer any amount in excess of the employer's tax liability.

The paid leave mandate expired at the end of 2020, so employers are no longer required to provide such leave. However, the tax credits were extended through September 30, 2021, for employers who voluntarily decided to continue to provide paid leave. For employers who chose to do so, antidiscrimination rules require that leave be provided to all employees.

Sick Leave Credits for April 1, 2021 Through September 30, 2021

Employers can qualify for a credit for up to ten total days of paid sick leave per employee from April 1, 2021 through September 30, 2021. The amount of the credit depends on whether the employee or a family member is sick:

- **If the employee is sick.** Employers qualify for a credit for up to ten days of full-pay for employees who can't work or telework because they had to self-isolate or quarantine, experienced COVID-19 symptoms and needed to obtain a diagnosis, were exposed to COVID-19 and unable to work pending test results, needed to get COVID-19 vaccinated, or were recovering from a vaccination. This credit is capped at $511 per day. Thus, the maximum credit is $5,110 per employee.

  EXAMPLE: Acme, Inc. has five employees. Acme provided them each with one day of paid sick leave to get COVID-19 vaccinations. Each employee was paid $500 per day, so the sick leave cost Acme $2,500. Acme is entitled to a sick leave credit for $2,500.

- **If the employee cares for others.** Employers can also get a sick leave credit for providing up to ten days paid leave to employees who couldn't work or telework because they had to care for a child under 18 years of age whose school or place of care was closed due to COVID-19, or were caring for any person subject to a quarantine order or advised by a health care provider to self-quarantine. This credit is equal to 67% of employee pay, capped at $200 per day.

Family Leave Credits for April 1, 2021 Through September 30, 2021

Employers can also receive a credit for up to 60 days of family leave for days employees couldn't work or telework for any of the same reasons listed above, which qualify for the sick leave credit. The family leave credit is equal to 67% of employee pay, capped at $200 per day. So, the maximum credit is $12,000.

Employers can take both the sick leave and family credits up to a maximum of 70 combined days per employee. But you cannot use both credits for the same day of paid leave. Thus, the maximum possible credit is $17,110 per employee.

Sick and Family Leave Credits for April 1, 2020 Through March 31, 2021

Sick leave and family leave credits are also available for paid leave taken during April 1, 2020 through March 31, 2021. The rules are largely the same as for the later credits except:

- COVID-19 vaccinations do not qualify for either credit, and
- the family leave credit is limited to 50 days, for a maximum of $10,000.

Sick leave and family leave days taken before April 1, 2021, don't count against the ten-day and 60-day limits for the credit during April 1, 2021 through September 30, 2021. The clock was effectively reset on April 1, 2021.

Claiming the Credits

Employers did not have to wait until they filed their taxes for the year to collect these credits. Instead, they could reduce their employer Medicare payroll tax payments up to the amount of the credit. If the credit exceeded this amount, they could file a request for an accelerated payment of the credit from the IRS on Form 7200, *Advance Payments of Credits Due to COVID-19*. Any unclaimed credits can be deducted from employer income. Because these are refundable credits, the IRS pays the employer any amount of the credit that exceeds the employer's tax liability.

Reimbursing Employees for Business-Related Expenditures

When you own a business, you generally pay all your business expenses yourself, including expenses you incur to enable your employees to do their work—for example, office space, tools, and equipment. However, there may be times when an employee must pay for a work-related expense. Most commonly, this occurs when an employee is driving or traveling, while on the job. Sometimes, depending on the circumstances, an employee could end up paying for almost any work-related expense—for example, an employee might pay for office supplies or parking at a client's office.

All these employee payments have important tax consequences, whatever form they take. The rules discussed below apply whether the expenses are incurred by an employee who is not related to you or by an employee who is your spouse or child. They also apply to a business owner who has incorporated the business and works as its employee.

Accountable Plans

The best way to reimburse or otherwise pay your employees for any work-related expenses is to use an accountable plan. When you pay employees for their expenses under an accountable plan, two great things happen:

- You don't have to pay payroll taxes on the payments.
- The employees won't have to include the payments in their taxable income.

Moreover, the amounts you pay will be deductible by you, just like your other business expenses, subject to the same rules.

Requirements for an Accountable Plan

An accountable plan is an arrangement in which you agree to reimburse or advance employee expenses only if the employee:

- pays or incurs expenses that qualify as deductible business expenses for your business while performing services as your employee
- adequately accounts to you for the expenses within a reasonable period of time, and
- returns to you within a reasonable time any amounts received in excess of the actual expenses incurred.

These payments to employees can be made through advances, direct reimbursements, charges to a company credit card, or direct billings to the employer.

These strict rules are imposed to prevent employees from seeking reimbursement for personal expenses (or nonexistent phony expenses) under the guise that they were business expenses. Employees used to do this all the time to avoid paying income tax on the reimbursed amounts (employees must count employer reimbursements for their personal expenses as income, but not reimbursements for the employer's business expenses).

An accountable plan need not be in writing (although it's not a bad idea). All you need to do is set up procedures for your employees to follow that meet the requirements.

Employees Must Document Expenses

Your employees must give you the same documentation for a work-related expense that the IRS requires of you when you claim that expense for your business. This documentation should be provided within 60 days after the expense was incurred.

You need thorough documentation for car, travel, and meal expenses—these are the expenses the IRS is really concerned about. However, you can ease up on the documentation requirements if you pay employees a per diem (per day) allowance equal to or less than the per diem rates the federal government pays its workers while traveling. You can find these rates at www.gsa.gov (look for the link to "Per Diem Rates"). If you use this method, the IRS will assume that the amounts for lodging, meals, and incidental expenses are accurate without any further documentation. The employee need only substantiate the time, place, and business purpose of the expense. The same holds true if you pay the standard mileage rate for an employee who uses a personal car for business. (See Chapter 8 for more about deducting car expenses.)

However, per diem rates may not be used for an employee who:
- owns more than 10% of the stock in an incorporated business, or
- is a close relative of a 10% or more owner—a brother, sister, parent, spouse, grandparent, or other lineal ancestor or descendent.

In these instances, employees must keep track of the actual cost of all business-related expenses that they want to get reimbursed for by their employer. Any per diem rate reimbursement for a 10% or more owner or owner's relative must be counted as taxable wages for the employee.

The documentation requirements are less onerous for other types of expenses. Nevertheless, the employee must still document the amount of money spent and show that it was for your business. For example, an employee who pays for a repair to an office computer out of his or her own pocket should save the receipt and write "repair of office computer" or something similar to show the business purpose of the payment. It's not sufficient for an employee to submit an expense report with vague categories or descriptions such as "travel" or "miscellaneous business expenses."

Returning Excess Payments

Employees who are advanced or reimbursed more than they actually spent for business expenses must return the excess payments to the employer within a reasonable time. The IRS says a reasonable time is 120 days after an expense is incurred. Any amounts not returned are treated as taxable wages for the employee and must be added to the employee's income for tax purposes. This means that you, the employer, must pay payroll tax on those amounts.

> **EXAMPLE:** You give your employee a $1,000 advance to cover her expenses for a short business trip. When she gets back, she gives you an expense report and documentation showing she only spent $900 for business while on the trip. If she doesn't return the extra $100 within 120 days after the trip, it will be considered wages for tax purposes and you'll have to pay payroll tax on the amount.

Covid-19-Related Disaster Relief Payments to Employees

The COVID-19 pandemic was declared a national emergency on March 13, 2020. As a result, employers were allowed to reimburse or pay employees for reasonable and necessary personal, family, living, or funeral expenses they incurred due to the pandemic emergency. (I.R.C. § 139(b)(2).). Such qualified disaster relief payments may include, but are not limited to:

- uninsured and unreimbursed medical expenses, including co-pays, deductibles, prescription, and over-the-counter medications
- health expenses that are not medical expenses such as hand sanitizer, home disinfectant supplies, vitamins, and supplements

Covid-19-Related Disaster Relief Payments to Employees (continued)

- increased expenses due to being quarantined at home—for example, increased utility expenses
- expenses for setting up or maintaining a home office—for example, faster Internet connections, computers, monitors, laptops, printers, office supplies
- housing for additional family members
- nonperishable food purchases
- increased childcare expenses, including tutoring due to school closings
- increased commuting costs—for example, taking a taxi or an Uber to work instead of public mass transit, and
- funeral expenses for family members arising from the pandemic.

However, employers can't make tax-free wage replacement payments to employees—for example, paid sick leave or other leave, or payment for lost wages. Also not included are expenses covered by insurance.

The payments can be made to full or part-time employees. There is no dollar limit on such payments. The only limit is that they be necessary and reasonable. Moreover, unlike most employee fringe benefits, qualified disaster payments are not subject to antidiscrimination rules—they may be provided to some employees, but not others.

Employees are not required to substantiate their actual expenses provided the payments can be reasonably expected to be commensurate with the expenses incurred. Employers are not required to have a formal written reimbursement plan or other documentation. Nevertheless, employers should keep records of the amount paid and to whom.

Qualified disaster relief payments are tax free to the employee. They are not taxable wages or included in gross income. They should not be included as wages in an employee's W-2 form. Nor need they be reported to the IRS on Form 1099-NEC. The employer may deduct the payments as an employee benefit program.

Unaccountable Plans

Any payments you make to employees for business-related expenses that do not comply with the accountable plan rules are deemed to be made under an unaccountable plan. These payments are considered to be employee wages, which means all of the following:

- The employee must report the payments as income on his or her tax return and pay tax on them.
- The employee may not deduct the expenses. (See "No Deduction for Unreimbursed Employee Expenses," below.)
- You (the employer) may deduct the payments as wages paid to an employee.
- You (the employer) must withhold the employee's income taxes and share of Social Security and Medicare taxes from the payments.
- You (the employer) must pay the employer's 7.65% share of the employee's Social Security and Medicare taxes on the payments.

This is a tax disaster for the employee and not a good result for the employer, either, because you will have to pay Social Security and Medicare tax that you could have avoided if the payments had been made under an accountable plan.

No Deduction for Unreimbursed Employee Expenses

In most states, unless you've agreed to do so, you have no legal obligation to reimburse or pay employees for job-related expenses they incur. In the past, employees were entitled to deduct from their own income ordinary and necessary expenses arising from their employment that were not reimbursed by their employers. However, this miscellaneous itemized deduction was eliminated by the Tax Cuts and Jobs Act starting in 2018 through 2025. Thus, employees who pay job-related expenses get no deduction for them. They should seek reimbursement or an increase in salary to help pay for these costs.

> ⓘ **CAUTION**
> **Some states require reimbursement.** Check with your state's labor department to find out the rules for reimbursing employee expenses. You might find that you are legally required to repay employees. In California, for example, employers must reimburse employees for all expenses or losses they incur as a direct consequence of carrying out their job duties. (Cal. Lab. Code § 2802.) States with similar requirements include Illinois, Iowa, Montana, New Hampshire, and Pennsylvania. In addition, the federal Fair Labor Standards Act (FLSA) prohibits employers from requiring employees to pay for job-related expenses if doing so would cause the employee's wage rate to fall below the minimum wage or overtime compensation rate.

Employing Your Family or Yourself

Whoever said "never hire your relatives" must not have read the tax code. The tax law promotes family togetherness by making it highly advantageous for small business owners to hire their spouses or children. If you're single and have no children, you're out of luck.

Employing Your Children

Believe it or not, your children can be a great tax savings device. If you hire your children as employees to do legitimate work in your business, you may deduct their salaries from your business income as a business expense. Your child will have to pay tax on the salary only to the extent it exceeds the standard deduction amount for the year: $12,550 in 2021. Moreover, if your child is under 18, you won't have to withhold or pay any FICA (Social Security or Medicare) tax on the salary (subject to a couple of exceptions).

These rules allow you to shift part of your business income from your own tax bracket to your child's bracket, which should be much lower than yours (unless you earn little or no income). This can result in substantial tax savings.

For example, in 2021, a child need only pay a 10% tax on taxable earned income up to $9,950—taxable income means total income minus the standard deduction. Thus, a child could earn up to $22,500 and pay only a 10% income tax on $9,950 of it—that's only $995 in tax on $22,500 in income.

No Payroll Taxes

As mentioned above, one of the advantages of hiring your child is that you need not pay FICA taxes for your child under the age of 18 who works in your trade or business, or your partnership if it's owned solely by you and your spouse.

> **EXAMPLE:** Lisa, a 16-year-old, makes deliveries for her mother's mail order business, which is operated as a sole proprietorship. Although Lisa is her mother's employee, her mother need not pay FICA taxes on her salary until she turns 18.

Moreover, you need not pay federal unemployment (FUTA) taxes for services performed by your child who is under 21 years old.

However, these rules do not apply—and you must pay both FICA and FUTA—if you hire your child to work for:

- your corporation, or
- your partnership, unless all the partners are parents of the child.

> **EXAMPLE:** Ron works in a computer repair business that is co-owned by his mother and her partner, Ralph, who is no relation to the family. FICA and FUTA taxes must be paid for Ron because he is working for a partnership and not all of the partners are his parents.

You need not pay FICA or FUTA if you've formed a one-member limited liability company and hire your child to work for it. For tax purposes, a one-member LLC is a "disregarded entity"—that is, it's treated as if it didn't exist.

No Withholding

In addition, if your child has no unearned income (for example, interest or dividend income), you must withhold income taxes from your child's pay only if it exceeds the standard deduction for the year. The standard deduction was $12,550 in 2021 and is adjusted every year for inflation. Children who are paid less than this amount need not pay any income taxes on their earnings.

> **EXAMPLE:** Connie, a 15-year-old girl, is paid $4,000 a year to help out in her parents' bakery shop. She has no income from interest or any other unearned income. Her parents need not withhold income taxes from Connie's salary because she has no unearned income and her salary was less than the standard deduction amount for the year.

However, you must withhold income taxes if your child has more than $350 in unearned income for the year and his or her total income exceeds $1,100 (in 2021).

> **EXAMPLE:** If Connie (from the above example) is paid $4,000 in salary and has $500 in interest income, her parents must withhold income taxes from her salary because she has more than $350 in unearned income and her total income for the year was more than $1,100.

Employing Your Spouse

You don't get the benefits of income shifting when you employ your spouse in your business, because your income is combined when you file a joint tax return. You'll also have to pay FICA taxes on your spouse's wages, so you get no savings there, either. You need not pay FUTA tax if you employ your spouse in your unincorporated business. This tax is usually less than $50 per year, however, so this is not much of a savings.

The real advantage of hiring your spouse is in the realm of employee benefits. You can provide your spouse with any or all of the employee benefits discussed in "Tax Deductions for Employee Pay and Benefits," above. You'll get a tax deduction for the cost of the benefit, and your spouse doesn't have to declare the benefit as income, provided the IRS requirements are satisfied. This is a particularly valuable tool for health insurance—you can give your spouse health insurance coverage as an employee benefit. (See Chapter 13 for a detailed discussion.)

Another benefit of hiring your spouse is that you can both go on business trips and deduct the cost as a business expense, as long as your spouse's presence was necessary (for your business, not for you personally).

If you work at an outside office or other workspace, no law says your spouse must work there too. After all, having your spouse spend all day with you at your office might constitute too much togetherness. Fortunately, your spouse can work at home—for example, by doing accounting, collections, or marketing work for the family business. All these activities can easily be conducted from a home office.

Having your spouse work at home has tax benefits as well. If you set up a home office for your spouse that is used exclusively for business purposes, you'll get a home office deduction. Your spouse has no outside office, so the home office will easily pass the convenience of the employer test. (See Chapter 7.) Moreover, you can currently deduct with bonus depreciation, Section 179, and the de minimis safe harbor the cost of office furniture, computers, additional phone lines, copiers, fax machines, and other business equipment you buy for your spouse's use on the job.

Rules to Follow When Employing Your Family

The IRS is well aware of the tax benefits of hiring a child or spouse, so it's on the lookout for taxpayers who claim the benefit without really having their family members work in their businesses. If the IRS concludes that your children or spouse aren't really employees, you'll lose your tax deductions for their salary and benefits. And they'll have to pay tax on their benefits. To avoid this, you should follow these simple rules.

Rule 1: Your Child or Spouse Must Be a Real Employee

First of all, your spouse or children must be bona fide employees. Their work must be ordinary and necessary for your business, and their pay must be for services actually performed. Their services don't have to be indispensable, only common, accepted, helpful, and appropriate for your business. Any real work for your business can qualify—for example, you could employ your child or spouse to clean your office, answer the phone, stuff envelopes, input data, or make deliveries (a child may only make deliveries by foot or bicycle, not by car). You get no business deductions when you pay your child for personal services, such as babysitting or mowing your lawn at home. On the other hand, money you pay for yard work performed on business property could be deductible as a business expense.

The IRS won't believe that an extremely young child is a legitimate employee. How young is too young? The IRS has accepted that a seven-year-old child may be an employee but probably won't believe that children younger than seven are performing any useful work for your business.

In addition, where one spouse solely owns a business (usually as a sole proprietor) and the other spouse works as his or her employee, the spouse who owns the business must substantially control the business in terms of management decisions and the employee-spouse must be under that spouse's direction and control. If the employee-spouse has an equal say in the affairs of the business, provides substantially equal services to the business, and contributes capital to the business, that spouse *cannot be treated as an employee.*

You should keep track of the work and hours your children or spouse perform by having them fill out timesheets or timecards. You can find these in stationery stores or make a timesheet yourself. There are also many timesheet apps you can use. It should list the date, the services performed, and the time spent performing the services. Although not legally required, it's also a good idea to have your spouse or child sign a written employment agreement specifying job duties and hours. These duties should be related only to your business.

Rule 2: Compensation Must Be Reasonable

When you hire your children, it is advantageous (tax wise) to pay them as much as possible. That way, you can shift as much of your income as possible to your children, who are probably in a much lower income tax bracket. Conversely, you want to pay your spouse as little as possible, because you get no benefits from income shifting. This is because you and your spouse are in the same income tax bracket (assuming you file a joint return, as the vast majority of married people do). Moreover, your spouse will have to pay the employee's share of Social Security taxes on his or her salary—an amount that is not tax deductible. This tax is 7.65% up to the annual ceiling. (As your spouse's employer, you'll have to pay employment taxes on your spouse's salary as well, but these taxes are deductible business expenses.) The absolute minimum you can pay your spouse is the minimum wage in your area. On the other hand, at higher income levels, the pass-through tax deduction is based on the amount you pay your employees; so, to maximize this deduction, you might want to pay your spouse more. (See Chapter 10.)

However, you can't just pay any amount you choose: Your spouse's and/or your child's total compensation must be reasonable. Total compensation means the sum of the salary plus all the fringe benefits you provide your spouse, including health insurance and medical expense reimbursements, if any. This is determined by comparing the amount paid with the value of the services performed. You should have no problem as long as you pay no more than what you'd pay a stranger for the same work—don't try paying your child $100 per hour for office cleaning just to get a big tax deduction. Find out what workers performing similar services in your area are being paid. For example, if you plan to hire your teenager to do computer inputting, check with an employment agency or temp agency in your area to see what these workers are being paid.

To prove how much you paid (and that you actually paid it), you should pay your child or spouse by check or electronic deposit, not cash. Do this once or twice a month as you would for any other employee. The funds should be deposited in a bank account in your child's or spouse's name. Your child's bank account may be a trust account.

Rule 3: Comply With Legal Requirements for Employers

You must comply with most of the same legal requirements when you hire a child or spouse as you do when you hire a stranger. These rules are explained in detail in Publication 15, Circular E, *Employer's Tax Guide*, and Publication 929, *Tax Rules for Children and Dependents*. You can download them from the IRS website at www.irs.gov.

Employing Yourself

If you are a sole proprietor, partner in a partnership, or member of a limited liability company (LLC), you are not an employee of your business. You are a business owner. However, if you have incorporated your business, whether as a regular C corporation or an S corporation, you must be an employee of your corporation if you actively work in the business. In effect, you will be employing yourself. This has important tax consequences.

Your Company Must Pay Payroll Taxes

Your incorporated business must treat you just like any other employee for tax purposes. This means it must withhold income and FICA taxes from your pay and pay half of your FICA tax itself. It must also pay FUTA taxes for you. It gets a tax deduction for its contributions, the same as any other employer. (See "Tax Deductions for Employee Pay and Benefits," above.) Your corporation—not you personally—must pay these payroll taxes.

You can't avoid having your corporation pay payroll taxes by working for free. You must pay yourself at least a reasonable salary—what similar companies pay for the same services.

Tax Deductions for Your Salary and Benefits

When you're an employee, your salary is deductible by your incorporated business as a business expense. However, you must pay income tax on your salary, so there is no real tax savings.

But being an employee can have an upside. You'll be eligible for all of the tax-advantaged employee benefits discussed in "Tax Deductions for Employee Pay and Benefits," above. This means your corporation can provide you with benefits like health insurance and deduct the expense. (See Chapter 13 for more on deducting medical expenses.) If your corporation is a regular C corporation, you won't have to pay income tax on the value of your employee benefits. However, most employees of S corporations must pay tax on their employee benefits, so you probably won't get a tax benefit. The only exception is for employees of an S corporation who own less than 2% of the corporate stock. It isn't likely you'll have this little stock in your own S corporation.

Your Employee Expenses

Your corporation should reimburse you or pay directly for any expenses you incur while working for your corporation—for example, when you travel on company business.

If you comply with the requirements for an accountable plan, your corporation gets to deduct the expense and you don't have to count the reimbursement as income to you. If you fail to follow the rules, any reimbursements must be treated as employee income subject to tax.

You may not deduct any expenses you incur as an employee on your own personal tax return. This deduction was eliminated by the Tax Cuts and Jobs Act starting in 2018 through 2025.

Tax Deductions When You Hire Independent Contractors

As far as tax deductions are concerned, hiring independent contractors is very simple. Most of the time, the amounts you pay to an IC to perform services for your business will be deductible as business operating expenses. These expenses are deductible as long as they are ordinary, necessary, and reasonable in amount.

> EXAMPLE: Emily, a graphic designer, hires Don, an attorney, to sue a client who failed to pay her. He collects $5,000, and she pays him $1,500 of this amount. The $1,500 is an ordinary and necessary business operating expense—Emily may deduct it from her business income for the year.

Of course, you get no business deduction if you hire an IC to perform personal services.

> EXAMPLE: Emily pays lawyer Don $2,000 to write her personal will. This is a personal expense. Emily cannot deduct the $2,000 from her business income.

If you hire an IC to perform services on your behalf in the start-up phase of your business, to manufacture inventory, or as part of a long-term asset purchase, the rules for those types of expense must be followed. (See "Tax Deductions for Employee Pay and Benefits," above.)

> EXAMPLE: Don hires Ralph, a business broker, to help him find a good bakery shop to buy. After a long search, Ralph finds the right shop and Don buys it for $200,000. He pays Ralph a $12,000 broker's fee. This fee is a business start-up expense. Don may deduct $5,000 of the total fee during the first year he's in business and the remaining $7,000 over the first 180 months he's in business.

No Deduction for an IC's Taxes

When you hire an independent contractor, you don't have to withhold or pay any state or federal payroll taxes on the IC's behalf. Therefore, you get no deductions for the IC's taxes; the IC is responsible for paying them.

However, if you pay an unincorporated IC by cash, check, or direct deposit $600 or more during the year for business-related services, you must:

- obtain the IC's taxpayer identification number, and
- file IRS Form 1099-NEC, telling the IRS how much you paid the IC (before 2020, Form 1099-MISC was filed instead of Form 1099-NEC).

The IRS may impose a $270 fine per violation if you intentionally fail to file a Form 1099 when required. But, far more serious, you'll be subject to severe penalties if the IRS later audits you and determines that you misclassified the worker.

RESOURCE
For a detailed discussion of how to file a 1099 form and the consequences of not filing one, see *Working With Independent Contractors*, by Stephen Fishman (Nolo).

Paying Independent Contractors' Expenses

Independent contractors often incur expenses while performing services for their clients—for example, for travel, photocopying, phone calls, or materials. Many ICs want their clients to separately reimburse them for such expenses. The best practice is not to do this. It's better to pay ICs enough so they can cover their own expenses, rather than paying them less and having them bill you separately for expenses. This is because ICs who pay their own expenses are less likely to be viewed as your employees by the IRS or other government agencies.

However, it's customary in some businesses and professions for the client to reimburse the IC for expenses. For example, a lawyer who handles a business lawsuit will usually seek reimbursement for expenses such as photocopying, court reporters, and travel. If this is the case, you may pay these reimbursements.

When you reimburse an IC for a business-related expense, you, not the IC, get the deduction for the expense. You should not include the amount of the reimbursement on the 1099-NEC form you must file with the IRS reporting how much you paid the IC. The reimbursement is not considered income for the IC. Make sure to require ICs to document expenses with receipts, and save them in case the IRS questions the payments.

You may reimburse an IC for business-related travel expenses and deduct the expense, but make sure proper documentation is provided. Only 50% of meal expenses while travelling are deductible. It is unclear whether meals consumed other than while travelling are deductible. (See Chapter 14.)

Retirement Deductions

When you own your own business, it's up to you to establish and fund your own pension plan to supplement the Social Security benefits you'll receive when you retire. The tax law helps you do this by providing tax deductions and other income tax benefits for your retirement account contributions and earnings.

This chapter provides a general overview of the retirement plan choices you have as a small business owner. Choosing what type of account to establish is just as important as deciding what to invest in once you open your account—if not more so. Once you set up your retirement account, you can always change your investments within the account with little or no difficulty. But changing the type of retirement account you have may prove difficult and costly. So it's best to spend some time up front learning about your choices and deciding which plan will best meet your needs.

RESOURCE

For additional information on the tax aspects of retirement, see:

- *IRAs, 401(k)s & Other Retirement Plans: Strategies for Taking Your Money Out,* by Twila Slesnick and John C. Suttle (Nolo)
- IRS Publication 560, *Retirement Plans for Small Business,* and
- IRS Publication 590, *Individual Retirement Arrangements (IRAs).*

CAUTION

You should get professional help with your plan if you have employees (other than a spouse). Having employees makes it much more complicated to set up a retirement plan. (See "Having Employees Complicates Matters—Tremendously," below.) Because of the many complex issues raised by having employees, any business owner with employees should turn to a professional consultant for help in choosing, establishing, and administering a retirement plan.

Why You Need a Retirement Plan (or Plans)

In all likelihood, you will receive Social Security benefits when you retire. However, Social Security will probably cover only half of your needs—possibly less, depending upon your retirement lifestyle. You'll need to make up this shortfall with your own retirement investments.

When it comes to saving for retirement, small business owners are better off than employees of most companies. This is because the government allows small businesses to set up retirement accounts specifically designed for small business owners. These accounts provide enormous tax benefits that are intended to maximize the money you can save during your working years for your retirement years. The amount you are allowed to contribute each year to your retirement account depends upon the type of account you establish and how much money you earn. If your business doesn't earn money, you won't be able to make any contributions—you need income to fund retirement accounts.

The two biggest benefits that most of these plans provide—tax deductions for plan contributions and tax deferral on investment earnings—are discussed in more detail below.

Tax Deduction

Retirement accounts that comply with IRS requirements are called "tax qualified."

You can deduct the amount you contribute to a tax-qualified retirement account from your income taxes (except for Roth IRAs and Roth 401(k)s). If you are a sole proprietor, a partner in a partnership, or an LLC member, you can deduct from your personal income contributions you make to a retirement account. If you have incorporated your business, the corporation can deduct as a business expense contributions that it makes on your behalf. Either way, you or your business get a substantial income tax savings with these contributions.

EXAMPLE: Art, a sole proprietor, contributes $10,000 this year to a qualified retirement account. He can deduct the entire amount from his personal income taxes. Because Art is in the 24% tax bracket, he saves $2,400 in income taxes for the year (24% × $10,000), and he has also saved $10,000 toward his retirement.

Tax Deferral

In addition to the tax deduction you receive for putting money into a retirement account, another tremendous tax benefit to retirement accounts is tax deferral. When you earn money on an investment, you usually must pay taxes on those earnings in the same year that you earn the money. For example, you must pay taxes on the interest you earn on a savings account or certificate of deposit in the year when the interest accrues. And when you sell an investment at a profit, you must pay income tax in that year on the gain you receive. For example, you must pay tax on the profit you earn from selling stock in the year that you sell the stock.

A different rule applies, however, for earnings you receive from a tax-qualified retirement account. You do not pay taxes on investment earnings from retirement accounts until you withdraw the funds. Because most people withdraw these funds at retirement, they are often in a lower income tax bracket when they pay tax on these earnings. This can result in substantial tax savings for people who would have had to pay higher taxes on these earnings if they paid as the earnings accumulated.

CAUTION

Retirement accounts have restrictions on withdrawals. The tax deferral benefits you receive by putting your money in a retirement account come at a price: You're not supposed to withdraw the money until you are 59½ years old; and, after you turn 72, you must withdraw a certain minimum amount each year and pay tax on it (but, due to the COVID-19 pandemic, no such withdrawals were required for 2020). Stiff penalties are imposed if you fail to follow these rules. So, if you aren't prepared to give up your right to use this money freely, you should think about a taxable account instead where there are no restrictions on your use of your money. You should also consider a Roth IRA or Roth 401(k)—you can withdraw your contributions to these accounts (but not earnings) at any time without penalty (see below).

RESOURCE

For detailed guidance on distributions from retirement accounts, refer to *IRAs, 401(k)s & Other Retirement Plans: Strategies for Taking Your Money Out,* **by Twila Slesnick and John C. Suttle (Nolo).**

Having Employees Complicates Matters—Tremendously

If you own your own business and have no employees (other than your spouse), you can probably choose, establish, and administer your own retirement plan with little or no assistance. The instant you add employees to the mix, however, virtually every aspect of your plan becomes more complex. This is primarily due to something called "nondiscrimination rules." These rules are designed to ensure that your retirement plan benefits all employees, not just you. In general, the laws prohibit you from doing the following:

- making disproportionately large contributions for some plan participants (like yourself) and not for others
- unfairly excluding certain employees from participating in the plan, or
- unfairly withholding benefits from former employees or their beneficiaries.

If the IRS finds the plan to be discriminatory at any time (usually during an audit), the plan could be disqualified—that is, determined not to satisfy IRS rules. If this happens, you and your employees will owe income tax and probably penalties, as well.

Having employees also increases the plan's reporting requirements. You must provide employees with a summary of the terms of the plan, notification of any changes you make, and an annual report of contributions. And you must file an annual tax return. Because of all the complex issues raised by having employees, any business owner with employees (other than a spouse) should seek professional help when creating a retirement plan.

Special Retirement Account Withdrawal Rules for 2020

Ordinarily, if you withdraw money from an IRA, a 401(k), or another tax-qualified retirement plan before age 59½, you must pay a 10% early withdrawal penalty plus regular income tax on the amount. However, due to the COVID-19 pandemic, Congress eliminated the penalty for pandemic-related withdrawals for 2020. You could withdraw up to $100,000 from your plan during 2020 without paying the 10% penalty if you:

- your spouse, or dependent were diagnosed with COVID-19
- experienced adverse financial consequences because you were quarantined, furloughed, laid off, or forced to reduce work hours due to COVID-19
- were unable to work because of a lack of child care due to COVID-19 and experienced adverse financial consequences as a result, or
- own or operate a business that closed or reduced operating hours due to COVID-19.

There were no income limits on who could make such withdrawals. And you could use the money for any purpose.

You can't make such penalty-free withdrawals after 2020.

Ordinarily, when you withdraw money from a retirement plan (other than a Roth IRA or Roth 401(k)) you must pay all the tax due that year. However, you have three years to pay the income tax on your up-to-$100,000 2020 withdrawals. You can spread your tax payments equally over the three years, starting in 2020.

Moreover, you don't have to pay any tax at all on your withdrawal if you pay the entire amount back within three years of the withdrawal date. You can pay the money back in a lump sum or with multiple recontributions.

Individual Retirement Accounts—IRAs

The simplest type of tax-deferred retirement account is the individual retirement account, or" IRA." An IRA is a retirement account established by an individual, not a business. You can have an IRA whether you're a business owner or an employee in someone else's business. Moreover, you can establish an IRA for yourself as an individual and also set up one or more of the other types of retirement plans discussed below, which are just for businesses.

An IRA is a trust or custodial account set up for the benefit of an individual or his or her beneficiaries. The trustee or custodian administers the account. The trustee can be a bank, mutual fund, or brokerage firm, or another financial institution (such as an insurance company).

IRAs are extremely easy to set up and administer. You need a written IRA agreement but don't need to file any tax forms with the IRS. The financial institution you use to set up your account will usually ask you to complete IRS Form 5305, *Traditional Individual Retirement Trust Account*, which serves as an IRA agreement and meets all of the IRS requirements. Keep the form in your records—you don't file it with the IRS.

Most financial institutions offer an array of IRA accounts that provide for different types of investments. You can invest your IRA money in just about anything: stocks, bonds, mutual funds, treasury bills and notes, and bank certificates of deposit. However, you can't invest in collectibles such as art, antiques, stamps, or other personal property.

You can establish as many IRA accounts as you want, but there is a maximum combined amount of money you can contribute to all of your IRA accounts each year. This amount goes up every year. Maximum contributions are shown in the chart below. The limit is adjusted each year for inflation in $500 increments.

There are different limits for workers who are at least 50 years old. Anyone at least 50 years old at the end of the year can make increased annual contributions of $1,000 per year. This rule is intended to allow older people to catch up with younger folks, who will have more years to make contributions at the higher levels.

Annual IRA Contribution Limits		
Tax Year	Under Age 50	Aged 50 or Over
2021	$6,000	$7,000

If you are married, you can double the contribution limits. For example, a married couple under 50 can contribute up to $6,000 per spouse into their IRAs, or a total of $12,000. This is true even if one spouse isn't working. To take advantage of doubling, you must file a joint tax return, and the working spouse must earn at least as much as the combined IRA contribution.

Traditional IRAs

The two different types of IRAs that you can choose from are:
- traditional IRAs, and
- Roth IRAs.

Traditional IRAs have been around since 1974. Anybody who has earned income (from a job, business, or alimony) can have a traditional IRA. As stated above, you can deduct your annual contributions to your IRA from your taxable income. If neither you nor your spouse (if you have one) has another retirement plan, you may deduct your contributions no matter how high your income is.

However, there are income limits on your deductions if you are covered by another retirement plan. For these purposes, being covered by another plan means you have one of the self-employed plans described below (or are covered by an employer plan).

These limits are based on your and your spouse's annual modified adjusted gross income (MAGI for short). Your MAGI is your adjusted gross income before it is reduced by your IRA contributions and certain other more unusual items. These limits are set forth in the following chart.

Annual Income Limits for IRA Deductions				
Tax Year	Married Filing Jointly		Single Taxpayer	
	Full Deduction	Partial Deduction	Full Deduction	Partial Deduction
2021	Under $105,000	$105,000–125,000	Under $66,000	$66,000–$76,000

If you aren't covered by a retirement plan at work, but your spouse (with whom you file jointly) is covered, you get a full IRA deduction if your MAGI is under $198,000. Your deduction is phased out between $198,000 and $208,000, and eliminated completely if your MAGI is over $208,000.

You can still contribute to an IRA even if you can't take a deduction. This is called a "nondeductible IRA." Your money will grow in the account tax free; and, when you make withdrawals, you'll only have to pay tax on your account earnings, not the amount of your contributions (which have already been taxed). However, figuring out how much is taxable and how much is tax free can be a big accounting headache.

For 2020 and later, there is no age limit on making contributions to IRAs.

There are time restrictions on when you can (and when you must) withdraw money from your IRA. You are not supposed to withdraw any money from your IRA until you reach age 59½, unless you die or become disabled. Under the normal tax rules, you are required to start withdrawing at least a minimum amount of your money by April 1 of the year after the year you turn 72 (but, due to the COVID-19 pandemic, no such withdrawals were required for 2020). Once you start withdrawing money from your IRA, the amount you withdraw will be included in your regular income for income tax purposes.

As a general rule, if you make early withdrawals, you must pay regular income tax on the amount you take out, plus a 10% federal tax penalty. There are some exceptions to this early withdrawal penalty (for example, if you withdraw money to purchase a first home or pay educational expenses, the penalty doesn't apply—subject to dollar limits). To learn about these and other exceptions in detail, see *IRAs, 401(k)s & Other Retirement Plans: Strategies for Taking Your Money Out*, by Twila Slesnick and John C. Suttle (Nolo). (Penalty-free withdrawals of up to $100,000 due to the COVID-19 pandemic were permitted during 2020; see "Special Retirement Account Withdrawal Rules for 2020," above.)

Roth IRAs

Like traditional IRAs, Roth IRAs are tax deferred and allow your retirement savings to grow without any tax burden. Unlike traditional IRAs, however, your contributions to Roth IRAs are not tax deductible. Instead, you get to withdraw your money from the account tax free when you retire.

Once you have established your account, your ability to contribute to it will be affected by changes in your income level. If you are single and your income reaches $125,000 in 2021, your ability to contribute to your Roth IRA will begin to phase out. Once your income reaches $140,000, you will no longer be able to make contributions. If you are married and filing a joint return with your spouse, your ability to contribute to your account will start to phase out when your income reaches $198,000, and you will be prohibited from making any contributions at all when your income reaches $208,000. These are the 2021 limits. The limits are adjusted for inflation each year.

You can withdraw the money you contributed to a Roth IRA penalty free anytime—you already paid tax on it so the government doesn't care. But the earnings on your investments in a Roth IRA are a different matter. You can't withdraw these until after five years. Early withdrawals of your earnings are subject to income tax and early distribution penalties. You are not, however, required to make withdrawals when you reach age 72. Because Roth IRA withdrawals are tax free, the government doesn't care if you leave your money in your account indefinitely. However, your investment earnings will be tax free on withdrawal only if you leave it in your Roth IRA for at least five years.

Is the Roth IRA a good deal? If your tax rate when you retire is higher than your tax rate before retirement, you'll probably be better off with a Roth IRA than a traditional IRA because you won't have to pay tax on your withdrawals at the higher rates. The opposite is true if your taxes go down when you retire. The catch is that nobody can know for sure what their tax rate will be when they retire. You can find several online calculators that will help you compare your results with a Roth IRA versus traditional IRA at www.choosetosave.org/calculators. Much more information on Roth IRAs can be found at www.rothira.com.

Roth IRA Conversions

If the Roth IRA sounds attractive to you, and you already have a traditional IRA, you may convert it to a Roth IRA. This can vastly increase the amount of money in your Roth IRA. However, when you convert to a Roth IRA, you'll have to pay income tax on the amount of the conversion. For example, if you convert $20,000 from your traditional IRA to a Roth IRA, you'll have to add $20,000 to your taxable income for the year. If you were in the 25% bracket, this would add $5,000 to your income taxes. One way to keep these taxes down is to convert only a portion of your traditional IRAs into a Roth each year for several years instead of doing it all at once.

Whether a Roth conversion is a good idea or not depends on many factors, including your age, your current tax rate, and your tax rate upon retirement. You can find an online calculator at www.dinkytown.net/retirement.html that allows you to compare the results when you convert to a Roth versus leaving your traditional IRAs alone. You may not undo a Roth IRA conversion, called a "Roth recharacterization." Thus, once you elect to convert a traditional IRA to a Roth you must pay the income tax due. You can't get out of it by changing your mind and undoing the conversion.

Employer IRAs

You can establish an employer IRA as long as you are in business and earn a profit. You don't have to have employees working for you, and it doesn't matter how your business is organized: You can be a sole proprietor, a partner in a partnership, a member of a limited liability company, or an owner of a regular or S corporation.

The great advantage of employer IRAs is that you can contribute more than you can with traditional IRAs and Roth IRAs, both of which have lower annual contribution limits. And as long as you meet the requirements for establishing an employer IRA, you can have this type of IRA in addition to one or more individual IRAs.

There are two kinds of employer IRAs to choose from: SEP-IRAs and SIMPLE IRAs.

SEP-IRAs

SEP-IRAs are designed for the self-employed. Any person who receives self-employment income from providing a service can establish a SEP-IRA. It doesn't matter whether you work full time or part time. You can even have a SEP-IRA if you are covered by a retirement plan at a full-time employee job.

A SEP-IRA is a simplified employee pension. It's very similar to an IRA, except that you can contribute more money under this plan. Instead of being limited to a $6,000 to $7,000 annual contribution (2021), you can invest up to 20% of your net profit from self-employment every year, up to a maximum of $58,000 a year in 2021. You don't have to make contributions every year, and your contributions can vary from year to year. As with other IRAs, you can invest your money in almost anything (stocks, bonds, notes, or mutual funds).

You can deduct your contributions to SEP-IRAs from your income taxes, and the interest on your SEP-IRA investments accrues tax free until you withdraw the money. Withdrawals from SEP-IRAs are subject to the same rules that apply to traditional IRAs. This means that if you withdraw your money from your SEP-IRA before you reach age 59½, you'll have to pay a 10% tax penalty plus regular income taxes on your withdrawal, unless an exception applies. And you must begin to withdraw your money by April 1 of the year after the year you turn 72 (but, due to the COVID-19 pandemic, no such withdrawals were required for 2020).

SIMPLE IRAs

Self-employed people and companies with fewer than 100 employees can set up SIMPLE IRAs. If you establish a SIMPLE IRA, you are not allowed to have any other retirement plans for your business (although you may still have an individual IRA). SIMPLE IRAs are easy to set up and administer and will enable you to make larger annual contributions than a SEP or Keogh plan if you earn less than $10,000 per year from your business.

SIMPLE IRAs may be established only by an employer on behalf of its employees. If you are a sole proprietor, you are deemed to employ yourself for these purposes and may establish a SIMPLE IRA in your own name as the employer. If you are a partner in a partnership, an LLC member, or the owner of an incorporated business, the SIMPLE IRA must be established by your business, not you personally.

Contributions to SIMPLE IRAs are divided into two parts. You may contribute:

- up to 100% of your net income from your business up to an annual limit—the contribution limit is $13,500 for 2021 ($16,500 if you are 50 or older), and
- a matching contribution that can equal 3% of your net business income.

If you're an employee of your incorporated business, your first contribution (called a salary reduction contribution) comes from your salary, and the matching contribution is paid by your business.

The limits on contributions to SIMPLE IRAs might seem very low, but they could work to your advantage if you earn a small income from your business—for example, if you only work at it part time. This is because you can contribute an amount equal to 100% of your earnings, up to the $13,500 or $16,500 limits. Thus, for example, if your net earnings are only $10,000, you could contribute the entire amount (plus a 3% employer contribution). You can't do this with any of the other plans because their percentage limits are much lower. For example, you may contribute only 20% of your net self-employment income to a SEP-IRA or Keogh, so you would be limited to a $2,000 contribution if you had a $10,000 profit.

The money in a SIMPLE IRA can be invested like any other IRA. Withdrawals from SIMPLE IRAs are subject to the same rules as traditional IRAs, with one big exception: Early withdrawals from SIMPLE IRAs are subject to a 25% tax penalty if the withdrawal is made within two years after the date you first contributed to your account. Other early withdrawals are subject to a 10% penalty, the same as traditional IRAs, unless an exception applies. (Penalty-free withdrawals of up to $100,000 due to the COVID-19 pandemic were permitted during 2020. See "Special Retirement Account Withdrawal Rules for 2020" above.)

Keogh Plans

Keogh plans—named after the Congressman who sponsored the legislation that created them—are only for business owners who are sole proprietors, partners in partnerships, or LLC members. You can't have a Keogh if you incorporate your business.

Keoghs require more paperwork to set up than employer IRAs, but they also offer more options: You can contribute more to these plans and still get an income tax deduction for your contributions.

Types of Keogh Plans

The two basic types of Keogh plans are:
- defined contribution plans, in which benefits are based on the amount contributed to and accumulated in the plan, and
- defined benefit plans, which provide for a set benefit upon retirement.

There are two types of defined contribution plans: profit-sharing plans and money purchase plans. These plans can be used separately or in tandem with one another.

Setting Up a Keogh Plan

As with individual IRAs and employer IRAs, you can set up a Keogh plan at most banks, brokerage houses, mutual funds, and other financial institutions, as well as trade or professional organizations. You can also choose among a huge array of investments for your money.

To set up your plan, you must adopt a written Keogh plan and set up a trust or custodial account with your plan provider to invest your funds. Your plan provider will ordinarily have an IRS-approved master or prototype Keogh plan for you to sign. You can also have a special plan drawn up for you, but this is expensive and unnecessary for most small business owners.

Profit Sharing Plans

You can contribute up to 20% of your net self-employment income to a profit-sharing Keogh plan, up to a maximum of $58,000 per year in 2021. You can contribute any amount up to the limit each year or not contribute at all.

Money Purchase Plans

In a money purchase plan, you contribute a fixed percentage of your net self-employment earnings every year. You decide how much to contribute each year. Make sure you will be able to afford the contributions each year because you can't skip them, even if your business earns no profit for the year. In return for giving up flexibility, you can contribute a higher percentage of your earnings with a money purchase plan: the lesser of 25% of your compensation or $58,000 in 2021 (the same maximum amount as the profit-sharing plan).

Withdrawing Your Money

You may begin to withdraw your money from your Keogh plan after you reach age 59½. If you have a profit-sharing plan, early withdrawals are permitted without penalty in cases of financial hardship, if you become disabled, or if you have to pay health expenses in excess of 7.5% of your adjusted gross income. If you have a money purchase plan, early withdrawals are permitted if you become disabled, leave your business after you turn 55, or make child support or alimony payments from the plan under a court order. Otherwise, early withdrawals from profit-sharing and money purchase Keogh plans are subject to a 10% penalty. (However, penalty-free withdrawals of up to $100,000 due to the COVID-19 pandemic were permitted during 2020; see "Special Retirement Account Withdrawal Rules for 2020," above.)

Solo 401(k) Plans

Most people have heard of 401(k) plans—they are retirement plans established by businesses for their employees. A 401(k) is a type of profit-sharing plan in which a business's employees make plan contributions from their salaries and the business makes a matching contribution. These plans are complex to establish and administer and are generally used only by larger businesses. Until recently, self-employed people and businesses without employees rarely used them, because they offered no benefit over other profit-sharing plans that are much easier to set up and run.

However, things have changed. Now, any business owner who has no employees (other than a spouse) can establish a solo self-employed 401(k) plan (also called a "one-person" or "individual" 401(k)). Solo 401(k) plans are designed specifically for business owners without employees.

Solo 401(k) plans have the following advantages over other retirement plans:

- You can make very large contributions—as much as 20% of your net profit from self-employment, plus an elective deferral contribution of up to $19,500 in 2021. The maximum contribution per year is $58,000 (2021) (the same maximum amount as for profit-sharing and money purchase plans discussed in "Keogh Plans," above). Business owners over 50 may make additional catch-up contributions of up to $6,500 per year that are not counted toward the $58,000 limit.

- You can borrow up to 50% of your vested account balance up to $50,000 from your solo 401(k) plan), as long as you repay the loan within five years (you cannot borrow from a traditional IRA, Roth IRA, SEP-IRA, or SIMPLE IRA).

As with other plans, you must pay a 10% penalty tax on withdrawals you make before age 59½, but you may make penalty-free early withdrawals for reasons of personal hardship (defined as an "immediate financial need" that can't be met any other way).

You can set up a solo 401(k) plan at most banks, brokerage houses, mutual funds, and other financial institutions and invest the money in a variety of ways. You must adopt a written plan and set up a trust or custodial account with your plan provider to invest your funds. Financial institutions that offer solo 401(k) plans have preapproved ready-made plans that you can use.

CAUTION

Beware of retirement account deadlines. If you want to establish any of the retirement accounts discussed in this chapter and take a tax deduction for the year, you must meet specific deadlines. The deadlines vary according to the type of account you set up, as shown in the following chart. Once you establish your account, you have until the due date of your tax return for the year (April 15 of the following year, plus any filing extensions) to contribute to your account and take a deduction. (For 2021, the due date for filing individual 2020 tax returns was extended to May 17 due to the COVID-19 pandemic; the extended filing date remained October 15, 2021.)

Retirement Account Deadlines	
Plan Type	Deadline for Establishing Plan
Traditional IRA	Due date of tax return (April 15)
Roth IRA	Due date of tax return (April 15 plus extensions)
SEP-IRA	Due date of tax return (April 15 plus extensions)
SIMPLE IRA	October 1
Keogh Profit Sharing Plan	December 31
Keogh Money Purchase Plan	December 31
Keogh Defined Benefit Plan	December 31
401(k) Plan	December 31

Medical Expenses

Whaen you own your own business, you don't have an employer to provide you with health insurance. Unless you can obtain coverage through a spouse whose employer provides family coverage, you must obtain health insurance and pay for it and other health care costs on your own.

This chapter explains how the Affordable Care Act (ACA) affects small business owners, and the array of tax deductions and strategies available to them to help lower their health care costs.

The Affordable Care Act (ACA)

The Patient Protection and Affordable Care Act (ACA) enacted by Congress in 2010 (also referred to as "Obamacare") took effect in 2014. The ACA affects all businesses, no matter how large or small. However, it has been particularly significant for the self-employed—especially those who have had trouble obtaining affordable health insurance. Congress has tweaked the ACA and eliminated one of its major provisions— the individual mandate. Otherwise, the ACA remains largely in place. Here are the key things to know about the ACA:

- Starting in 2019, individuals who fail to obtain health insurance for themselves and their dependents were no longer required to pay a penalty to the IRS (but a few states impose penalties).
- It requires larger businesses to offer their employees health coverage or pay substantial penalties.
- It imposes minimum standards for health coverage.
- You can obtain health coverage through a health insurance exchange.
- You might qualify for a premium tax credit to help you pay for your coverage. For 2021 and 2022, this credit is available to many higher-income individuals.

 RESOURCE
For more information on all aspects of the ACA, see
www.healthcare.gov.

Federal Individual Health Insurance Mandate Terminated

One of the ACA's principal features was the individual health insurance mandate. Subject to certain exceptions, all Americans were required to obtain at least minimal comprehensive health insurance coverage or pay a penalty to the IRS. Congress effectively eliminated the individual mandate starting in 2019 by reducing the penalty for noncompliance to zero. Thus, during 2019 and later, individuals who fail to obtain health coverage are not penalized by the federal government. As far as the federal government is concerned, an individual's decision whether to obtain health insurance is purely voluntary, just as it was before the ACA was enacted.

However, some states have enacted their own statewide health care individual mandates. These include California, the District of Columbia, Massachusetts, New Jersey, Rhode Island, and Vermont. If you live in any of these states, you may have to pay a penalty to the state if you don't have health insurance. Other states are considering implementing their own mandates.

The Employer Mandate

The ACA's employer mandate has not been changed. Businesses with at least 50 full-time employees (or a combination of full-time and part-time employees that's "equivalent" to at least 50 full-time employees) are required to provide at least 95% of their full-time employees and their families with "minimum essential healthcare coverage," or pay a tax penalty. Employers who provide no coverage at all must pay a penalty to the IRS equal to $3,750 per year per employee (excluding the first 30 employees). The penalty is smaller for employers who provide coverage that doesn't meet the minimum standards. Employees can be required to help contribute toward their coverage, but the amount of any employee contributions is capped at 9.83% of household income.

For detailed guidance on how to determine whether your business has more than 50 full-time employees for the ACA's purposes, visit the IRS ACA Information Center for Applicable Large Employers (ALEs) at www.irs.gov/affordable-care-act/employers/aca-information-center-for-applicable-large-employers-ales.

Smaller employers—those with fewer than 50 full-time equivalent employees—are not subject to the employer mandate. However, if they do elect to provide their employees with health coverage, they may qualify for tax credits. (See "Tax Credits for Employee Health Insurance," below.) Moreover, smaller employers are able to purchase coverage through state small business health insurance exchanges (also called "SHOP exchanges"). This can help keep their costs down because they'll become part of a much larger risk pool.

ACA Health Insurance Rules

To help everyone obtain coverage, the ACA imposed the following rules on all health insurers and the coverage they provide.

No preexisting condition exclusions. First, health insurers are not allowed to use your health status to deny you coverage. This means you can purchase health insurance regardless of any current or past health conditions.

Insurance premium rates. Insurers may vary their premiums based on the following factors only: your age (older people may be charged up to 300% more than the young), tobacco use, geography, and the number of family members covered. They may not charge you more based on your health status.

Minimal comprehensive coverage. All health insurers must offer comprehensive health insurance that provides at least the following ten essential health benefits:

- ambulatory ("walk-in") patient services
- emergency services
- hospitalization
- maternity/newborn care
- mental health and substance use disorder services (including behavioral health treatment)

- prescription drugs
- rehab and habilitative services/devices
- lab services
- preventive/wellness services and chronic disease management, and
- pediatric services (including oral and vision care).

No rescission. Your insurer can't cancel your insurance if you get sick.

No dollar caps. Health insurers cannot impose lifetime or annual dollar limits on their coverage. So, no matter how much your health care costs, your insurer must pay for it all once you've paid your total annual out-of-pocket limit.

State Health Insurance Exchanges

Online health insurance exchanges (also called "marketplaces") have been established to help individuals and small businesses obtain health coverage.

Several states have established their own online health care exchanges that they run themselves or with help from the federal government. The states that don't have their own marketplace use the federal government's insurance exchange at www.healthcare.gov. Links to the appropriate online exchange are available at: www.healthcare.gov/get-coverage. The states and federal government have also established call centers for those who prefer to obtain information from a person over the phone.

You aren't required to obtain your health insurance through your state's exchange. You can obtain it on your own or through an insurance broker. You might have more choices if you shop outside your state's exchange. However, you must obtain your insurance through your state exchange to qualify for health insurance premium credits.

Open Enrollment Periods

Under the ACA's rules, unless you have a "qualifying life event" as described below, individual nongroup coverage for yourself and your dependents can be obtained only if you apply during the annual open enrollment period. This is so whether you obtain coverage from your state health insurance exchange or directly from a private health insurer.

Ordinarily, in most states, the open enrollment period is November 1 to December 15 for coverage to start the following year; but some states have longer open enrollment periods. However, during 2021, the open enrollment period was extended to make it easier for people to sign up for coverage during the COVID-19 pandemic. In most states, the extended enrollment period was February 15, 2021 through August 15, 2021. That is, you could sign up as late as August 2021 for 2021 coverage. The open enrollment period for 2022 coverage is scheduled to go back to normal, so you'll have to sign up by December 15, 2021, for coverage to begin in January 2022.

Qualifying Life Events

After the open enrollment period ends, individual nongroup health insurance coverage is available for purchase only for individuals who have a "qualifying life event" during the year. This includes:

- losing your existing health insurance coverage—for example, because you quit your job, were laid off, or your work hours were reduced below the level required for you to qualify for employer-provided coverage
- getting married, divorced, or legally separated
- giving birth to or adopting a child
- losing your coverage because you moved to another state or a part of the same state outside of your health plan service area
- losing eligibility for Medicaid—for example, because your income grew
- no longer being eligible to receive coverage as someone else's dependent—for example, you turn 26 and are no longer eligible for coverage through your parents' plan
- being timely enrolled in coverage through your state exchange, and income increases or decreases enough to change your eligibility for subsidies, or
- becoming a U.S. citizen.

Once a qualifying life event occurs, you have 60 days to obtain individual coverage, either through your state health insurance exchange or private insurers. This period is called your "special enrollment opportunity."

Note carefully that the following are not qualifying life events:
- getting sick
- getting pregnant
- losing your coverage because you didn't pay your premiums, or
- voluntarily quitting your existing health coverage.

Thus, for example, you can't go without coverage past the open enrollment deadline and then decide you want to enroll because you get sick (or get pregnant; but after you have a child, you can obtain coverage).

Medicaid Enrollment

You can enroll in Medicaid or the Children's Health Insurance Program (CHIP) in your state at any time. There is no open enrollment period for these programs. Medicaid is publicly funded health care for low-income and disabled Americans. The Medicaid eligibility rules vary from state to state. In 36 states and the District of Columbia, adults can get Medicaid if their income is up to 138% of the federal poverty level. This is $17,774 a year for individuals, or $36,570 for a family of four. Eligibility is determined by current monthly income, so individuals can qualify even if their annual income is over these levels. For more information, see www.healthcare.gov/medicaid-chip.

Health Insurance Premium Tax Credits

To help people afford this coverage, the ACA provides a premium assistance credit for those who purchase health insurance from a state exchange and are not eligible for other affordable coverage, for example, through a spouse's employer. The purpose of the credits is to ensure that people don't have to spend more than a specified percentage of their household income on health insurance.

As originally designed, the premium tax credit was only for low and moderate income people whose household income was between 100% and 400% of the federal poverty level (FPL). For example, based on the 2020 FPL, the credit was available in 2020 only for individuals with household incomes below $51,040 and families of four with incomes below $104,800. If you earned one dollar more than these limits, you got no credit.

However, Congress removed the 400% of FPL limit for 2021 and 2022. During these years, Americans who earn over 400% of the federal poverty level are required to pay no more than 8.5% of their household income for ACA health insurance. Regardless of how high their income, they are entitled to a premium tax credit to the extent the cost of the silver benchmark plan in their area exceeds 8.5% of their household income. Those with incomes under 400% of the federal poverty level are required to pay less than 8.5% of their income for health insurance, based on a sliding scale.

As a result of these changes, many self-employed business owners will qualify for premium tax credits for the first time; others will get larger credits. For example, if your income is $100,000, you are required to pay no more than $8,500 for ACA coverage. If a silver plan for your family costs $15,000, you are entitled to a $6,500 premium tax credit. You can get an estimate of the credit you qualify for using the Kaiser Health Reform Health Insurance Marketplace Calculator (https://kff.org/interactive/subsidy-calculator).

The old rules are scheduled to return in 2023, although this could change. But for 2021–2022 at least, the new rules represent the most significant upgrade the ACA has received since it was adopted in 2010. If you already have ACA coverage, you might be able to switch to a more expensive policy with better coverage if you now qualify for the tax credits. If you obtain individual health coverage outside your health exchange, you should consider whether it's worthwhile to switch to ACA coverage.

To obtain the ACA credit, you must: (1) obtain your health insurance through your state exchange, (2) file a joint return if you're married, and (3) not have access to affordable health coverage elsewhere, like through an employer or spouse's employer.

Although they are called "credits," these payments are really a government-funded subsidy. You don't need to owe any income taxes to receive the credit. Moreover, unless you direct otherwise, the full credit amount for the year is paid by the federal government directly to your health insurance company when you enroll in your health insurance plan. This means that you do not need to wait until your taxes have been filed and processed to receive the credit; nor do you need to pay the full premium when you purchase health insurance and then wait to be reimbursed.

The Personal Deduction for Medical Expenses

All taxpayers—whether or not they own a business—are entitled to a personal income tax deduction for medical and dental expenses for themselves and their dependents. Eligible expenses include both health insurance premiums and out-of-pocket expenses not covered by insurance. However, two significant limitations on the deduction make it virtually useless (unusable) for most taxpayers.

To take the personal deduction, you must comply with both of the following requirements:

- You must itemize your deductions on IRS Schedule A. You can itemize deductions only if all of your itemized deductions exceed the standard deduction for the year. The Tax Cuts and Jobs Act greatly increased the standard deduction to $25,100 for joint returns and $12,550 for single returns in 2021. Itemized deductions include medical expenses, home mortgage interest, state and local taxes (up to a $10,000 annual limit), charitable contributions, and a few others. As a result, only 10% of taxpayers itemize.

- All taxpayers who itemize can deduct the amount of their medical and dental expenses that is more than 7.5% of their adjusted gross income (AGI). (Your AGI is your net business income and other taxable income, minus deductions for retirement contributions and one-half of your self-employment taxes, plus a few other items (as shown at the bottom of your Form 1040).)

EXAMPLE: Al is a self-employed interior decorator whose adjusted gross income for 2021 is $100,000. He pays $1,000 per month for health insurance for himself and his wife. He spends another $4,000 in out-of-pocket medical and dental expenses for the year, for a total $16,000 in medical expenses. Al may deduct his medical expenses only if all of his itemized deductions exceed the $25,100 standard deduction for the year. If they do exceed the standard deduction, his personal medical expense deduction is limited to the amount he paid that's more than $7,500 (7.5% × $100,000 = $7,500). Because he paid a total of $16,000 in medical expenses for the year, his deduction is limited to $8,500.

As you can see, unless your medical expenses are substantial, the 7.5% limitation eats up much of your deduction. The more money you make, the less you can deduct. For this reason, most business owners need to look elsewhere for meaningful medical expense deductions.

Deducting Health Insurance Costs

Health insurance premiums are the largest medical expense most people pay. There are several ways that business owners can deduct these costs.

Personal Income Tax Deduction for the Self-Employed

Self-employed people are allowed to deduct health insurance premiums (including dental and long-term care coverage) for themselves, their spouses, their dependents, and their children under age 27. Self-employed people who have Medicare coverage may deduct their Medicare premiums as part of the self-employed health insurance deduction—this includes all Medicare parts (not just Part B). This insurance can also cover their children up to age 26, whether or not they are dependents. For these purposes, a child includes a son, daughter, stepchild, adopted child, or eligible foster child. Sole proprietors, partners in partnerships, LLC members, and S corporation shareholders who own more than 2% of the company stock can use this deduction. Basically, any business owner, other than the owner of a regular C corporation, can take this deduction. And you get the deduction whether you purchase your health insurance policy as an individual or have your business obtain it. It's important to understand, however, that this is not a business deduction. It is a special personal deduction for the self-employed. Ordinarily, this deduction applies only to your federal, state, and local income taxes, not to your self-employment taxes.

EXAMPLE: Kim is a sole proprietor who pays $10,000 each year for health insurance for herself, her husband, and her three children. Her business earns far more than this amount in profit each year. Every year, she may deduct her $10,000 annual health insurance expenses from her gross income for federal and

294 DEDUCT IT! LOWER YOUR SMALL BUSINESS TAXES

state income tax purposes. Because her combined federal and state income tax rate is 30%, this saves her $3,000 in income taxes each year. Kim may not deduct her premiums from her income when she figures her self-employment taxes.

S corporation owners, partners in partnerships, and owners of multi-member LLCs taxed as partnerships, can take this deduction only if their business pays for the health insurance directly or reimburses them for their payments. The amount of the payments must be reported as wages on an S corporation owner's W-2 form, and as guaranteed payments on the K-1 form provided to partners and multimember LLC owners by the partnership or LLC.

Business Income Limitation

There is a significant limitation on the health insurance deduction for the self-employed: You may deduct only as much as you earn from your business. If your business earns no money or incurs a loss, you get no deduction. Thus, if Kim from the above example earned only $3,000 in profit from her business, her self-employed deduction would be limited to that amount; she wouldn't be able to deduct the remaining $7,000 in premiums she paid for the year.

If your business is organized as an S corporation, your deduction is limited to the amount of wages you are paid by your corporation.

If you have more than one business, you cannot combine the income from all your businesses for purposes of the income limit. You may only use the income from a single business you designate to be the health insurance plan sponsor.

Designating Your Plan Sponsor

If you purchase your health insurance plan in the name of one of your businesses, that business will be the sponsor. However, the IRS says you may purchase your health coverage in your own name and still get the self-employed health insurance deduction. (IRS Chief Counsel Memo 200524001.) This might be advantageous because it allows you to pick which of your businesses will be the sponsor at the start of each year.

Obviously, you should pick the business you think will earn the most money that year.

Moreover, if you have more than one business, you can have one purchase medical insurance and the other purchase dental insurance and deduct 100% of the premiums for each policy, subject to the income limits discussed above. This will be helpful if no single business earns enough income for you to deduct both policies through one business.

> **EXAMPLE:** Robert is a sole proprietor medical doctor who has a sideline business running a medical lab. He purchases a medical insurance policy for himself and his family with his medical practice as the sponsor. He also purchases a dental insurance plan with his lab business as the sponsor. He may deduct 100% of the premiums for each policy, subject to the income limits.

No Other Health Insurance Coverage

You may not take the self-employed health insurance deduction if you are eligible to participate in a health insurance plan maintained by your employer or your spouse's employer. This rule applies separately to plans that provide long-term care insurance and those that do not. Thus, for example, if your spouse has employer-provided health insurance that does not include long-term care, you may purchase your own long-term care policy and deduct the premiums.

Tax Reporting

Because the self-employed health insurance deduction is a personal deduction, you take this deduction directly on your Form 1040 (it does not go on your Schedule C if you're a sole proprietor). If you itemize your deductions and do not claim 100% of your self-employed health insurance costs on your Form 1040, you may include the rest with all other medical expenses on Schedule A, subject to the 10% limit. You would have to do this, for example, if your health insurance premiums exceeded your business income.

Deducting Health Insurance as a Business Expense

You can deduct health insurance costs as a currently deductible business expense if your business pays them on behalf of an employee. The benefit to treating these costs as a business expense is that you can deduct them from your business income for tax purposes. The premiums are an employee fringe benefit and are not taxable income for the employee. Thus, if you are an employee of your business, you can have your business pay your health insurance premiums and then deduct the cost as a business expense, reducing both your income and your self-employment taxes.

> EXAMPLE: Mona, a sole proprietor data miner, hires Milt to work as an employee in her business. She pays $250 per month to provide Milt with health insurance. The payments are a business expense that she can deduct from her business income. Milt need not count the value of the insurance as income or pay any tax on it. Mona deducts her $3,000 annual payments for Milt's insurance from her business income for both income tax and self-employment tax purposes. The $3,000 deduction saves her $720 in income taxes (she's in the 24% income tax bracket; 24% × $3,000 = $720). She also saves $459 in self-employment taxes (15.3% × $3,000 = $459).

Sole Proprietors, LLCs, S Corporations, Partnerships, and LLPs

Unfortunately, if (like the majority of small business owners) you are a sole proprietor, partner in a partnership, LLC member (taxed as a partnership or sole proprietor), limited liability partnership, or S corporation shareholder with more than 2% of the company stock, you cannot be an employee of your own business for health insurance purposes. If your partnership, LLC, or S corporation buys health insurance on your behalf, it may deduct the cost as a business expense, but it must also add the amount to your taxable income.

If your business is organized as a partnership or multimember LLC, the premiums are ordinarily treated as a guaranteed payment. The business lists the payment on the Schedule K-1 it provides the IRS and you showing your income from the business. You'll then have to pay income and self-employment tax on the amount.

You can still take the self-employed health insurance tax deduction, discussed above, which will effectively wipe out the extra income tax you had to pay. But the self-employed health insurance deduction is a personal deduction, not a business deduction, and thus does not reduce your business income for self-employment tax purposes.

> EXAMPLE: Jim is a co-owner of a consulting firm organized as a multimember LLC. The firm spends $10,000 for health insurance for Jim. It treats the money as a guaranteed payment and lists it as income to Jim on the K-1 form it provides the IRS. The LLC gets to deduct the payment as a business expense. Jim must pay income and self-employment tax on the $10,000. However, he may also deduct the $10,000 from his income tax as a personal deduction using the self-employed health insurance deduction. The net result is that Jim only pays self-employment tax on the $10,000. The same result would have been achieved if Jim had purchased his health insurance himself.

Partnerships, multimember LLCs, and LLPs can avoid having to report health insurance payments as income if they don't take a tax deduction for them. This will have the same tax result and make things simpler.

If your business is an S corporation, the insurance costs are added to your employee compensation and are deducted as such by the corporation. However, you have to pay only income taxes on that amount, not employment taxes or unemployment tax. Again, if you qualify, you may take the self-employed health insurance deduction and wipe out the extra income tax you had to pay. To qualify for the deduction, your medical insurance must be either: (1) established by your S corporation, in its own name, and paid for with its funds, or (2) if purchased in your own name, your S corporation either directly pays for the health insurance, or reimburses you for it, and includes the premium payments as wages on your IRS Form W-2, *Wage and Tax Statement*. (IRS Notice 2008-1.) You cannot qualify for the deduction if your S corporation neither pays for the insurance directly with its own funds nor reimburses you for your payments.

C Corporations

If your business is organized as a C corporation (or you form an LLC and elect to be taxed as a C corporation), you ordinarily will work as its employee and will be entitled to the full menu of tax-free employee fringe benefits, including health insurance. This means the corporation can purchase health insurance for you, deduct the cost as a business expense, and not have to include the cost in your employee compensation. Your health insurance is completely tax free.

If you want to convert your health insurance premiums to a tax-free fringe benefit and you don't have a C corporation, you must form one to run your business and have the corporation hire you as its employee. You can do this even if you're running a one-person business.

As an employee of a C corporation, you must be paid a salary, and your corporation must pay Social Security and Medicare taxes on your behalf. Your corporation deducts your health insurance premiums from its taxes—you don't deduct them from your personal taxes. Because you own the corporation, you get the benefit from the deduction.

There are disadvantages to incorporating, however. Incorporating costs money, you'll have to comply with more burdensome bookkeeping requirements, and you will have a more complex tax return. You'll also have to pay state and federal unemployment taxes for yourself—a tax you don't need to pay if you're not an employee of your business. And, depending on your state's requirements, you may have to provide yourself with workers' compensation coverage.

Because your health insurance is 100% deductible from your income taxes, it may not be worthwhile to incorporate just to save on Social Security and Medicare taxes. This is particularly true if your employee income would substantially exceed the Social Security tax ceiling: $142,800 in 2021. If you're in this situation, think about obtaining an HRA instead. (See "Adopting a Health Reimbursement Arrangement," below.)

Disability Insurance

Disability insurance pays a monthly benefit to employees who are unable to work due to sickness or injury. You may provide disability insurance to your employees, including your spouse, as an employee benefit and deduct the premiums as a business expense. If your business is a C corporation, it may deduct disability payments made for you, its employee. However, any employees who collect disability benefits must include them in their taxable income.

Employing Your Spouse

If you're a sole proprietor or have formed an entity other than an S corporation to run your business, there's another way you can deduct health insurance costs as a business expense: Hire your spouse to work in your business as an employee and provide him or her with health insurance. The insurance should be purchased in the name of the spouse-employee, not in the employer's name. The policy can cover your spouse, you, your children, and other dependents as well. Moreover, this insurance can cover your children up to age 26, whether or not they are your dependents. Then you can deduct the cost of the health insurance as a business expense.

> EXAMPLE: Joe is a self-employed optometrist. He hires his wife, Martha, to work as his employee assistant. He pays her $25,000 per year and provides her with a health insurance policy covering both of them and their two children. The annual policy premiums are $10,000. Joe may deduct the $10,000 as a business expense for his optometry practice, listing it as an expense on his Schedule C. He gets to deduct the $10,000 not only from his $150,000 income for income tax purposes, but also from his self-employment income.

If you do this and you're self-employed, *you should not* take the health insurance deduction for self-employed people discussed above. You're better off tax wise deducting all your health insurance premiums as a business expense, because a business deduction reduces the amount of your income subject to self-employment taxes. The self-employed health insurance deduction is a personal deduction, not a business deduction, and thus does not reduce your business income for self-employment tax purposes.

Your Spouse May Not Be Your Partner

A marriage might be a partnership, but you can't be partners with your spouse in your business and also claim your spouse is your employee for purposes of health insurance deductions. If your spouse co-owns the business with you, your spouse is treated as self-employed—not an employee— for purposes of health insurance. Your spouse is a co-owner if you file partnership returns for your business (IRS Form 1065) listing your spouse as a partner, or if your spouse has made a substantial financial investment in your business with the spouse's own money.

Alternatively, spouses who jointly own a business may elect to be taxed as a "qualified joint venture." When this is done, both spouses are treated as sole proprietors for tax purposes. See Chapter 1 for more details.

There are a couple of catches to this deduction. This method ordinarily doesn't work if you have an S corporation because your spouse is deemed to be a shareholder of the corporation along with you and can't also be a corporate employee. In addition, your spouse must be a bona fide employee. In other words, he or she must do real work in your business, you must pay applicable payroll taxes, and you must otherwise treat your spouse like any other employee. (See Chapter 11 for a detailed discussion.)

You'll probably want to pay your spouse as low a salary as possible, because both of you will have to pay Social Security and Medicare taxes on that salary (but not on employee benefits like health insurance and medical expense reimbursements). You should, however, regularly pay your spouse at least some cash wages, or the IRS could claim your spouse is not a real employee. You can make the cash wages a relatively small part of your spouse's total compensation—wages plus fringe benefits like your medical reimbursement plan.

No matter how you pay your spouse, that person's total compensation must be reasonable—that is, you can't pay more than your spouse's services are worth. For example, you can't pay your spouse at a rate of $100 per hour for simple clerical work. Total compensation means the sum of the salary plus all the fringe benefits you pay your spouse, including health insurance and medical expense reimbursements, if any. (See "Adopting a Health Reimbursement Arrangement," below.)

Of course, if you're single, you won't be able to hire a spouse to take advantage of this method for turning health insurance costs into a business expense. However, if you're a single parent, you could hire your child and deduct the cost of your child's health insurance as a business expense. But your child's policy cannot also cover you or other family members.

Sick and Family Leave Tax Credits for the Self-Employed

In response to the COVID-19 pandemic, Congress enacted special sick leave and family leave tax credits for the self-employed. These credits are available only if you couldn't work due to COVID-19 or needed to care for a family member because of the disease. Technically, two separate sets of credits exist: one for April 1, 2021 through September 30, 2021 and one for April 1, 2020 through March 31, 2021. However, both are very similar.

Credits for April 1, 2021 Through September 30, 2021

Here are the rules for April 1, 2021 through September 30, 2021.

Sick Leave Credit

You can qualify for a credit for up to ten total days of sick leave during April 1, 2021 through September 30, 2021. The amount of the credit depends on whether you're sick or someone else is:

- **If you're sick.** You qualify for a credit of up to $511 per day if you can't work or telework because you have to self-isolate or quarantine, are experiencing COVID-19 symptoms and need to obtain a diagnosis, have been exposed to COVID-19 and are unable to work pending test results, need to get COVID-19 vaccinated, or are recovering from a vaccination. This credit is equal to 100% of the average net self-employment income you earn per day, capped at $511 per day. Thus, the maximum credit is $5,110.

- **If you care for others.** You also qualify for a sick leave credit of up to $200 per day if you can't work or telework because you have to care for a child under 18 years of age whose school or place of care has been closed due to COVID-19, or you're caring for any person subject to a quarantine order or advised by a health care provider to self-quarantine. This credit is equal to 67% of the average self-employment income you earn per day, capped at $200 per day. So, the maximum credit is $2,000.

Family Leave Credit

You can also receive a credit for up to 60 days of family leave for days you can't work or telework for any of the same reasons listed above that qualify you for the sick leave credit. The family leave credit is equal to 67% of the average self-employment income you earn per day, capped at $200 per day. Thus, the maximum credit is $12,000.

Calculating Your Credit

If you qualify, you can take both the sick leave and family credits up to a maximum of 70 combined days. But you cannot use both credits for the same day of leave.

Determine your average daily net self-employment income by dividing your total net self-employment income for the year or the prior year by 260.

> **EXAMPLE:** Jane is a self-employed consultant whose net self-employment income for 2021 is $200,000. Her average daily net self-employment income is $769 ($200,000 ÷ 260 = $769), but her sick leave credit is capped at $511. She takes four days off during May 2021 to recover from the side effects of her second COVID-19 vaccination. She may claim a sick leave credit of four days x $511 = $2,044.

Credits for April 1, 2020 Through March 31, 2021

Sick leave and family leave credits are also available for leave taken during April 1, 2020 through March 31, 2021. The rules are largely the same as for the later credits except for these differences:

- COVID-19 vaccinations do not qualify for either credit.
- The family leave credit is limited to 50 days, for a maximum of $10,000.

Sick leave and family leave days taken before April 1, 2021, don't count against the ten-day and 60-day limits for the credit during April 1, 2021 through September 30, 2021. The clock is effectively reset on April 1, 2021.

Claiming the Credit

You claim these credits on new IRS Form 7202, *Credits for Sick Leave and Family Leave for Certain Self-Employed Individuals*, which you include with your Form 1040. These are both refundable tax credits, meaning you get the full amount even if it exceeds your tax liability for the year. So, for example, if you owe $1,000 in total taxes and qualify for a $2,500 credit, you won't have to pay any estimated taxes, and the IRS will send you a check for $1,500 after it processes your 2021 tax return.

Tax Credits for Employee Health Insurance

The previous section explained how you can deduct health insurance costs for employees—including your spouse—as a business expense. Tax deductions are all well and good, but here's something even better: tax credits. Unlike a deduction, a tax credit is a dollar-for-dollar reduction in the taxes you owe the IRS. In other words, a $1,000 credit saves you $1,000 on your taxes.

If your business has employees and provides them with health insurance coverage, you may qualify for the Small Business Health Care Tax Credit. The tax credit is available to eligible employers for two consecutive tax years.

This credit is equal to 50% of the premiums small employers pay for their employees' health insurance. For example, if your business paid $20,000 for employee health insurance in 2021, you'd be entitled to a whopping $10,000 tax refund.

To qualify for the credit, you must:

- have no more than 25 full-time equivalent employees
- pay your employees average annual full-time wages of more than $27,000 and less than $55,000
- pay at least 50% of the annual premiums for your employees' health insurance, and
- purchase your employees' health insurance through a Small Business Health Options Program (SHOP) Marketplace. (These are health insurance exchanges specifically designed for employers with 50 or fewer full-time employees: see www.healthcare.gov/small-businesses/employers.)

If you have questions about the Small Business Health Care Tax Credit, refer to the IRS's website at www.irs.gov/affordable-care-act/employers/small-business-health-care-tax-credit-and-the-shop-marketplace.

Adopting a Health Reimbursement Arrangement

Health insurance usually doesn't cover all your medical expenses. For example, it doesn't cover deductibles or co-payments—that is, amounts you must pay yourself before your insurance coverage kicks in. Many costs aren't covered at all, including fertility treatment and optometric care. As a result, the average family of four pays about $3,500 a year in out-of-pocket health-related expenses. One way to deduct these expenses is to establish a health reimbursement arrangement (HRA).

An HRA is a plan under which an employer reimburses its employees for health or dental expenses. This can include health insurance, co-pays, and other medical expenses not covered by insurance.

These plans are usually self-funded—that is, the employer pays the expenses out of its own pocket, not through insurance.

Why would an employer do this? One good reason is that the reimbursements are tax-deductible business expenses for the employer. Also, the employee doesn't have to include the reimbursements as taxable income (as long as the employee has not taken a deduction for these amounts as a personal medical expense).

There are three different types of HRAs:

- spouse-only HRAs for businesses with one employee-spouse
- Individual Coverage HRAs (ICHRAs) for businesses with any number of employees, and
- Qualified Small Employer HRAs (QSEHRAs) for businesses with up to 50 employees.

Spousal Health Reimbursement Accounts

The Affordable Care Act (ACA) imposes various restrictions on the ability of employers to use HRAs. Businesses with more than one employee may establish HRAs only if they comply with the requirements for Qualified Small Employer Health Reimbursement Arrangements (QSEHRAs) discussed below. However, the ACA does not apply to HRAs established by businesses with only one employee. Thus, if you're married, you can hire your spouse as the sole employee of your business and provide him or her with an HRA that is not subject to the restrictions. However, this only works if your spouse is your only employee. And your business must be organized as a sole proprietorship, a partnership, an LLC, or a C corporation. This leaves out S corporations, but S corporations can take advantage of ICHRAs and QSEHRAs discussed below.

11 Steps to Audit-Proof Your Health Reimbursement Arrangement for Your Spouse

Your HRA must look like a legitimate business expense for IRS purposes. You must treat your spouse like a real employee and manage your plan in a businesslike manner.

1. Adopt a written HRA for your business.
2. Use time sheets to keep track of the hours your spouse works—these should show the date, work done, and time spent on that work.
3. Make sure your spouse's total compensation is reasonable—including health expense reimbursements. Determine usual pay rates for the work your employee-spouse does and retain those records.
4. Have your spouse open a separate bank account to use when he or she pays medical expenses or receives reimbursements from your business.
5. Comply with all payroll tax, unemployment insurance, and workers' compensation requirements for your spouse-employee.
6. Reimburse your spouse for covered expenses by check from a separate business bank account or pay the health care provider directly from your business account. Make a notation on the check that the payment is made under your HRA.
7. Never pay your spouse in cash.
8. Have your spouse submit all bills to be reimbursed or paid by your business at least twice a year. Keep all documentation showing the nature and amounts of the medical expenses paid for by your HRA— receipts, canceled checks, and so on, to show that you didn't reimburse your spouse too much and that the payments were for legitimate medical expenses.
9. Don't pay for expenses incurred before the date you adopted your HRA.
10. Your health policy generally should be purchased in the name of the employee-spouse, not in the name of the sole proprietor-spouse.
11. Claim your deduction on the correct tax form:
    • sole proprietors or owners of one-person LLCs—Schedule C, Line 14, "Employee benefit programs"
    • multimember LLCs and partnerships—Form 1065, Line 19, "Employee benefit programs," or
    • C corporations—Form 1120, Line 24, "Employee benefit programs."

Medical Expense Reimbursement Plan

[___*Your business name*___], ("Employer") and [___*employee's name*___] ("Employee") enter into this Health Reimbursement Arrangement ("HRA") under which Employer agrees to reimburse Employee for medical expenses incurred by Employee and Employee's spouse and dependents, subject to the conditions and limitations set forth below.

1. Uninsured Expenses

Employer will reimburse eligible Employee and Employee's spouse and dependents only for medical expenses that are not covered by health or accident insurance.

2. Medical Expenses Defined

Medical expenses are those expenses defined by Internal Revenue Code Sec. 213(d).

3. Eligible Employee

This plan is a one-employee plan that does not include group health insurance. All full- and part-time employees of Employer may participate in this plan, but should the plan cover more than one eligible employee, it will be amended to purchase qualified Affordable Care Act "group health coverage" as a plan component.

4. Dependent Defined

Dependent is defined by I.R.C. Sec. 152. It includes any member of an eligible Employee's family for whom the Employee and his or her spouse provide more than half of the financial support.

5. Submission of Claims

To obtain reimbursement under this HRA, Employee shall submit to Employer, at least annually, all bills for medical care, including those for accident or health insurance. Such bills and other claims for reimbursement shall be verified by Employer prior to reimbursement. Employer, in its sole discretion, may terminate Employee's right to reimbursement if the Employee fails to comply.

Medical Expense Reimbursement Plan (continued)

6. Payments

At its option, Employer may pay the medical expenses directly to the medical provider or by purchasing insurance that pays Employee's expenses. Such a direct payment or provision of such insurance shall relieve Employer of all further liability for the expense.

7. Effective Date; Plan Year

This HRA shall take effect on [_date_] and operates on a calendar-year basis thereafter. The HRA year is the same as the tax year of Employer. HRA records shall be kept on a calendar year basis.

8. Benefits Not Taxable

Employer intends that the benefits under this HRA shall qualify under I.R.C. Sec. 105 so as to be excludable from the gross income of the Employee covered by the HRA.

9. Termination

Employer may terminate this HRA at any time. Medical expenses incurred prior to the date of termination shall be reimbursed by Employer. Employer is under no obligation to provide advance notice of termination.

_____   _____

Employer's Signature   Date

_____   _____

Employee's Signature   Date

The plan may cover not only your spouse, but also you, your children, and other dependents. This allows your business to reimburse your and your family's out-of-pocket medical expenses and deduct the amounts as a business expense. And you need not include the reimbursements in your own taxable income. The IRS has ruled that this is perfectly legal. (Rev. Rul. 2002-45.)

> **EXAMPLE:** Jennifer has her own public relations business. She hires her husband Paul as an employee to work as her part-time assistant. She establishes an HRA covering Paul, herself, and their young child. Paul spends $12,000 for health insurance, co-pays, and uninsured health expenses. Jennifer reimburses Paul for the $12,000 as provided by their plan. Jennifer may deduct the $12,000 from her business income for the year, meaning she pays neither income nor self-employment tax on that amount. Paul need not include the $12,000 in his income—it's tax free to him. The deduction saves Jennifer and Paul $4,000 in taxes for the year.

CAUTION

Your spouse must be a legitimate employee. Your spouse must be a legitimate employee for your HRA to pass muster with the IRS. You can't simply hire your spouse on paper—he or she must do real work in your business. If you can't prove your spouse is a legitimate employee, the IRS will disallow your deductions in the event of an audit.

> **EXAMPLE:** Mr. Haeder, a sole proprietor attorney who practiced law in his home, claimed that he hired his wife as his employee to answer the telephone, greet visitors, type legal papers, and clean his office. Mrs. Haeder had no employment contract or set work schedule, did not maintain any time records, and did not directly or regularly receive a salary. Instead, Mr. Haeder paid her the maximum amount she could deduct as an IRA contribution. Annually, he transferred money in his brokerage account to an IRA in his wife's name. For all but one of the years eventually audited by the IRS, no W-2 was issued to Mrs. Haeder. Mr. Haeder sponsored an HRA that covered out-of-pocket expenses for his wife, her children, and her spouse— that is, himself. Mrs. Haeder submitted bills for out-of-pocket medical

expenses to her husband, which he reimbursed and attempted to deduct as business expenses. The IRS determined Mr. Haeder was not entitled to deduct the reimbursements under the plan, because Mrs. Haeder was not a bona fide employee. The tax court agreed, finding that there was no credible evidence that Mrs. Haeder performed any services other than those reasonably expected of a family member. (*Haeder v. Commissioner,* TC Memo 2001-7.)

Make sure to comply with all the legal requirements for hiring an employee, including providing workers' compensation insurance (required in many states), paying any state unemployment insurance premiums, and paying and withholding income tax. Your spouse-employee should also submit a weekly timesheet showing the date, work done, and time spent on that work. If this is too much trouble or too expensive, forget about establishing an HRA.

The total amount your spouse is reimbursed under your HRA can be the spouse's sole source of remuneration as your business's employee. But the total amount must be reasonable for the work the spouse does. If you don't pay your spouse-employee wages, you won't need to make payroll tax payments or filings. Some tax pros prefer that the spouse-employee be paid at least a nominal salary, for example, $1,000 per year or $100 per month, and a W-2 filed with the IRS as added proof of employment. But if your spouse is not your bona fide employee, paying such a small amount of wages won't be much help.

You also need to make sure that you and your spouse do not end up being partners (co-owners) in the business. Your spouse cannot be your partner and your employee in the same business. You must own the business and your spouse must work under your direction and control. Factors that indicate that your spouse is your partner include joint ownership of business assets, joint sharing of profits, and joint control over business operations.

Again, the HRA deduction is available only to your employees, not to you (the business owner). The only way you can qualify as an employee is if your business is a C corporation. (See "Deducting Health Insurance as a Business Expense," above.) However, if you don't have a spouse to employ, you could employ your child and provide him or her with an HRA. But the plan may not cover you or any other family members.

How to Establish a Spousal HRA

If a spousal HRA sounds attractive to you, you should act to establish one as early in the year as possible, because it applies only to medical expenses incurred after the date the plan is adopted. (Rev. Rul. 2002-58.) Forget about using an HRA to reimburse your spouse or yourself for expenses you have already incurred. If you do, the reimbursement must be added to your spouse's income for tax purposes, and you must pay employment tax on it.

A written HRA must be drawn up and adopted by your business. If your business is incorporated, the plan should be adopted by a corporate resolution approved by the corporation's board of directors. You can find a form for this purpose in *The Corporate Records Handbook: Meetings, Minutes & Resolutions*, by Anthony Mancuso (Nolo).

Sample Spousal HRA

A sample spousal HRA is provided above.

Individual Coverage HRAs (ICHRAs)

If your business has more than one employee, you may not establish a spousal HRA. However, the Affordable Care Act's rules were amended effective January 1, 2020 to allow businesses with multiple employees to establish Individual Coverage Health Reimbursement Arrangements (ICHRAs). ICHRAs appear to be the Goldilocks of HRAs: Unlike spousal HRAs, you can use them for any number of employees, and they are not subject to most of the restrictions imposed on QSEHRAs (see below).

ICHRAs may be used by any business of whatever size. And, there are no caps on benefits. Here's how they work.

Employees Obtain Individual Coverage

Employees must obtain their own individual health coverage to use ICHRAs. They can do this through their state health insurance exchange or obtain insurance elsewhere, including Medicare coverage. The employee can be the primary policyholder or covered under a family member's individual policy. Employees must prove they have coverage each year.

However, employees who have ICHRAs will not be eligible for ACA premium tax credits. In contrast, employees who have QSEHRAs may receive tax credits, but the amount of the credit is reduced by the amount of HRA benefits received.

Employer Provides Monthly Allowance

The employer sets a monthly allowance of tax-free money employees can use to pay for their health insurance coverage and other uninsured healthcare expenses. There are no caps on the amount of the allowance—it can be as big or small as desired.

Employer Reimburses Employees

Employees submit proof of their expenses and the employer reimburses them up to the allowance amount. The reimbursements are tax free to the employees and tax deductible by the employer.

Employers May Offer Different Allowances to Different Classes of Employees

Employers are not required to provide the same allowances to all employees. They can offer different amounts for different classes of employees, including:
- full-time
- part-time
- seasonal
- salaried
- hourly
- temporary employees working for a staffing firm
- employees covered under a collective bargaining agreement
- employees in a waiting period
- foreign employees who work abroad
- employees in different locations, based on rating areas, and
- a combination of two or more of the above.

HRA allowances must be the same for all employees within the same class. However, employers can make distinctions based on an employee's age or family size. For example, an employer can increase the allowance amount for older workers or those with more children or other dependents.

Establishing an ICHRA

The employer must give notice of the ICHRA to all employees at least 90 days before the beginning of the plan year. The notice must make clear that participating in the ICHRA makes the employee ineligible for ACA tax credits. The Department of Labor has created a model notice that employers may use. The notice and FAQs created by the IRS are at: www.irs.gov/newsroom/health-reimbursement-arrangements-hras.

Qualified Small Employer HRAs (QSEHRAs)

Another type of HRA for businesses with multiple employees is the Qualified Small Employer HRA, or QSEHRA. QSEHRAs became available in 2017. Unfortunately, there are far more restrictions on these plans than on spousal HRAs or individual HRAs. With a QSEHRA, an eligible small business can reimburse an employee's individually purchased health insurance and other deductible medical costs up to $5,300 per year for an individual and up to $10,700 for a family (these are the limits for 2021). The cost of the QSEHRA benefit must be entirely covered by the employer.

Which Employers May Offer QSEHRAs?

QSEHRAs may be offered only by employers with fewer than 50 full-time (or full-time equivalent) employees during the prior year and who do not offer a group health plan to any of their employees.

Which Employees May be Covered by QSEHRAs?

As with ICHRAs, only employees who obtain their own health insurance that meets the minimum requirements of the Affordable Care Act (called minimum essential coverage) may benefit from a QSEHRA. Reimbursements paid to an employee without such coverage must be included in the employee's taxable income. Minimum essential coverage includes all individually purchased private insurance, government insurance such as Medicare, and the employee's or spouse's job-based

314 | DEDUCT IT! LOWER YOUR SMALL BUSINESS TAXES

insurance. The employees must provide their employer with proof that they have such coverage. Employees must also substantiate all medical expenses that are reimbursed. Reimbursements made under a QSEHRA must be reported to the IRS on the employee's W-2.

All eligible employees must be covered by the QSEHRA. This includes all employees except those who:

- have not completed 90 days of service
- are under age 25
- are part-time or seasonal employees
- are covered by a collective bargaining agreement if health benefits were the subject of good-faith bargaining, or
- are nonresident aliens with no earned income from sources within the United States.

Thus, QSEHRA benefits cannot be offered to only a select group, such as to only a company's owner and top-level employees.

A QSEHRA plan may be used only for employees. It may not be used by sole proprietors, partners in partnerships, or members of limited liability companies (LLCs). However, until the IRS issues further guidance, a business organized as an S corporation may maintain a QSEHRA for its shareholder-employees who own more than 2% of the corporate stock.

How to Establish a QSEHRA

The employer begins a QSEHRA by giving all of its eligible employees written notice of the plan, which can also serve as the document establishing the plan. The notice must be given 90 days before the beginning of a plan year. The notice must:

- list the amount of the employee's permitted benefit for the year
- require the employee to provide information about the QSEHRA to any health insurance exchange to which the employee applies for advance payment of premium assistance tax credits to help pay for health insurance, and
- contain a warning that, if the employee is not covered under minimum essential coverage for any month, the employee may have to pay tax on any plan reimbursements.

An employer that fails to provide the required notice may be subject to a $50 per-employee, per-failure penalty, up to a $2,500 calendar year maximum for all such failures.

Health Savings Accounts

Another tax-advantaged method of buying health insurance has been available since 2004: Health Savings Accounts (HSAs). HSAs can save you taxes, but they're not for everybody.

What Are Health Savings Accounts?

The HSA concept is very simple: Instead of relying on health insurance to pay small or routine medical expenses, you pay them yourself. To help you do this, you establish a Health Savings Account with a health insurance company, bank, or other financial institution. Your contributions to the account are tax deductible, and you don't have to pay tax on the interest or other money you earn on the money in your account. You can withdraw the money in your HSA to pay almost any kind of health-related expense, and you don't have to pay any tax on these withdrawals.

In case you or a family member gets really sick, you must also obtain a health insurance policy with a high deductible—for 2021, at least $1,400 for individuals and $2,800 for families. The money in your HSA can be used to pay this large deductible and any co-payments you're required to make.

Using an HSA can save you money in two ways:
- You'll get a tax deduction for the money you deposit in your account.
- The premiums for your high-deductible health insurance policy may be lower than those for traditional comprehensive coverage policies or HMO coverage (perhaps as much as 40% lower).

Establishing Your HSA

To participate in the HSA program, you need two things:
- a high-deductible health plan that qualifies under the HSA rules, and
- an HSA account.

HSA-Qualified Plans

You can't have an HSA if you're covered by health insurance other than a high-deductible HSA plan—for example, if your spouse has family coverage for you from his or her job. So you might have to change your existing coverage. However, you may get your own HSA if you are not covered by your spouse's health insurance. In addition, people eligible to receive Medicare may not participate in the HSA program.

You need to obtain a bare-bones health plan that meets the HSA criteria (is "HSA qualified"). You may obtain coverage from a health maintenance organization, preferred provider organization, or traditional plan. The key feature of an HSA-qualified health plan is that it has a relatively high annual deductible (the amount you must pay out of your own pocket before your insurance kicks in). In 2021, the minimum annual deductible for a single person was $1,400, and $2,800 for families.

You can have a higher deductible if you wish, but there is an annual ceiling on the total amount you can have for your deductible plus other out-of-pocket expenses you're required to pay before your health plan provides coverage. (Such out-of-pocket expenses include co-payments, but do not include health insurance premiums.) For example, in 2021 the annual ceiling for an individual HSA plan was $7,000. This means that your annual deductible and other out-of-pocket expenses you're required to pay before your insurance kicks in cannot exceed that amount. Thus, if your annual deductible was $3,500, your other annual out-of-pocket expenses would have to be limited to $3,500. In 2021, the maximum limits were $7,000 for a single person and $14,000 for families. All these numbers are adjusted for inflation each year.

In addition, your health insurance plan must be HSA qualified. To become qualified, the insurer must agree to participate in the HSA program and give the roster of enrolled participants to the IRS. If your insurer fails to report to the IRS that you are enrolled in an HSA-qualified insurance plan, the IRS will not permit you to deduct your HSA contributions.

HSA-qualified health insurance policies should be clearly labeled as such on the cover page or declaration page of the policy. It might be possible to convert a high-deductible health insurance policy you already have to an HSA-qualified health insurance policy; ask your health insurer for details.

The premiums you pay for an HSA-qualified health plan are deductible to the same extent as any other health insurance premiums. This means that, if you're self-employed, you may deduct your entire premium from your federal income tax as a special personal deduction.

You can also deduct your contribution if your business is an LLC or a partnership or if you've formed an S corporation. If your partnership or multimember LLC makes the contribution for you, it must be reported as a distribution to you on your Schedule K-1. You still get the self-employed health insurance deduction but will have to pay tax on the distribution if it exceeds your basis (the value of your investment) in your LLC or partnership. Contributions by an S corporation to a shareholder-employee's HSA are treated as guaranteed payments. The S corporation may deduct them, but they must be included in the shareholder-employee's gross income and are subject to income tax. (IRS Notice 2005-8.)

If you've formed a C corporation and work as its employee, your corporation can make a contribution to your HSA and deduct the amount as employee compensation. The contribution is not taxable to you. (See "HSAs for Employees," below.)

HSA Account

Once you have an HSA-qualified health insurance policy, you may open your HSA account. An HSA must be established with a trustee. The HSA trustee keeps track of your deposits and withdrawals, produces annual statements, and reports your HSA deposits to the IRS.

Health insurers can administer both the health plan and the HSA. However, you don't have to have your HSA administered by your insurer. You can establish an HSA with banks, insurance companies, mutual funds, or other financial institutions offering HSA products.

Whoever administers your account will usually give you a checkbook or debit card to use to withdraw funds from the account. You can also make withdrawals by mail or in person.

Look at the plans offered by several companies to see which offers the best deal. Compare the fees charged to set up the account, as well as any other charges (some companies may charge an annual service fee, for example). Ask about special promotions and discounts. And find out how the account is invested.

HSAs and the ACA

The ACA has not eliminated HSAs. They can continue. Moreover, HSA-qualified health plans are offered on many state health exchanges. People who already have HSA-qualified plans and HSA accounts may keep them.

Making Contributions to Your HSA

When you have your HSA-qualified health plan and HSA account, you can start making contributions to your account. There is no minimum amount you are required to contribute each year; you may contribute nothing if you wish. If your business is a corporation, partnership, or LLC, you don't have to make all the contributions to your HSA from your personal funds. All or part of your annual contribution can be paid for by your business from its funds. But, as described in the following section, this changes how the contributions are deducted.

The maximum limits on how much you may contribute each year are:

- If you have individual coverage, the maximum you may contribute to your HSA each year is $3,600.
- If you have family coverage, the maximum you may contribute to your HSA each year is $7,200.

These maximums are for 2021 and are adjusted for inflation each year.

Taxpayers who have HSAs may make a one-time tax-free rollover of funds from their Individual Retirement Accounts (IRAs) to their HSA. The rollover amount is limited to the maximum HSA contribution for the year (minus any HSA contributions you've already made for the year).

Catch-Up Contributions

Individuals who are 55 to 65 years old can make additional optional tax-free catch-up contributions to their HSA accounts of up to $1,000 (see the chart below). This rule is intended to compensate for the fact that older folks won't have as many years to fund their accounts as younger taxpayers. If you're in this age group, it's wise to make these contributions if you can afford them, so your HSA account will have enough money to pay for future health expenses.

	Self Only	Family
Maximum Contribution	$3,600	$7,200
Catch-Up Contribution (55 and over)	$1,000	$1,000
Minimum Deductible	$1,400	$2,800
Maximum Out-of-Pocket Payments	$7,000	$14,000

Where to Invest Your HSA Contributions

The contributions you make to your HSA account may be invested just like IRA contributions. You can invest in almost anything: money market accounts, bank certificates of deposit, stocks, bonds, mutual funds, Treasury bills, and notes. However, you can't invest in collectibles such as art, antiques, postage stamps, or other personal property.

Deducting HSA Contributions

The amounts contributed each year to HSA accounts, up to the annual limit, are deductible from federal income taxes.

Individual Contributions

You can deduct HSA contributions made with your personal funds as a personal deduction on the first page of your IRS Form 1040. You deduct the amount from your gross income, just like a business deduction. This means you get the full deduction whether or not you itemize your personal deductions.

> EXAMPLE: In 2021, Martin, an actuary, establishes an HSA for himself and his family with a $3,000 deductible. He contributes the maximum amount to his

HSA account—$7,200. Because he is in the 24% federal income tax bracket, this saves him $1,728 in federal income tax for 2021.

Contributions by Your Business

If your business is a partnership or an LLC and it makes an HSA contribution for you as a distribution of partnership or LLC funds, it is reported as a cash distribution to you on your Schedule K-1 (Form 1065). You may take a personal deduction for the HSA contribution on your tax return (IRS Form 1040) and the contribution is not subject to income or self-employment taxes.

However, the tax result is very different if the contribution is made as a guaranteed payment to the partner or LLC member. A guaranteed payment is like a salary paid to a partner or an LLC member for services performed for the partnership or LLC. The amount of a guaranteed payment is determined without reference to the partnership's or LLC's income. The partnership or LLC deducts the guaranteed payment on its return and lists it as a guaranteed payment to you on your Schedule K-1 (Form 1065). You must pay income and self-employment tax on the amount. You may take a personal income tax deduction on your Form 1040 for the HSA contribution.

Contributions by an S corporation to a shareholder-employee's HSA are treated as wages subject to income tax, but they normally are not subject to employment taxes. The shareholder can deduct the contribution on his or her personal tax return (IRS Form 1040) as an HSA contribution.

If you've formed a C corporation and work as its employee, your corporation can make a contribution to your HSA and deduct the amount as employee compensation. The contribution is not taxable to you. However, if you have other employees, similar contributions must be made to their HSAs. You may also make contributions from your own fund.

Withdrawing HSA Funds

If you or a family member needs health care, you can withdraw money from your HSA to pay your deductible or any other medical expenses. You pay no federal tax on HSA withdrawals used to pay qualified medical expenses. However, you cannot deduct qualified medical expenses as an itemized deduction on Schedule A (Form 1040) that are equal to the tax-free distribution from your HSA.

Qualified medical expenses are broadly defined to include many types of expenses ordinarily not covered by health insurance—for example, dental or optometric care. This is one of the great advantages of the HSA program over traditional health insurance. (The lists in "What HSA Funds Can Be Used For," below, show the type of health expenses that can and cannot be paid with an HSA.)

No Approval Required

HSA participants need not obtain advance approval from their HSA trustee (whether their insurer or someone else) that an expense is a qualified medical expense before they withdraw funds from their accounts. You make that determination yourself. The trustee will report any distribution to you and the IRS on Form 1099-SA, *Distributions From an HSA, Archer MSA, or Medicare Advantage MSA*. You should keep records of your medical expenses to show that your withdrawals were for qualified medical expenses and are therefore excludable from your gross income.

However, you may not use HSA funds to purchase nonprescription medications.

Tax-Free Withdrawals

If you withdraw funds from your HSA to use for something other than qualified medical expenses, you must pay the regular income tax on the withdrawal plus a 20% penalty. For example, if you were in the 24% federal income tax bracket, you'd have to pay a 44% tax on your nonqualified withdrawals.

Once you reach the age of 65 or become disabled, you can withdraw your HSA funds for any reason without penalty. If you use the money for nonmedical expenses, you will have to pay regular income tax on the withdrawals. When you die, the money in your HSA account is transferred to the beneficiary you've named for the account. The transfer is tax free if the beneficiary is your surviving spouse. Other transfers are taxable.

If you elect to leave the HSA program, you can continue to keep your HSA account and withdraw money from it tax free for health care expenses. However, you won't be able to make any additional contributions to the account.

What HSA Funds Can Be Used For

Health insurance ordinarily may not be purchased with HSA funds. However, there are three exceptions to this general rule. HSA funds can be used to pay for:

- a health plan during any period of continuation coverage required under any federal law—for example, when you are terminated from your job and purchase continuing health insurance coverage from your employer's health insurer, which the insurer is legally required to make available to you under COBRA
- long-term health care insurance
- health insurance premiums you pay while you are receiving unemployment compensation
- Medicare expenses (but not Medigap), and
- retiree health expenses for individuals age 65 and over.

For a list of all the expenses that may be paid with HSA funds, see IRS Publication 969, *Health Savings Accounts and Other Tax-Favored Health Plans*. You can download it from the IRS website, at www.irs.gov.

HSAs for Employees

Employers may provide HSAs to their employees. Any business, no matter how small, may participate in the HSA program. The employer purchases an HSA-qualified health plan for its employees, and they establish their own individual HSA accounts. The employer may pay all or part of its employees' insurance premiums and make contributions to their HSA accounts. Employees may also make their own contributions to their individual accounts. The combined annual contributions of the employer and employee may not exceed the limits listed above.

HSAs are portable when an employee changes employers. Contributions and earnings belong to the account holder, not the employer. Employers are required to report amounts contributed to an HSA on the employee's Form W-2.

Health insurance payments and HSA contributions made by businesses on behalf of their employees are currently deductible business expenses. The employees do not have to report employer contributions to their HSA accounts as income. Employers deduct them on the "Employee benefit programs" line of their business income tax return. If filing Schedule C, this is in Part II, Line 14.

If you've formed a C corporation and work as its employee, your corporation may establish an HSA on your behalf and deduct its contributions on its own tax return. The contributions are not taxable to you, but you get no personal deduction for them. You do get a deduction, however, if you make contributions to your HSA account from your personal funds. You can't do this if you have an S corporation, an LLC, or a partnership, because owners of these entities are not considered employees for employment benefit purposes.

Hiring Your Spouse

If you're a sole proprietor or have formed any business entity other than an S corporation, you may hire your spouse as your employee and have your business pay for an HSA-qualified family health plan for your spouse, you, and your children and other dependents. Moreover, your HSA-qualified health plan can cover your children up to age 26, whether or not they are your dependents. Your spouse then establishes an HSA,

324 OF SMALL BUSINESS TAXES

which your business may fully fund each year. The money your business spends for your spouse's health insurance premiums and to fund the HSA is a fully deductible business expense. This allows you to reduce both your income and your self-employment taxes. (See "Personal Income Tax Deduction for the Self-Employed," above.)

Nondiscrimination Rules

If you have employees other than yourself, your spouse, or other family members, you'll need to comply with nondiscrimination rules—that is, you'll have to make comparable HSA contributions for all employees with HSA-qualified health coverage during the year. Contributions are considered comparable if they are either of the same amount or the same percentage of the deductible under the plan. The rule is applied separately to employees who work less than 30 hours per week. Employers who do not comply with these rules are subject to a 35% excise tax.

Tax Reporting for HSAs

You must report to the IRS each year how much you deposit to and withdraw from your HSA. You make the report using IRS Form 8889, *Health Savings Accounts (HSAs).* You'll also be required to keep a record of the name and address of each person or company whom you pay with funds from your HSA.

Additional Deductions

This chapter looks at some of the most common deductible operating expenses that small businesses incur. These are costs that a business is likely to incur in the normal course of running its operations, such as advertising expenses, insurance, and legal fees. You can deduct these costs as business operating expenses as long as they are ordinary, necessary, and reasonable in amount and meet the additional requirements discussed below.

Advertising

Almost any type of business-related advertising is a currently deductible business operating expense. You can deduct advertising to sell a particular product or service, to help establish goodwill for your business, or just to get your business known. Advertising includes expenses for:

- business cards
- brochures
- advertisements in the local yellow pages
- newspaper and magazine advertisements
- trade publication advertisements
- catalogs
- radio and television advertisements
- advertisements on the Internet, including Google adwords
- fees you pay to advertising and public relations agencies
- billboards
- package design costs, and
- signs and display racks.

However, advertising to influence government legislation is never deductible. "Help wanted" ads you place to recruit workers are not advertising costs, but you can deduct them as ordinary and necessary business operating expenses.

Goodwill Advertising

If it relates to business you reasonably expect to gain in the future, you can usually deduct the cost of institutional or "goodwill" advertising meant to keep your name before the public. Examples of goodwill advertising include:

- advertisements that encourage people to contribute to charities, such as the Red Cross or similar causes
- having your business sponsor a Little League baseball team, bowling team, or golf tournament
- giving away product samples, and
- holding contests and giving away prizes—for example, a car dealer can deduct the cost of giving a car away.

In one case, the tax court even allowed a gas station owner to deduct the cost of providing free beer to customers as an advertising expense. The court stated that a small business owner "can offer free beer to beer lovers" to improve business. (*Sullivan v. Commissioner*, TC Memo 1982-150.)

However, you can't deduct time and labor that you give away as an advertising expense, even though doing so promotes goodwill. You must actually spend money to have an advertising expense. For example, a lawyer who does pro bono work for indigent clients to advertise his law practice may not deduct the cost of his services as an advertising expense.

Giveaway Items

Giveaway items that you use to publicize your business (such as pens, coffee cups, T-shirts, refrigerator magnets, calendars, tote bags, and key chains) are deductible. However, you are not allowed to deduct more than $25 in business gifts to any one person each year. This limitation applies to advertising giveaway items unless they:

- cost $4 or less
- have your name clearly and permanently imprinted on them, and
- are one of a number of identical items you distribute widely.

Signs, display racks, and other promotional materials that you give away to other businesses to use on their premises do not count as gifts.

Website Development and Maintenance

The costs of developing and maintaining a website for a business vary widely. It can be relatively inexpensive if you use a standard template you purchase from a template company. However, the cost will be much higher if you want to create a custom design.

Many businesses currently deduct all website development and ongoing maintenance expenses as an advertising expense. However, some tax experts believe that the cost of initially setting up a website is a capital expense, not a currently deductible business operating expense, because the website is a long-term asset that benefits the business for more than one year. Under normal tax rules, capital expenses must be deducted over several years. Three years is the most common deduction period used for websites, because this is the same period as for software.

However, even if website development costs are capital expenses, they may be currently deducted in a single year under Section 179, which allows businesses to deduct a substantial amount of capital expenses in a single year (see Chapter 5).

Most tax experts agree that ongoing website hosting, maintenance, and updating costs are a currently deductible operating expense. Money you spend to get people to view your website, such as SEO (search engine optimization) campaigns, is also a currently deductible advertising expense.

Permanent Signs

Signs that have a useful life of less than one year—for example, paper or cardboard signs—are currently deductible as business operating expenses. However, a permanent metal or plastic sign that has a useful life of more than one year is a long-term business asset, which you cannot currently deduct as a business operating expense. Instead, you must either depreciate the cost over several years or deduct it in one year using 100% bonus depreciation, Section 179 expensing, or the de minimis safe harbor deduction. (See Chapter 5 for more on deducting long-term assets.)

Business Bad Debts

Business bad debts are debts that arise from your business activities, such as:

- lending money for a business purpose
- selling inventory on credit, or
- guaranteeing business-related loans.

You can currently deduct business bad debts as a business operating expense when they become wholly or partly worthless. However, to claim the deduction, you must incur an actual loss of money or have previously included the amount of the debt as income on your tax return. Because of this limitation, many small businesses are unable to deduct bad debts.

Three Requirements to Deduct Bad Debts

Three requirements must be satisfied to deduct a business bad debt as a business operating expense:

- You must have a bona fide business debt.
- The debt must be wholly or partly worthless.
- You must have suffered an economic loss from the debt.

A Bona Fide Business Debt

A bona fide debt exists when someone has a legal obligation to pay you a sum of money—for example, you sell goods or merchandise to a customer on credit. A bona fide debt also exists if written evidence supports it—for example, a signed promissory note or other writing stating the amount of the debt, when it is due, and the interest rate (if any). An oral promise to pay may also be legally enforceable but would be looked upon with suspicion by the IRS.

A business debt is a debt that is created or acquired in the course of your business or becomes worthless as part of your business. Your primary motive for incurring the debt must be business related. Debts taken on for personal or investment purposes are not business debts. (Remember, investing is not a business; see Chapter 1.)

EXAMPLE 1: Mark, an advertising agent, lends $10,000 to his brother-in-law, Scott, to invest in his bird diaper invention. Mark will get 25% of the profits if the invention proves successful. This is an investment, not a business debt.

EXAMPLE 2: Mark lends $10,000 to one of his best business clients to keep the client's business running. Because the main reason for the loan was business related (to keep his client in business so he will continue as a client), the debt is a business debt.

A Worthless Debt

A debt must be wholly or partly worthless to be deductible. A debt becomes worthless when there is no longer any chance that the amount owed will be paid back to you. You don't have to wait until a debt is due to determine that it is worthless, and you don't have to go to court to try to collect it. You just have to be able to show that you have taken reasonable steps to try to collect the debt or that collection efforts would be futile. For example:

- You've made repeated collection efforts that have proven unsuccessful.
- The debtor has filed for bankruptcy or already been through bankruptcy and had all or part of the debt discharged (forgiven) by the bankruptcy court.
- You've learned that the debtor has gone out of business, gone broke, died, or disappeared.

Keep all documentation that shows a debt is worthless, such as copies of unpaid invoices, collection letters you've sent the debtor, logs of collection calls you've made, bankruptcy notices, and credit reports.

You must deduct the entire amount of a bad debt in the year it becomes totally worthless. If only part of a business debt becomes worthless—for example, you received a partial payment before the debt became uncollectible—you can deduct the unpaid portion that year, or you can wait until the following year to deduct it. For example, if you think you might get paid more the next year, you can wait and see what your final bad debt amount is before you deduct it.

An Economic Loss

You are not automatically entitled to deduct a debt because the obligation has become worthless. To get a deduction, you must have suffered an economic loss. According to the IRS, you have a loss only when you:

- have already reported as business income the amount you were supposed to be paid
- paid out cash, or
- made credit sales of inventory that were not paid for.

These rules make it impossible to deduct some types of business debts.

Types of Bad Debts

Small businesses can incur many different types of business debts. The sections that follow discuss some of the more common ones.

Sales of Services

Unfortunately, if you're a cash basis taxpayer who sells services to your clients (like many small businesses), you can't claim a bad debt deduction if a client fails to pay you. As a cash basis taxpayer, you don't report income until you actually receive it. As a result, you don't have an economic loss (in the eyes of the IRS) when a client fails to pay.

> EXAMPLE: Bill, a self-employed consultant, works 50 hours for a client and bills the client $2,500. The client never pays. Bill is a cash basis taxpayer, so he doesn't report the $2,500 as income, because he never received it. As far as the IRS is concerned, Bill has no economic loss and cannot deduct the $2,500 the client failed to pay.

The IRS strictly enforces this rule (harsh as it might seem). Absent the rule, the IRS fears that businesses will inflate the value of their services in order to get a larger deduction.

Accrual basis taxpayers, on the other hand, report sales as income in the year the sales are made—not the year payment is received. These taxpayers can take a bad debt deduction if a client fails to pay for services rendered, because they have already reported the money due as income. Therefore, accrual taxpayers have an economic loss when their services are not paid for.

> EXAMPLE: Acme Consulting Co. bills a client $10,000 for consulting services it performed during the year. Because Acme is an accrual basis taxpayer, it characterizes the $10,000 as income on its books and includes this amount in its gross income in the year in which it billed for the services, even though Acme hasn't actually received payment. The client later files for bankruptcy, and the debt becomes worthless. Acme may take a business bad debt deduction to wipe out the $10,000 in income it previously charged on its books.

There's no point in trying to switch from cash basis to the accrual method to deduct bad debts. The accrual method doesn't result in lower taxes—the bad debt deduction merely wipes out a sale that was previously reported as income.

Credit Sales of Inventory

Most deductible business bad debts result from credit sales of inventory to customers. If you sell goods on credit to a customer and are not paid, you get a deduction whether you are an accrual or cash basis taxpayer. You deduct the cost of the inventory at the end of the year to determine the cost of goods sold for the year. (See Chapter 6 for more about deducting inventory.)

Cash Loans

Whether you are a cash or accrual basis taxpayer, cash loans you make for a business purpose are deductible as bad debts in the year they become worthless.

> EXAMPLE: John, an advertising agent, loaned $10,000 to one of his best business clients to keep the client's business running. The client later went bankrupt and could not repay him. John may deduct the $10,000 as a business bad debt.

Business Loan Guarantees

If you guarantee a debt that becomes worthless, it qualifies as a business bad debt only if you:

- made the guarantee in the course of your business
- have a legal duty to pay the debt
- made the guarantee before the debt became worthless, and
- received reasonable consideration (compensation) for the guarantee— you meet this requirement if the guarantee is for a good-faith business purpose or according to normal business practices.

EXAMPLE: Jane owns Jane's Dress Co. She guaranteed payment of a $20,000 note for Elegant Fashions, a dress outlet. Elegant Fashions is one of Jane's largest clients. Elegant later filed for bankruptcy and defaulted on the loan. Jane had to make full payment to the bank. She can take a business bad debt deduction, because her guarantee was made for a good-faith business purpose—her desire to retain one of her better clients and keep a sales outlet.

Loans or Guarantees to Your Corporation

If your business is incorporated, you cannot take a bad debt deduction for a loan to your corporation if the loan is actually a contribution to capital— that is, part of your investment in the business. You must be careful to treat a loan to your corporation in the same way that you treat a loan made to a business in which you have no ownership interest. You should have a signed promissory note from your corporation setting forth:

- the loan amount
- the interest rate—which should be a reasonable rate
- the due date, and
- a repayment schedule.

If you are a principal shareholder in a small corporation, you'll often be asked to personally guarantee corporate loans and other extensions of credit. Creditors do this because they want to be able to go after your personal assets if they can't collect from your corporation. If you end up having to make good on your guarantee and can't get repaid from your corporation, you will have a bad debt. You can deduct this bad debt as a business debt if your dominant motive for making the loan or guarantee was to protect your employment status and ensure your continuing receipt of a salary. If your primary motive was to protect your investment in the corporation, the debt is a personal debt. The IRS is more likely to think you are protecting your investment if you receive little or no salary from the corporation or your salary is not a major source of your overall income.

> **EXAMPLE:** Andre is employed by, and the sole shareholder of, Andre's Fashions, Inc. The corporation pays Andre a $75,000 annual salary, which is his sole source of income. Andre's Fashions applies for a $50,000 bank loan. Before approving the loan, the bank requires Andre to personally guarantee payment of the loan. Andre's Fashions defaults on the loan and Andre has to make full payment to the bank from his personal funds. Andre is entitled to a business bad debt deduction because his primary motive for guaranteeing the loan was to protect his job with his corporation, not to protect his investment in the corporation.

Personal Debts

The fact that a debt doesn't arise from your business doesn't mean it's not deductible. However, unlike business bad debts, personal bad debts are deductible only if they become wholly worthless. A deductible nonbusiness bad debt is classified as a short-term capital loss for tax purposes. As such, it is subject to the limitations on taking short-term capital losses: You can deduct such a loss against any short- or long-term capital gains you have for the year from the sale of capital assets (such as real estate and stocks). Any remaining amount of your loss is deductible only up to $3,000 per year against your other ordinary income. Nondeductible losses may be carried over to be deducted in future years.

Casualty Losses

Casualty losses are damage to property caused by fire, theft, vandalism, earthquake, storm, floods, terrorism, or some other "sudden, unexpected, or unusual event." There must be some external force involved for a loss to be a casualty loss. Thus, you get no deduction if you simply lose or misplace property or it breaks or wears out over time.

You may take a deduction for casualty losses to business property if, and only to the extent that, insurance doesn't reimburse you for the loss. However, unlike the case with personal casualty losses, you don't have to file an insurance claim to qualify for the business disaster loss deduction. In some cases, you could be better off not filing a claim if it will result in substantial increases in your insurance premiums or cancellation of your policy.

Amount of Deduction

The casualty loss deduction permits you to deduct an amount equal to the decline in value of property due to a casualty. How much you may deduct depends on whether the property involved was stolen or completely destroyed or only partially destroyed. If more than one item was stolen or wholly or partly destroyed, you must figure your deduction separately for each and then add them all together.

However, you may never deduct more than the property's adjusted basis. Your adjusted basis is the property's original cost, plus the value of any improvements, minus any deductions you took for depreciation or Section 179 expensing. (See Chapter 5.) Business personal property—computers and other equipment, for example—often has a zero adjusted basis because 100% of the cost can be deducted the year of purchase with 100% bonus depreciation (through 2022) or Section 179 expensing. In this event, the disaster loss deduction is zero. Business real property and passenger vehicles are less likely to have a zero adjusted basis when a disaster strikes.

In addition, you must always reduce your casualty losses by the amount of any insurance proceeds you actually receive or reasonably expect to receive. If the reimbursement turns out to be less than you expected, you can claim a loss the year you determine you'll receive no further reimbursement. Don't amend your original return for the prior year. If the reimbursement is larger than expected, you must include the amount in income for the year received to the extent a tax benefit was obtained from the excess loss claimed in the earlier year.

Total Loss

If the property is stolen or completely destroyed, your deduction is figured as follows: Adjusted Basis – Salvage Value / Insurance Proceeds = Casualty Loss. Obviously, if an item is stolen, there will be no salvage value.

> EXAMPLE: Sean's business computer is stolen from his apartment by a burglar. The computer cost $2,000. Sean has taken no tax deductions for it because he purchased it only two months ago, so his adjusted basis is $2,000. Sean is a renter and has no insurance covering the loss. Sean's casualty loss is $2,000. ($2,000 Adjusted Basis – $0 Salvage Value – $0 Insurance Proceeds = $2,000.)

Partial Loss

If the property is only partly destroyed, your casualty loss deduction is the lesser of the decrease in the property's fair market value or its adjusted basis, reduced by any insurance you receive or expect to receive.

> EXAMPLE: Assume that Sean's computer from the example above is partly destroyed due to a small fire in his home. Its fair market value in its partly damaged state is $500. Because he spent $2,000 for it, the decrease in its fair market value is $1,500. The computer's adjusted basis is $2,000. He received no insurance proceeds. Thus, his casualty loss is $1,500.

Inventory

You don't have to treat damage to or loss of inventory as a casualty loss. Instead, you may deduct it on your Schedule C as part of your cost of goods sold. (See Chapter 6 for a detailed discussion of inventory.) This is advantageous because it reduces your income for self-employment tax purposes, which casualty losses do not. However, if you do this, you must include any insurance proceeds you receive for the inventory loss in your gross income for the year.

Casualty Gains

If the total insurance compensation and/or other reimbursement you receive is more than the adjusted basis in the destroyed or damaged property, you'll have a casualty gain, not a loss. This is common with business personal property that is often fully expensed or depreciated. However, you can defer the gain by purchasing replacement property of equal or greater value. Your basis in the replacement property is its cost reduced by the amount of unrecognized casualty gain.

Personal Property

Uninsured casualty losses to personal property—that is, property you don't use for your business—can also be deductible from your income tax. However, during 2018 through 2025, you can qualify for a personal casualty loss deduction only if your loss is caused by a federally declared disaster. Other casualty losses to personal property—for example, uninsured losses due to ordinary house fires—are not deductible. For this reason, it is wise to have adequate homeowners' or renters' insurance to fully cover such losses.

As a general rule, uninsured losses caused by a federally declared disaster are an itemized deduction and are deductible only to the extent they exceed 10% of your adjusted gross income for the year. For example, if you have $10,000 in total casualty losses and 10% of your AGI is $7,000, your loss is limited to $3,000. In addition, your loss is deductible only to the extent it exceeds $100—in other words, you must reduce your loss by $100. This reduction applies to each total casualty or theft loss. It does not matter how many pieces of property are involved in an event. Only a single $100 reduction applies.

However, special rules allow you to deduct uninsured disaster losses sustained from January 1, 2018 to February 25, 2021, due to a federally declared major disaster. Such losses in excess of $500 can be deducted without itemizing and are not subject to the 10% of AGI floor.

Losses Due to the COVID-19 Pandemic

Ordinarily, casualty losses involve physical damage to tangible property such as a building. However, some losses caused by the COVID-19 pandemic could also be deductible casualty losses. To be deductible, such losses must:

- not be reimbursed through insurance or otherwise
- be evidenced by "closed and completed transactions," and
- be related to the disaster and sustained in the same year.

Such losses could include business inventory sold at a loss, thrown away because it spoiled or expired, or donated to charity. However, inventory losses can already be deducted as cost of goods sold. If you do so, you may not also take a casualty loss deduction. Other possible casualty deductions due to the COVID-19 pandemic include monetary losses directly attributable to the pandemic, such as termination payments made to cancel contracts, loss of deposits paid for preplanned business travel or events, or payments to cancel leases and other expenses to close a business.

Because the COVID-19 pandemic was declared a national disaster by the federal government, taxpayers have the option of deducting their 2021 losses in 2020 instead of 2021 and obtaining a refund for taxes paid in that year. (I.R.C. § 165(i).) You should consult with a tax professional to see if you qualify for this deduction, and, if so, when and how to take it.

Damage to Your Home Office

If you take the home office deduction, you may deduct losses due to damage or destruction of your home office as part of your deduction. However, your loss is reduced by any insurance proceeds you receive or expect to receive.

You can deduct casualty losses that affect your entire house as an indirect home office expense. The amount of your deduction is based on your home office use percentage.

> **EXAMPLE:** Dana's home is completely destroyed by a fire. Her fire insurance only covered 80% of her loss. Her home office took up 20% of her home. She can deduct 20% of her total casualty loss as an indirect home office deduction.

You can fully deduct casualty losses that affect only your home office—for example, if only your home office is burned in a fire—as direct home office expenses. However, you can't deduct as a business expense casualty losses that don't affect your home office at all—for example, if your kitchen is destroyed by fire.

If the loss involves business property that is in your home office but is not part of your home—for example, a burglar steals your home office computer—it's not part of the home office deduction.

(See Chapter 7 for a detailed discussion of the home office deduction.)

Tax Reporting

You report casualty losses to business property on part B of IRS Form 4684, *Casualties and Thefts*, and then transfer the deductible casualty loss to Form 4797, *Sales of Business Property*, and the first page of your Form 1040. The amount of your deductible casualty loss is subtracted from your adjusted gross income for the year. However, casualty losses are not deducted from your self-employment income for Social Security and Medicare tax purposes. These reporting requirements are different from the reporting for other deductions covered in this chapter, which are reported on IRS Schedule C, Form 1040.

Partnerships, S corporations, and LLCs must also fill out Form 4797. The amount of the loss is taken into account when calculating the entity's total business income for the year. This amount is reported on the entity's information tax return (Form 1065 for partnerships and LLCs; Form 1120-S for S corporations). C corporations deduct their casualty losses on their own tax returns (Form 1120).

If you take a casualty loss as part of your home office deduction, you must include it on Form 8829, *Expenses for Business Use of Your Home.*

Charitable Contributions

Many businesses have unsold inventory they want to get rid of. One easy way is to give the inventory to charity. This can result in a charitable tax deduction. The tax treatment of donations depends on how the business making the donation is legally organized.

Contributions by Sole Proprietors, LLCs, Partnerships, and S Corporations

If you are a sole proprietor, a partner in a partnership, an LLC member, or an S corporation shareholder, the IRS treats any charitable contributions your business makes as a personal contribution by you and your co-owners. As such, the contributions are not business expenses—you can deduct them only as a personal charitable contribution. Ordinarily, you may deduct charitable contributions only if you itemize your personal deductions on your tax return. However, special temporary rules allow you to deduct $300 in cash contributions to public charities without itemizing during 2020. During 2021, married couples who file jointly may each deduct $300 for a $600 total deduction. This deduction is scheduled to end after 2021. You may deduct additional contributions of money or property contributions (including inventory) only if you itemize your personal deductions on your personal tax return; they are subject to certain income limitations. You can deduct the lesser of the cost of donated inventory or its fair market value on the day it's donated.

EXAMPLE: Michele owns a clothing store as a sole proprietor. In December, she donates some unsold inventory to the Salvation Army. The clothing has a fair market value of $2,000, but it cost Jane only $1,000. Jane may only deduct $1,000 as a charitable contribution (assuming she itemizes her deductions).

There is an enhanced deduction for donations of food inventory to a public charity or an operating foundation that uses the food to care for the ill, needy, or infants. The deduction is the food's tax basis (cost) plus half the difference between its fair market value and basis, up to twice the basis. Cash basis taxpayers who do not keep inventories (including many farmers and some other small businesses) are allowed to deduct half the fair market value under the enhanced food inventory deduction, plus deducting the cost as a business expense. This enhanced deduction is limited to 25% of net business income for 2020–2021, 15% for other years. Charitable contributions are treated very differently for C corporations. C corporations can deduct charitable deductions as a business expense on their own corporate tax returns. Ordinarily, C corporations may deduct no more than 10% of their adjusted gross income for charitable donations; but, for 2020–2021, they may deduct 25% of AGI. C corporations are also subject to the rule regarding the lesser of cost or fair market value. C corporations also get an enhanced deduction when they contribute inventory (both food and nonfood) to a public charity or an operating foundation that uses the items to care for the ill, needy, or infants. The corporation may add 50% of the difference between the inventory's tax basis (cost) and fair market value (up to twice the basis) to the deduction amount. This makes inventory contributions particularly attractive for C corporations.

There are several organizations that specialize in facilitating charitable donations of unsold inventory by corporations, including the National Association for the Exchange of Industrial Resources (NAEIR) at www.naeir.org.

RESOURCE
For detailed guidance on tax deductions for charitable contributions, refer to *Every Nonprofit's Tax Guide: How to Keep Your Tax-Exempt Status & Avoid IRS Problems*, by Stephen Fishman (Nolo).

Clothing

You can deduct the cost of clothing if all below are true:
- It is essential for your business.
- It is not suitable for ordinary street wear.
- You don't wear the clothing outside of business.

Thus, for example, you may deduct the cost of uniforms or special work clothes not suitable for personal wear, such as nurse's uniforms, theatrical costumes, and special sanitary clothing, or clothing with a company logo. But clothing that you can wear on the street is not deductible—for example, you can't deduct the cost of business suits. Courts have also disallowed deductions for a tennis pro outfit and a house painting uniform because both of these could be worn on the street. If your clothing is deductible, you may also deduct the cost of dry cleaning and other care.

Dues and Subscriptions

Dues you pay to professional, business, and civic organizations are deductible business expenses, as long as the organization's main purpose is not to provide entertainment facilities to members. This includes dues paid to:
- bar associations, medical associations, and other professional organizations
- trade associations, local chambers of commerce, real estate boards, and business leagues, and
- civic or public service organizations, such as a Rotary or Lions club.

You get no deduction for dues you pay to belong to other types of social, business, or recreational clubs—for example, country clubs or athletic clubs. (See Chapter 10.) For this reason, it's best not to use the word "dues" on your tax return, because the IRS may question the expense. Use other words to describe the deduction—for example, if you're deducting membership dues for a trade organization, list the expense as "trade association membership fees."

You may deduct as a business expense subscriptions to professional, technical, and trade journals that deal with your business field.

Education Expenses

What about deducting the cost of business-related education—for example, a college course or seminar? Such expenses may be deductible, but only in strictly limited circumstances. To qualify for an education deduction, you must be able to show that the education:

- maintains or improves skills required in your existing business, or
- is required by law or regulation to maintain your professional status.

Lifetime Learning Credit

Instead of taking a tax deduction for your business-related education expenses, you may qualify for the lifetime learning credit. A tax credit is a dollar-for-dollar reduction in your tax liability, so it's even better than a tax deduction.

The lifetime learning credit can be used to help pay for any undergraduate or graduate level education, including nondegree education, to acquire or improve job skills (for example a continuing education course). If you qualify, your credit equals 20% of the first $10,000 of postsecondary tuition and fees you pay during the year, for a maximum credit of $2,000 per tax return. However, the credit is phased out and then eliminated at certain income levels: It begins to go down if your modified adjusted gross income is more than $59,000 ($119,000 for a joint return), and you cannot claim the credit at all if your MAGI is more than $69,000 ($139,000 for a joint return). These are the limits for 2021. The limits are adjusted for inflation each year.

You can take this credit not only for yourself, but for a dependent child (or children) for whom you claim a tax exemption, or your spouse as well (if you file jointly). And it can be taken any number of times. However, you can't take the credit if you've already deducted the education cost as a business expense.

> EXAMPLE: Bill, a self-employed real estate broker with a $40,000 AGI, spends $2,000 on continuing real estate education courses during the year. He may take a $400 lifetime learning credit (20% × $2,000 = $400).

Because of these restrictions, it is usually not possible to deduct undergraduate and graduate tuition. Instead, this deduction is usually used by professionals like doctors and accountants, who can deduct the cost of continuing professional education.

> EXAMPLE: Sue is a self-employed attorney. Every year, she is required by law to attend 12 hours of continuing education to keep her status as an active member of the state bar. The legal seminars she attends to satisfy this requirement are deductible education expenses.

If you qualify, deductible education expenses include tuition, fees, books, and other learning materials. They also include transportation and travel (see below). You may also deduct expenses you pay to educate or train your employees.

Can You Deduct Your MBA?

You ordinarily can't deduct the cost of obtaining a degree that leads to a professional license or certification—for example, a law degree, medical degree, or dental degree. However, it may be possible to deduct the cost of obtaining an MBA (a master's degree in business administration) because an MBA is a more general course of study that does not lead to a professional license or certification. The decisive factor is whether you were already established in your trade or business before you obtained the MBA. If so, it is deductible.

In one highly publicized case, for example, a registered nurse was allowed to deduct her $15,000 tuition cost of obtaining an MBA with a health care management specialization. She worked for many years as a quality control coordinator at various hospitals. The court held that, while the MBA may have improved her skill set, she was already performing the tasks and activities of her trade or business before commencing the MBA program, and continued to do so after receiving the degree. (*Lori A. Singleton-Clarke v. Commissioner*, TC Summ. Op. 2009-182 (2009).)

Starting a New Business

You cannot currently deduct education expenses you incur to qualify for a *new* business or profession. For example, courts have held that IRS agents could not deduct the cost of going to law school, because a law degree would qualify them for a new business—being a lawyer. (*Jeffrey L. Weiler*, 54 TC 398 (1970).) On the other hand, a practicing dentist was allowed to deduct the cost of being educated in orthodontia, because becoming an orthodontist did not constitute the practice of a new business or profession for a dentist. (Rev. Rul. 74-78.)

Minimum Educational Requirements

You cannot deduct the cost required to meet the minimum or basic level educational requirements for a business or profession. Thus, for example, you can't deduct the expense of going to law school or medical school.

Traveling for Education

Local transportation expenses paid to get to and from a deductible educational activity are deductible. This includes transportation between either your home or business and the educational activity. Going to or from home to an educational activity does not constitute nondeductible commuting. If you drive, you may deduct your actual expenses or use the standard mileage rate. (See Chapter 8 for more on deducting car expenses.)

No law that says you must take your education courses as close to home as possible. You may travel outside your geographic area for education, even if the same or a similar educational activity is available near your home or place of business. Companies and groups that sponsor educational events are well aware of this rule and take advantage of it by offering courses and seminars at resorts and other enjoyable vacation spots, such as Hawaii and California. Deductible travel expenses may include airfare or other transportation, lodging, and meals.

You cannot claim travel itself as an education deduction. You must travel to some sort of educational activity. For example, an architect could not deduct the cost of a trip to Paris because he studied the local architecture while he was there—but he could deduct a trip to Paris to attend a seminar on French architecture.

Entertainment and Meals

The Tax Cuts and Jobs Act made major changes to the longstanding deductions for business-related entertainment and meals. Starting in 2018, most business-related entertainment is not deductible. However, business-related meals remain deductible, and this deduction has been substantially enhanced for 2021–2022.

Entertainment

For decades, taxpayers were allowed to partly deduct the cost of entertainment, amusement, or recreation if the purpose was to generate income or provide other specific business benefits. The Tax Cuts and Jobs Act eliminated all such deductions starting in 2018. (I.R.C. § 274(a).) So, you may not deduct country club or skiing outings; theater or sporting event tickets; entertainment at night clubs; hunting, fishing, or similar trips; or other vacation trips. This is true even if the expenses result in a specific business benefit, such as landing a new client. Nondeductible entertainment expenses also include membership fees and dues for any club organized for business, pleasure, recreation, or other social purposes, and any entertainment facility fees.

However, a few types of entertainment remain wholly or partly deductible, including 100% of:

- the cost of entertainment provided as part of a company recreational or social activity—for example, a picnic or holiday party for your employees
- entertainment expenses for business meetings of employees, stockholders, agents, or directors—for example, the costs of renting a conference room in a hotel for such a meeting
- expenses for entertainment goods, services, and facilities that you sell to customers
- expenses for goods, services, and facilities you or your business makes available to the general public, and
- the cost of any entertainment or recreation expenses included as part of an employee's compensation and reported as such on the employee's W-2.

Meals

Business-related meals have long been a deductible expense. This continues, even after enactment of the Tax Cuts and Jobs Act. Historically, food and beverage expenses have been closely scrutinized by the IRS because of past abuses by taxpayers. For this reason, it is wise to keep good records of such expenses. See Chapter 15.

Meals with Clients, Prospects, and Others

When the Tax Cuts and Jobs Act eliminated the deduction for business-related entertainment, many feared it also eliminated deductions for client and prospect meals because such meals were deducted as an entertainment expense. However, the IRS has adopted regulations providing that most business-related food and beverage expenses remain deductible. (IRS Reg. 1.274-12.) Under the IRS regulations, food and beverage costs are deductible as a business expense if:

- the expense is not lavish or extravagant under the circumstances
- the taxpayer, or an employee of the taxpayer, is present when the items are consumed, and
- the food or beverages are provided to a business associate.

You or an employee need to be present at the meal to take this deduction. Moreover, the food or beverages must be furnished to a "business associate." This is any person you could reasonably expect to engage or deal with in the active conduct of your business, including current or prospective customers, clients, suppliers, employees, agents, partners, or professional advisers.

The meal need not be indispensable to be "ordinary and necessary," it just needs to be helpful to your business. The IRS does not require that you actually close a deal or get some other specific business benefit to take this deduction.

Although the meal may not be "lavish or extravagant," there is no dollar limit on how much you can spend; nor are you barred from eating at deluxe restaurants. You must use your common sense to determine if a meal is too lavish under the circumstances. In practice, the IRS will rarely second-guess you on this, especially if you have good documentation for the expense.

> **EXAMPLE:** Ivan, a sole proprietor consultant, has a meeting with a prospective client at a nice restaurant because the prospective client will like getting a free lunch. While at the lunch they discuss business, but don't close any deals. He pays $200 for the lunch, including a $35 tip. The cost of the lunch is a deductible business expense.

Limits on Meal Expense Deduction

Ordinarily, you may only deduct 50% of the total cost of a business meal, including food, beverages, tax, and tip. For example, if a meal costs $100, you may deduct $50. However, Congress enacted a special rule for 2021 and 2022 to help restaurants recover from the COVID-19 pandemic. During these years, you may deduct 100% of the cost of business meals and beverages purchased from restaurants. (IRC 274(n)(2)(D).)

For these purposes, a "restaurant" is a business that prepares and sells food or beverages to retail customers for immediate consumption, which includes everything from high-end French restaurants to McDonald's and Starbucks.

You don't have to eat the food at the restaurant to get the 100% deduction. You can order restaurant take-out and deduct the full cost. Likewise, you can deduct 100% of the cost of business meals ordered from restaurants through delivery services like Grubhub or Uber Eats.

"Restaurants" do not include businesses that predominantly sell prepackaged food or beverages for later consumption, like grocery stores, liquor stores, drug stores, specialty food stores, and vending machines. Food or beverages purchased from these places are still subject to the 50% limitation.

Because of these rules, you should separately track your total costs for meals and beverages purchased from restaurants and those for meals from other places like grocery stores and liquor stores.

Meals Combined with Entertainment

Special rules apply when food and beverages are provided during an entertainment activity to which you take a business associate. For these purposes, "entertainment" includes any activity generally considered to be entertainment, amusement, or recreation, like entertaining at bars, theaters, country clubs, golf and athletic clubs, sporting events, and on hunting, fishing, vacation, and similar trips.

The cost of the entertainment activity itself is not deductible. But food and beverages provided during an entertainment activity are deductible if they are purchased separately from the entertainment or listed separately on the receipt. (IRS Reg. 1.274-11.)

Entertainment and Meal Deductions—2018 and Later			
Type of Expense	Percentage Deductible		
	100%	50%	0%
Entertainment			
Company recreational or social activity—e.g.: • golf outings for all employees • holiday parties for all employees	✓		
Meetings of employees, stockholders, agents, or directors	✓		
Entertaining clients or customers			✓
Tickets—e.g.: • sporting events • theater • concerts			✓
Club dues or membership fees—e.g.: • country clubs • social clubs • athletic or sporting clubs			✓
Entertainment facility fees—e.g.: • skybox lease fees • golfing fees			✓

Meals		
Meals with clients, prospects, employees, and others (100% deduction for meals in restaurants 2021–2022)	✓	✓
Recreational employee meals—e.g.: • holiday parties • employee picnics	✓	
Meals at employer's business premises (100% deduction for meals from restaurants 2021–2022)	✓	✓
Meals while traveling overnight for business (100% deduction for meals in restaurants 2021–2022)	✓	✓
Meals at meetings of employees, stockholders, agents, or directors	✓	
Meals provided to general public	✓	
Meals sold to customers	✓	

EXAMPLE: You treat a client to a baseball game (which you also attend) and pay for beers and hot dogs while at the game. Because you paid for the beer and food separately, you can deduct the cost. You can't deduct the cost of the tickets. The food and beers purchased from a concession stand are 100% deductible during 2021–2022.

What if the cost of tickets for an entertainment event like a ball game includes the cost of food and beverages? The food and beverages are not deductible unless separately listed on the bill or invoice.

Other Meals

Other types of meals that remain deductible after the passage of the Tax Cuts and Jobs Act include:

- meals you consume while you travel for business—a business travel expense deduction, not an entertainment deduction (see Chapter 9) (100% deductible if purchased from restaurants during 2021–2022, otherwise 50% deductible)

- 100% of the cost of meals provided to employees as part of a company recreational or social activity—for example, food for an employee picnic or holiday party (may not include only highly compensated employees)
- meal expenses for business meetings of employees, stockholders, agents, or directors (may not include food at restaurants, but may include food for off-site meetings at hotels or other places business meetings are normally held)
- 50% of the cost of meals served to employees on business premises —for example, donuts, bagels, coffee, or even an employee cafeteria (100% deduction for meals purchased from restaurants during 2021-2022)
- 100% of the cost of meals sold to customers—for example, food costs for restaurants, food at an event or a workshop patrons pay to attend (food part of the cost), and
- 100% of the cost of meals made available to the general public— for example, by a realtor who provides free snacks at an open house, or a financial adviser who puts on a free educational dinner seminar for potential clients.

Gifts

If you give someone a gift for business purposes, your business expense deduction is limited to $25 per person per year. Any amount over the $25 limit is not deductible. If this amount seems awfully low, that's because it was established in 1954!

> **EXAMPLE:** Lisa, a self-employed marketing consultant, gives a $200 Christmas gift to her best client. She may deduct $25 of the cost.

A gift to a member of a customer's family is treated as a gift to the customer, unless you have a legitimate nonbusiness connection to the family member. If you and your spouse both give gifts, you are treated as one taxpayer—it doesn't matter if you work together or have separate businesses.

The $25 limit applies only to gifts to individuals. It doesn't apply if you give a gift to an entire company, unless the gift is intended for a particular person or group of people within the company. Such company-wide gifts are deductible in any amount, as long as they are reasonable.

> **EXAMPLE:** Bob sells products to the Acme Company. Just before Christmas, he drops off a $100 cheese basket at the company's reception area for all of Acme's employees. He also delivers an identical basket to Acme's president. The first basket left in the reception area is a company-wide gift, not subject to the $25 limit. The basket for Acme's president is a personal gift and therefore is subject to the limit.

Insurance for Your Business

You can deduct the premiums you pay for any insurance you buy for your business as a business operating expense. This includes:

- medical insurance for your employees (see Chapter 13)
- fire, theft, and flood insurance for business property
- credit insurance that covers losses from business debts
- liability insurance
- professional malpractice insurance—for example, medical or legal malpractice insurance
- workers' compensation insurance you are required by state law to provide your employees (if you are an employee of an S corporation, the corporation can deduct workers' comp payments made on your behalf, but they must be included in your employee wages)
- business interruption insurance
- life insurance covering a corporation's officers and directors if you are not a direct beneficiary under the policy, and
- unemployment insurance contributions (either as insurance costs or business taxes, depending on how they are characterized by your state's laws).

Homeowners' Insurance for Your Home Office

If you have a home office and qualify for the home office deduction, you may deduct the home office percentage of your homeowners' or renters' insurance premiums. For example, if your home office takes up 20% of your home, you may deduct 20% of the premiums. You can deduct 100% of any special coverage that you add to your homeowners' or renters' policy for your home office and/or business property. For example, if you add an endorsement to your policy to cover business property, you can deduct 100% of the cost.

Car Insurance

If you use the actual expense method to deduct your car expenses, you can deduct as a business expense the cost of insurance that covers liability, damages, and other losses for vehicles used in your business. If you use a vehicle only for business, you can deduct 100% of your insurance costs. If you operate a vehicle for both business and personal use, you can deduct only the part of the insurance premiums that applies to the business use of your vehicle. For example, if you use a car 60% for business and 40% for personal reasons, you can deduct 60% of your insurance costs. (See Chapter 8.)

If you use the standard mileage rate to deduct your car expenses, you get no separate deduction for insurance. Your insurance costs are included in the standard rate. (See Chapter 8.)

Interest on Business Loans

Interest you pay on business loans is usually a currently deductible business expense. It makes no difference whether you pay the interest on a bank loan, personal loan, credit card, line of credit, car loan, or real estate mortgage. Nor does it matter whether the collateral you used to get the loan was business or personal property. If you use the money for business, the interest you pay to get that money is a deductible business expense. It's how you use the money that counts, not how you get it. Borrowed money is used for business when you buy something with the money that's deductible as a business expense.

> **EXAMPLE:** Max, the sole proprietor owner of a small construction company, borrows $50,000 from the bank to buy new construction equipment. He pays 6% interest on the loan. His annual interest is deductible on his Schedule C, Form 1040, because it is for a business loan.

Your deduction begins only when you spend the borrowed funds for business purposes. You get no business deduction for interest you pay on money that you keep in the bank. Money in the bank is considered an investment—at best, you might be able to deduct the interest you pay on the money as an investment expense.

How to Eliminate Nondeductible Personal Interest

Because interest on money you borrow for personal purposes—like buying clothes or taking vacations—is not deductible, you should avoid paying this type of interest whenever possible. If you own a business, you can do this by borrowing money to pay your business expense and then using the money your business earns to pay off your personal debt. By doing this, you "replace" your nondeductible personal interest expense with deductible business expenses.

Home Offices

If you are a homeowner and take the home office deduction, you can deduct the home office percentage of your home mortgage interest as a business expense. (See Chapter 7 for a detailed discussion of the home office deduction.)

Car Loans

If you use your car for business, you can deduct the interest that you pay on your car loan as an interest expense. You can take this deduction whether you deduct your car expenses using the actual expense method or the standard mileage rate, because the standard mileage rate was not intended to encompass interest on a car loan.

If you use your car only for business, you can deduct all of the interest you pay. If you use it for both business and personal reasons, you can deduct the business percentage of the interest. For example, if you use your car 60% of the time for business, you can deduct 60% of the interest you pay on your car loan.

Loans to Buy a Business

If you borrow money to buy an interest in an S corporation, a partnership, or an LLC, it's wise to seek an accountant's help to figure out how to deduct the interest on your loan. It must be allocated among the company's assets and, depending on what assets the business owns, the interest might be deductible either as a business expense or as an investment expense, which is more limited.

Interest on money you borrow to buy stock in a C corporation is always treated as investment interest. This is true even if the corporation is small (also "called closely" held) and its stock is not publicly traded.

Loans From Relatives and Friends

If you borrow money from a relative or friend and use it for business purposes, you may deduct the interest you pay on the loan as a business expense. However, the IRS is very suspicious of loans between family members and friends. You need to carefully document these transactions. Treat the loan like any other business loan: Sign a promissory note, pay a reasonable rate of interest, and follow a repayment schedule. Keep your canceled loan payment checks to prove you really paid the interest.

Interest You Can't Deduct

You can't deduct interest:

- on loans used for personal purposes
- on debts your business doesn't owe
- on overdue taxes (only C corporations can deduct this interest)
- that you pay with funds borrowed from the original lender through a second loan (but you can deduct the interest once you start making payments on the new loan)
- that you prepay if you're a cash basis taxpayer (but you may deduct it the next year)
- on money borrowed to pay taxes or fund retirement plans, or
- on loans of more than $50,000 that are borrowed on a life insurance policy on yourself or another owner or employee of your business.

Get Separate Credit Cards for Your Business and Car Expenses

If you use the same credit card for your business and nonbusiness expenses, you are theoretically entitled to a business deduction for the credit card interest on your business expenses. However, you'll have a very difficult time calculating exactly how much of the interest you pay is for business expenses. To avoid this problem, use a separate credit card for business. This can be a special business credit card, but it doesn't have to be. You can simply designate one of your ordinary credit cards for business use. If you drive for business and use the actual expense method to take your deduction, it's a good idea to use another credit card just for car expenses. This will make it much easier to keep track of what you spend on your car.

Always pay your personal credit cards first, because you can't deduct the interest you pay on those costs.

Points and other loan origination fees that you pay to get a mortgage on business property are not deductible business expenses. You must add these costs to the cost of the building and deduct them over time using depreciation. The same is true for interest on construction loans if you are in the business of building houses or other real property. Manufacturers of substantial amounts of goods—defined as goods worth $1 million or more, with an estimated production period of more than one year—must also depreciate the interest on money borrowed to produce their goods.

Limitation on Deducting Interest by Larger Businesses

Prior to 2018, businesses could deduct 100% of the interest they paid without limit. However, starting in 2018, the Tax Cuts and Jobs Act limited this deduction to 30% of adjusted taxable income for all businesses with average gross receipts of $25 million or more. But, due to the COVID-19 pandemic, Congress increased this amount to 50% for 2019 and 2020 (2020 only for partnerships). For these purposes, adjusted taxable income means taxable income without including (1) nonbusiness income or deductions, (2) business interest income or expenses, (3) net operating losses, (4) pass-through deductions, and (5) for tax years before 2022, depreciation deductions. Undeductible interest must be carried forward to be deducted in any number of future years.

Businesses whose average gross receipts over the prior three years are less than $25 million are not subject to this limitation and may deduct 100% of their interest expense each year. In addition, real property businesses with more than $25 million in gross receipts may elect out of the limitation by agreeing to depreciate their real property over a somewhat longer period.

Legal and Professional Services

You can deduct fees that you pay to attorneys, accountants, consultants, and other professionals as business expenses if the fees are paid for work related to your business.

EXAMPLE: Ira, a freelance writer, hires attorney Jake to represent him in a libel suit. The legal fees Ira pays Jake are a deductible business expense.

Legal and professional fees that you pay for personal purposes generally are not deductible. For example, you can't deduct the legal fees you incur if you get divorced or you sue someone for a traffic accident injury. Nor are the fees that you pay to write your will deductible, even if the will covers business property that you own.

Buying Long-Term Property

If you pay legal or other fees in the course of buying long-term business property, you must add the amount of the fee to the tax basis (cost) of the property. You may deduct this cost over several years through depreciation or deduct it in one year under I.R.C. Sec. 179. (See Chapter 5 for more on depreciation.)

Starting a Business

Legal and accounting fees that you pay to start a business are deductible only as business start-up expenses. You can deduct $5,000 of start-up expenses the first year you're in business and any excess amounts over 180 months. The same holds true for incorporation fees or fees that you pay to form a partnership or an LLC. (See Chapter 3 for more on start-up expenses.)

Accounting Fees

You can deduct any accounting fees that you pay for your business as a deductible business expense—for example, fees you pay an accountant to set up or keep your business books, prepare your business tax return, or give you tax advice for your business. During 2018 through 2025, you may not deduct tax preparation fees for your personal taxes as a miscellaneous itemized deduction. Thus, you should have your tax preparer bill you separately for preparing the business portion of your tax return.

Self-employed taxpayers may deduct the cost of having an accountant or other tax professional complete the business portion of their tax returns—Schedule C and other business tax forms—but they cannot deduct the time the preparer spends on the personal part of their returns. If you are self-employed and pay a tax preparer to complete your Form 1040 income tax return, make sure that you get an itemized bill showing the portion of the tax preparation fee allocated to preparing your Schedule C (and any other business tax forms attached to your Form 1040).

Taxes and Licenses

Most taxes that you pay in the course of your business are deductible.

Income Taxes

Federal income taxes that you pay on your business income are not deductible. However, a corporation or partnership can deduct state or local income taxes it pays. Individuals may deduct state and local income taxes only as an itemized deduction on Schedule A, Form 1040. This is a personal, not a business, deduction. However, an individual can deduct state tax on gross business income as a business expense. This tax is a federally deductible business operating expense. Of course, you can't deduct state taxes from your income for state income tax purposes.

Self-Employment Taxes

If you are a sole proprietor, a partner in a partnership, or an LLC member, you may deduct one-half of your self-employment taxes from your total net business income. This deduction reduces the amount of income on which you must pay personal income tax. It's an adjustment to gross income, not a business deduction. You don't list it on your Schedule C; instead, you take it on Page One of your Form 1040.

The self-employment tax is a 15.3% tax, so your deduction is equal to 7.65% of your income. To figure out your income after taking this deduction, multiply your net business income by 92.35% or 0.9235.

EXAMPLE: Billie, a self-employed consultant, earned $70,000 from her business and had $20,000 in business expenses. Her net business income was $50,000. She multiplies this amount by 0.9235 to determine her net self-employment income, which is $46,175. This is the amount on which Billie must pay federal income tax.

This deduction is intended to help ease the tax burden on the self-employed.

Employment Taxes

If you have employees, you must pay half of their Social Security and Medicare taxes from your own funds and withhold the other half from their pay. Employment taxes (also known as "payroll taxes") consist of a 12.4% Social Security tax on income up to an annual ceiling. In 2021, the annual Social Security ceiling was $142,800. Medicare taxes are levied at a 2.9% rate up to an annual ceiling—$200,000 for single taxpayers and $250,000 for marrieds filing jointly; all income above the ceiling is taxed at a 3.8% rate. This combines to a total 15.3% tax on employment income up to the Social Security tax ceiling. You may deduct half of this amount as a business expense. You should treat the taxes you withhold from your employees' pay as wages paid to your employees on your tax return.

EXAMPLE: You pay your employee $20,000 a year. However, after you withhold employment taxes, your employee receives $18,470. You also pay an additional $1,530 in employment taxes from your own funds. You should deduct the full $20,000 salary as employee wages and deduct the $1,530 as employment taxes paid.

Sales Taxes

You may not deduct state and local sales taxes on your goods and services that you are required to collect from the buyer and turn over to your state or local government. Do not include these taxes in gross receipts or sales.

However, you may deduct sales taxes that you pay when you purchase goods or services for your business. The amount of the tax is added to the cost of the goods or services for purposes of your deduction for the item.

> **EXAMPLE:** Jean, a self-employed carpenter, buys $100 worth of nails from the local hardware store. She has to pay $7.50 in state and local sales taxes on the purchase. She may take a $107.50 deduction for the nails. She claims the deduction on her Schedule C as a purchase of supplies.

If you buy a long-term business asset, the sales taxes must be added to its basis (cost) for purposes of regular or bonus depreciation or expensing under I.R.C. Sec. 179.

> **EXAMPLE:** Jean buys a $3,000 power saw for her carpentry business. She pays $150 in state and local sales tax. The saw has a useful life of more than one year and is therefore a long-term business asset for tax purposes. She can't currently deduct the cost as a business operating expense. Instead, Jean must depreciate the cost over several years or deduct the full cost in one year using 100% bonus depreciation or Section 179 expensing. The total cost to be depreciated or expensed is $3,150.

Real Property Taxes

You can deduct your current year's state and local property taxes on business real property as business expenses. However, if you prepay the next year's property taxes, you may not deduct the prepaid amount until the following year.

Home Offices

The only real property of most small business owners is their home. If you are a homeowner and take the home office deduction, you may deduct the home office percentage of your property taxes as a business deduction. This can be advantageous because the personal itemized deduction for homeowners' property taxes for a first and second home during 2018 through 2025 is limited to $10,000. Any property tax you deduct as part of your home office deduction doesn't count toward this limit. Additionally, the Tax Cuts and Jobs Act nearly doubled the standard deduction, with the result that many homeowners are unable to itemize and are therefore unable to deduct any property tax as a personal itemized deduction. You may deduct the home office portion of your property as a business deduction whether or not you itemize.

Charges for Services

Water bills, sewer charges, and other service charges assessed against your business property are not real estate taxes, but they are deductible as business expenses. If you have a home office, you can deduct your home office percentage of these items.

However, real estate taxes imposed to fund specific local benefits, such as streets, sewer lines, and water mains, are not deductible as business expenses. Because these benefits increase the value of your property, you should add what you pay for them to the tax basis (cost for tax purposes) of your property.

Buying and Selling Real Estate

When real estate is sold, the real estate taxes must be divided between the buyer and seller according to how many days of the tax year each held ownership of the property. You'll usually find information on this in the settlement statement you receive at the property closing.

Other Taxes

Other deductible taxes include:
- excise taxes—for example, Hawaii imposes a general excise tax on businesses ranging from 0.5% to 4% of gross receipts
- state unemployment compensation taxes or state disability contributions
- corporate franchise taxes
- occupational taxes charged at a flat rate by your city or county for the privilege of doing business, and
- state and local taxes on personal property—for example, equipment or machinery that you use in your business.

You can deduct taxes on gasoline, diesel fuel, and other motor fuels that you use in your business. However, these taxes are usually included as part of the cost of the fuel. For this reason, you usually do not deduct these taxes separately on your return. However, you may be entitled to a tax credit for federal excise tax that you pay on fuels used for certain purposes—for example, farming or off-highway business use.

License Fees

License fees imposed on your business by your local or state government are deductible business expenses.

15

Record Keeping and Accounting

When you incur business expenses, you get tax deductions and save money on your taxes. But those deductions are only as good as the records you keep to back them up.

By far the most common reason taxpayers lose deductions when they get audited by the IRS is failure to keep proper records. Any expense you forget to deduct, or lose after an IRS audit because you can't back it up, costs you dearly. Every $100 in unclaimed deductions costs the average midlevel-income person (in a 24% tax bracket) $43 in additional federal and state income and self-employment taxes.

Luckily, it's not difficult to keep records of your business expenses. In this chapter, we'll show you how to document your expenditures so you won't end up losing your hard-earned business deductions.

What Records Do You Need?

If you're a sole proprietor with no employees, you need just two types of records for tax purposes:

- a record of your business income and expenses, and
- supporting documents for your income and expenses.

You need records of your income and expenses to figure out whether your business earned a taxable profit or incurred a deductible loss during the year. You'll also have to summarize your income and expenses in your tax return (IRS Schedule C).

You need receipts and other supporting documents, such as credit card records and canceled checks, in case you're audited by the IRS. These supporting documents enable you to prove to the IRS that your claimed expenses are genuine. Some expenses—travel and entertainment, for example—require particularly stringent documentation. Without this paper trail, you'll lose valuable deductions in the event of an audit. Remember, if you're audited, it's up to you to prove that your deductions are legitimate.

These aren't necessarily all the records you'll need. For example, if you make or sell merchandise, you will also have to keep inventory records. And if you have employees, you must create and keep a number of records, including payroll tax records, withholding records, and employment tax returns. Also, special record-keeping requirements must be followed if you've formed a corporation, limited liability company with two or more owners, or partnership.

Business Checkbook and Credit Cards

Before you even think about what type of record-keeping system you'll use, you should set up a separate checking account for your business (if you haven't done so already). Your business checkbook will serve as your basic source of information for recording your business expenses and income.

A separate business checkbook is legally required if you've formed a corporation, a partnership, or an LLC. Keeping a separate business account is not legally required if you're a sole proprietor, but it will provide many important benefits:

- Your canceled checks or bank statements showing electronic payments made from the account will serve as proof that you actually paid for your claimed expenses.
- It will be much easier for you to keep track of your business income and expenses if you pay them from a separate account.
- Your business account will clearly separate your personal and business finances; this will prove very helpful if you're audited by the IRS.
- Your business account will help convince the IRS that you are running a business and not engaged in a hobby. Hobbyists don't generally have separate bank accounts for their hobbies. This is a huge benefit if you incur losses from your business, because losses from hobbies are not fully deductible. (See Chapter 2 for more on the hobby loss rule.)

Deposit all your business receipts (checks you receive from clients, for example) into the account and make all business-related payments electronically or by check from the account (other than those you make by credit card). Don't use your business account to pay for personal expenses or your personal account to pay for business items. To withdraw money for personal use, write a check to yourself or transfer funds into your personal checking account.

Setting Up Your Bank Account

Your business checking account should be in your business name. If you're a sole proprietor, this can be your own name. If you've formed a corporation, partnership, or limited liability company, the account should be in your corporate, partnership, or company name.

You don't need to open your business checking account at the same bank where you have your personal checking account. Shop around and open your account with the bank that offers you the best services at the lowest price.

If you're doing business under your own name, consider opening up a second account in that name and using it solely for your business instead of a separate business account. You'll usually pay less for a personal account than for a business account.

If you're a sole proprietor doing business under an assumed name, you'll likely have to give your bank a copy of your fictitious business name statement.

If you've incorporated your business, call your bank and ask what documentation is required to open the account. You will probably need to show the bank a corporate resolution authorizing the opening of a bank account and showing the names of the people authorized to sign checks. Typically, you will also have to fill out, and impress your corporate seal on, a separate bank account authorization form provided by your bank. You will also need to have a federal employer identification number.

Similarly, if you've established a partnership or limited liability company, you'll likely have to show the bank a resolution authorizing the account.

You may also want to establish interest-bearing accounts for your business in which you place cash you don't immediately need. For example, you may decide to set up a business savings account or a money market mutual fund in your business name.

Use a Separate Credit Card for Business

Use a separate credit card for business expenses instead of putting both personal and business items on one card. Credit card interest for business purchases is 100% deductible, while interest for personal purchases is not deductible at all. (See Chapter 2.) Using a separate card for business purchases will make it much easier for you to keep track of how much interest you've paid for business purchases. The card doesn't have to be in your business name. It can just be one of your personal credit cards. Always use your business checking account to pay your business credit card bill.

Records of Your Business Income and Expenses

When people talk about "keeping the books," they mean keeping a record of a business's income and expenses. You may be surprised to learn that, if you're a sole proprietor, the IRS does not require you to use any particular type of record-keeping system. It says that "you may choose any record-keeping system suited to your business that clearly shows your income and expenses."

Such records can take a variety of forms and be kept in a variety of ways—some simple, some complex.

Paper Versus Electronic Records

The first choice you need to make is whether to keep paper records you create by hand or to use computerized electronic record keeping. Either method is acceptable to the IRS.

Hiring a Bookkeeper

If you really hate record keeping, you always have the option of hiring someone to keep your records for you. You should have no problem finding a bookkeeper through referrals from friends or colleagues, sources such as Craigslist, or the phone listings. However, if you decide to use a bookkeeper, you should still continue to write all your business checks and make deposits yourself. Giving such authority to a bookkeeper can lead to embezzlement.

Although it might seem old-fashioned, many small business owners keep their records by hand on paper, especially when they are first starting out. You can use a columnar pad, notebook paper, or blank ledger books. There are also "one-write systems" that allow you to write checks and keep track of expenses simultaneously. Go to your local stationery store and you'll find what you need.

Manual bookkeeping may take a bit more time than using a computer, but has the advantage of simplicity. You'll always be better off using handwritten ledger sheets, which are easy to create and understand and simple to keep up to date, instead of a complicated computer program that you don't understand or use properly.

RESOURCE

For an excellent guide to small business bookkeeping by hand, refer to *Small Time Operator*, by Bernard B. Kamoroff (Lyons Press).

If you want to use electronic record keeping, many options are available to choose from. These range from simple checkbook programs to sophisticated accounting software. We won't discuss how to use these programs in detail. You'll need to read the manual or tutorial that comes with the program you choose. Various books and websites also explain how to use them. However, if you're not prepared to invest the time to use a computer program correctly, don't use it!

You can create your own spreadsheet to keep track of your expenses and income with a program such as *Excel*. Many templates are available to help you do this; or you can customize your own spreadsheet. See the discussion of how to track business expenses to see what you should include in your spreadsheet.

A personal finance program such as *Quicken* may be perfectly adequate for a one-owner service business. These programs are easy to use because they work off of a computerized checkbook. When you buy something for your business, you write a check using the program. It automatically inputs the data into a computerized check register, and you print out the check using your computer (payments can also be made online). You'll have to input credit card and cash payments separately.

You create a list of expense categories just like you do when you create a ledger sheet or spreadsheet. Programs like *Quicken* come with preselected categories, but these are not adequate for many businesses, so you'll probably have to create your own. The expense category is automatically noted in your register when you write a check.

Before You Purchase an Online Program

You don't want to spend your hard-earned money on a financial program only to discover that you don't like it. Before you purchase a program, do some research:

- Talk to others in similar businesses to find out what they use— if they don't like a program, ask them why.
- Think carefully about how many features you need—the more complex the program, the harder it will be to learn and use it.
- Obtain a demo version you can try out for free to see if you like it— you can usually download one from the software company's website.

A list and comparison of most available accounting software packages and online subscription services can be found at https://en.wikipedia.org/wiki/Comparison_of_accounting_software.

The program can then take this information and automatically create income and expense reports—that is, it will show you the amounts you've spent or earned for each category. This serves the same purpose as the expense journal. It can also create profit and loss statements. *Quicken* provides all the tools many small service businesses need. However, if your business involves selling goods or maintaining an inventory, or if you have employees, you'll need a more sophisticated program.

Small business accounting programs, such as *QuickBooks* by Intuit, *FreshBooks,* and *Sage 50cloud Accounting,* can do everything personal financial software can do and much more, including: bills, downloading credit card and bank transactions, reconciling bank accounts, generating sophisticated reports, creating budgets, tracking inventory, tracking employee time and calculating payroll withholding, generating invoices and keeping track of accounts receivable, and maintaining fixed asset records.

These programs are more expensive than personal finance software and are harder to learn to use. If you don't need their advanced features, there is no reason to use them.

Online bookkeeping relies on a Web-based computer application rather than desktop bookkeeping software. Your data is stored online in the "cloud" by the online bookkeeping service. This way you won't lose your data if your home computer is stolen or destroyed. Popular online accounting services that charge a monthly fee include *FreshBooks*, *QuickBooks Self-Employed*, *QuickBooks Online*, *Sage*, *Zoho Books*, *Outright*, *Xero*, *FreeAgent*, *Cheqbook*, *Sage Intacct*, *Clear Books*, and *Wave*.

Tracking Your Business Expenses

You can track your expenses by creating an expense journal that summarizes all your business expenses by category. This will show what you buy for your business and how much you spent. It's very easy to do this. You can create your journal on paper or you can set up a computer spreadsheet program, such as *Excel*, to do it. Or, if you already have or would prefer to use a financial computer program such as *Quicken*, you can do that instead.

To decide what your expense categories should be, sit down with your bills and receipts and sort them into categorized piles. IRS Schedule C, the tax form sole proprietors must use to list their expenses, contains categories of business expenses. These categories are a good place to start when you devise your own list, because you'll have to use the ones that apply to you when you complete your Schedule C for your taxes. The Schedule C categories include:

- advertising
- bad debts
- car and truck expenses
- commissions and fees
- depletion (rarely used by most small businesses)
- depreciation and Section 179 expense deductions
- employee benefit programs
- insurance (other than health)
- interest
- legal and professional services

- office expenses
- pension and profit-sharing plans
- rent or lease—vehicles, machinery, and equipment
- rent or lease—other business property
- repairs and maintenance
- supplies
- taxes and licenses
- travel
- utilities, and
- wages.

The Schedule C list of business categories is by no means exhaustive. (In fact, it used to contain more categories.) It just gives you an idea of how to break down your expenses. Depending on the nature of your business, you may not need all these categories or you might have others. For example, a graphic designer might have categories for printing and typesetting expenses, or a writer might have a category for agent fees.

You should always include a final category called "Miscellaneous" for various and sundry expenses that are not easily pigeonholed. However, you should use this category sparingly, to account for less than 10% of your total expenses. Unlike "travel" or "advertising," "miscellaneous" is not a type of business expense. It's just a place to lump together different types of expenses that don't fit into another category.

Entertainment Expenses No Longer Deductible

As a result of the Tax Cuts and Jobs Act, entertainment expenses are no longer deductible starting in 2018. For example, you may not deduct athletic or theater tickets for clients. There is no need to document these nondeductible expenses. (See Chapter 14 for more details.)

You can add or delete expense categories as you go along—for example, if you find your miscellaneous category contains many items for a particular type of expense, add it as an expense category. You don't need a category for automobile expenses, because these expenses require a different kind of documentation for tax purposes.

In separate columns, list the check number, date, and name of the person or company paid for each payment. If you pay by credit card or cash, indicate it in the check number column.

Once a month, go through your check register, credit card slips, receipts, and other expense records and record the required information for each transaction. Also, total the amounts for each category when you come to the end of the page and keep a running total of what you've spent for each category for the year to date.

Supporting Documents

The IRS lives by the maxim that "figures lie and liars figure." It knows very well that you can claim anything in your books and on your tax returns, because you create or complete them yourself. For this reason, the IRS requires that you have documents to support the deductions you claim on your tax return. In the absence of a supporting document, an IRS auditor may conclude that an item you claim as a business expense is really a personal expense, or that you never bought the item at all. Either way, your deduction will be disallowed.

The supporting documents you need depend on the type of deduction involved. However, at a minimum, every deduction should be supported by documentation showing what, how much, and who. That is, your supporting documents should show:

- what you purchased for your business
- how much you paid for it, and
- whom (or what company) you bought it from.

Additional record-keeping requirements must be met for deductions for local transportation, travel, meal, and gift deductions, as well as for certain long-term assets that you buy for your business. ("Records Required for Specific Expenses," below, covers these rules.)

You can meet the what, how much, and who requirements by keeping the following types of documentation:

- canceled checks
- sales receipts
- account statements

- credit card sales slips
- invoices, or
- petty cash slips for small cash payments.

Make Digital Copies of Your Receipts

According to an old Chinese proverb, "The palest ink is more reliable than the most retentive memory." However, when it comes to receipts, ink is no longer so reliable. Receipts printed on thermal paper (as most are) fade over time. By the time the IRS audits your return, you might find that all or most of the paper receipts you've carefully retained in your files are unreadable.

Because of the fading problem, you should photocopy your receipts if you intend to rely on hard copies. Obviously, this is time consuming and annoying. But there is an easier alternative: Make digital copies of your receipts and throw away the hard copies. Many smartphone apps are available for this purpose. Two of the most popular are *Shoeboxed.com* and *Expensify.com*. Using these and other similar apps, you can add notes and then upload the digital photos to an online account for permanent storage. These apps can even automatically categorize your expenses, and you can export your data to *QuickBooks, Quicken, Excel, FreshBooks,* and other accounting software.

Keep your supporting documents in a safe place. If you don't have a lot of receipts and other documents to save, you can simply keep them all in a single folder. If you have a lot of supporting documents to save or are the type of person who likes to be extremely well organized, separate your documents by category—for example, income, travel expenses, or equipment purchases. You can use a separate file folder for each category or get an accordion file with multiple pockets.

Canceled Check + Receipt = Proof of Deduction

Manny, a self-employed photographer, buys a $500 digital camera for his business from the local electronics store. He writes a check for the amount and is given a receipt. How does he prove to the IRS that he has a $500 business expense?

Could Manny simply save his canceled check when it's returned from his bank? Many people carefully save all their canceled checks (some keep them for decades), apparently believing that a canceled check is all the proof they need to show that a purchase was a legitimate business expense. This is not the case. All a canceled check proves is that you spent money for something. It doesn't show what you bought. Of course, you can write a note on your check stating what you purchased, but why should the IRS believe what you write on your checks yourself?

MANNY FARBER	**2345**
123 SHADY LANE	
ANYTOWN, IL 12345	Date Feb. 1, 20XX 12-34/5780
Pay to the order of Acme Camera Store	$ 500.00
Five hundred and 00/100	Dollars
Piggy Bank	
100 Main Street	
Anytown, IL 12345	
Memo Digital Camera	Manny Farber
⑈ 578000358⑈ 5355⑈05556⑈05555 ⑈	

Does Manny's sales receipt prove he bought his camera for his business? Again, no. A sales receipt only proves that somebody purchased the item listed in the receipt. It does not show who purchased it. Again, you could write a note on the receipt stating that you bought the item. But you could easily lie. Indeed, for all the IRS knows, you could hang around stores and pick up receipts people throw away to give yourself tax deductions. There are also websites that, for a fee, will create legitimate-looking fake receipts.

However, when you put a canceled check together with a sales receipt (or an invoice, a cash register tape, or a similar document), you have concrete proof that you purchased the item listed in the receipt. The check proves that you bought something, and the receipt proves what that something is.

509257

CUSTOMER'S ORDER NO. 14601				DATE February 1, 20XX			
NAME							
ADDRESS							
CITY, STATE, ZIP							

SOLD BY SF	CASH	C.O.D.	CHARGE	ON ACCT.	MDSE. RETD.	PAID OUT

	QUAN.	DESCRIPTION	PRICE	AMOUNT
1	1	Minolta Digital Camera	500	500
2				
3				
4				
5				
6				
7				
8				
9				
10				
11			Total	500
12				
RECEIVED BY				

KEEP THIS SLIP FOR REFERENCE

This doesn't necessarily prove that you bought the item for your business, but it's a good start. Often, the face of a receipt, the sales slip, or the payee's name on your canceled check will strongly indicate that the item you purchased was for your business. But if it's not clear, note what the purchase was for on the document. Such a note is not proof of how you used the item, but it will be helpful. For some types of items that you use for both business and personal purposes—cameras are one example— you might be required to keep careful records of your use. (See "Records Required for Specified Expenses," below.)

Credit Cards

Using a credit card is a great way to pay business expenses. The credit card slip will prove that you bought the item listed on the slip. You'll also have a monthly statement to back up your credit card slips. You should use a separate credit card for your business.

Account Statements

Sometimes, you'll need to use an account statement to prove an expense. Some banks no longer return canceled checks, or you may pay for something with an ATM card or another electronic funds transfer method. Moreover, you may not always have a credit card slip when you pay by credit card—for example, when you buy an item over the Internet. In these events, the IRS will accept an account statement as proof that you purchased the item. The chart below shows what type of information you need on an account statement.

Proving Payments With Bank Statements	
If payment is by:	**The statement must show:**
Check	Check number Amount Payee's name Date the check amount was posted to the account by the bank
Electronic funds transfer	Amount transferred Payee's name Date the amount transferred was posted to the account by the bank
Credit card	Amount charged Payee's name Transaction date

Records Required for Specific Expenses

The IRS is particularly suspicious of business deductions people take for local transportation, travel, meals, and gift expenses. It knows that many people wildly inflate these deductions—either because they're dishonest or because they haven't kept good records and make estimates of how much they think they must have spent. For this reason, special record-keeping requirements apply to these deductions. Likewise, there are special requirements for long-term assets that can be used for both personal and business purposes. If you fail to comply with the requirements discussed below, the IRS may disallow the deduction, even if it was legitimate.

Automobile Mileage and Expense Records

If you use a car or other vehicle for business purposes other than just commuting to and from work, you're entitled to take a deduction for gas and other auto expenses. You can either deduct the actual cost of your gas and other expenses or take the standard rate deduction based on the number of business miles you drive. (See Chapter 8 for more on car expenses.)

Either way, you must keep a record of:
- your mileage
- the dates of your business trips
- the places you drove for business, and
- the business purpose for your trips.

The last three items are relatively easy to keep track of. You can record the information in your appointment book, calendar, or day planner. Or, you can record it in a mileage log.

No Documentation Needed for Utilitarian Vehicles

All this documentation is not required for vehicles that ordinarily are not driven for personal use—for example, ambulances, hearses, trucks weighing more than 14,000 pounds, cement mixers, cranes, tractors, garbage trucks, dump trucks, forklifts, moving vans, and delivery trucks with seating for only the driver or seating for only the driver plus a folding jump seat. But you still need to keep track of your gas, repair, and other expenses.

Calculating your mileage takes more work. The IRS wants to know the total number of miles you drove during the year for business, commuting, and personal driving other than commuting. Commuting is travel from your home to your office or other principal place of business. If you work from a home office, you'll have no commuting mileage. (See Chapter 8 for more on commuting and automobile expenses.) Personal miles other than commuting include all the driving you do other than from home to your office—for example, to the grocery store, on a personal vacation, or to visit friends or relatives.

Claiming a Car Is Used Solely for Business

If you use a car 100% for business, you don't need to keep track of your personal or commuting miles. However, you can successfully claim to use a car 100% for business only if you:

- work out of a tax-deductible home office
- have at least two cars, and
- use one car just for business trips.

If you don't work from a home office, your trips from your home to your outside office are nonbusiness commuting, so the car you take from your home to your office is not used 100% for business, even if you drive it only for business after you get to your office and then drive straight home.

To keep track of your business driving you can use either a paper mileage logbook that you keep in your car or an electronic application. Logbooks are available in any stationery store and there are dozens of smartphone apps that you can use to record your mileage. Many of these apps use GPS tracking to automatically calculate your mileage for each trip.

Whichever you choose, there are several ways to keep track of your mileage; some are easy, and some are a bit more complicated.

52-Week Mileage Log

The hardest way to track your mileage—and the way the IRS would like you to do it—is to keep track of every mile you drive every day, 52 weeks a year, using a mileage logbook or business diary. This means you'll list every trip you take, whether for business, commuting, or personal reasons. If you enjoy record keeping, go ahead and use this method. But there are easier ways.

Tracking Business Mileage

An easier way to keep track of your mileage is to record your mileage only when you use your car for business. If you record your mileage with an electronic app, check the manual to see how to implement this system. If you use a paper mileage logbook, here's what to do:

- Note your odometer reading in the logbook at the beginning and end of every year that you use the car for business. (If you don't know your January 1 odometer reading for this year, you might be able to estimate it by looking at auto repair receipts that note your mileage.)
- Record your mileage and note the business purpose for the trip every time you use your car for business.
- Add up your business mileage when you get to the end of each page in the logbook. (This way, you'll have to add only the page totals at the end of the year instead of all the individual entries.)
- If you commute to your office or other workplace, figure out how many miles you drive each way and note in your appointment book how many times you drive to the office each week.

At the end of the year, your logbook will show the total business miles you drove during the year. You calculate the total miles you drove during the year by subtracting your January 1 odometer reading from your December 31 reading.

If you use the actual expense method, you must also calculate your percentage of business use of the car. You do this by dividing your business miles by your total miles.

> **EXAMPLE:** Yolanda, a self-employed salesperson, uses her car extensively for business. At the beginning of the year, her odometer reading was 34,201 miles. On December 31, it was 58,907 miles. Her total mileage for the year was therefore 24,706. She recorded 62 business trips in her mileage logbook for a total of 9,280 miles. Her business use percentage of her car is 37% (9,290 ÷ 24,706 = 0.376). Yolanda commuted to her office every day, 50 weeks a year. She determined that her office was ten miles from her home. So Yolanda had 5,000 miles of commuting mileage for the year.

Sampling Method

An even easier way to track your mileage is to use a sampling method. Under this method, you keep track of your business mileage for a sample portion of the year and use your figures for that period to extrapolate your business mileage for the whole year.

This method assumes that you drive about the same amount for business throughout the year. To back up this assumption, you must scrupulously keep an appointment book showing your business appointments all year long. If you don't want to keep an appointment book, don't use the sampling method.

Your sample period must be at least 90 days—for example, the first three months of the year. Alternatively, you may sample one week each month—for example, the first week of every month. You don't have to use the first three months of the year or the first week of every month; you could use any other three-month period or the second, third, or fourth week of every month. Use whatever works best—you want your sample period to be as representative as possible of the business travel you do throughout the year.

You must keep track of the total miles you drove during the year by taking odometer readings on January 1 and December 31 and deducting any atypical mileage before applying your sample results.

> EXAMPLE: Tom, a traveling salesman, uses the sample method to compute his mileage, keeping track of his business miles for the first three months of the year. He drove 6,000 miles during that time and had 4,000 business miles. His business use percentage of his car was 67%. From his January 1 and December 31 odometer readings, Tom knows he drove a total of 27,000 miles during the year. However, Tom drove to the Grand Canyon for vacation, so he deducts this 1,000-mile trip from his total. This leaves him with 26,000 total miles for the year. To calculate his total business miles, he multiplies the yearlong total by the business use percentage of his car: 67% × 26,000 = 17,420. Tom claims 17,420 business miles on his tax return.

Keeping Track of Actual Expenses

If you take the deduction for your actual auto expenses instead of the standard rate (or are thinking about switching to this method), keep receipts for all of your auto-related expenses, including gasoline, oil, tires, repairs, and insurance. At tax time, add them up to determine how large your deduction will be if you use the actual expense method. Also add in the amount you're entitled to deduct for depreciation of your auto. (See Chapter 8 for more on calculating automobile deductions.)

Use a Credit Card for Gas

If you use the actual expense method for car expenses, use a credit card when you buy gas. It's best to designate a separate card for this purpose. The monthly statements you receive will serve as your gas receipts. If you pay cash for gas, you must either get a receipt or make a note of the amount in your mileage logbook.

Costs for business-related parking (other than at your office) and for tolls are separately deductible whether you use the standard rate or the actual expense method. Get and keep receipts for these expenses.

Travel and Gift Expenses

Deductions for travel (including meals while traveling) and gifts are hot-button items for the IRS because they have been greatly abused by many taxpayers. You need to have more records for these expenses than for almost any others, and they will be closely scrutinized if you're audited.

Whenever you incur an expense for travel (including meals while traveling), or gifts you must document the following four facts:

- **The amount.** How much you spent, including tax and tip for meals. Document the amount of each separate travel expense, such as airfare, lodging, and meals. However, the cost of meals and incidental expenses may be combined on a daily basis by category—for example, daily meal, gas, taxi, or Uber expenses.

- **The time and place.** The dates of departure and return for travel, the date and place of meals, or the date and description of gifts. Make sure to note if a meal is purchased from a restaurant; these meals are 100% deducible during 2021–2022.
- **The business purpose.** The business reason for travel or the business benefit derived (or expected to be derived) from it. The business benefit derived (or expected to be derived) as a result of a gift.
- **The business relationship.** If meals or gifts are involved, show the business relationship of the people at the meal or receiving the gift—for example, list their names and occupations and any other information needed to establish their business relation to you.

The IRS does not require that you keep receipts, canceled checks, credit card slips, or any other supporting documents for travel expenses (including meals while traveling), or gifts that cost less than $75. However, you must still document the facts listed above. This exception does not apply to lodging—that is, hotel or similar costs—when you travel for business. You do need receipts for these expenses, even if they are less than $75.

All this record keeping is not as hard as it sounds. You can record the facts you have to document in a variety of ways. The information doesn't have to be all in one place. Information that is shown on a receipt, a canceled check, or another item need not be duplicated in a log, appointment book, calendar, or account book. Thus, for example, you can record the facts with:

- a receipt, credit card slip, or similar document alone
- a receipt combined with an appointment book entry, or
- an appointment book entry alone (for expenses less than $75).

However you document your expense, you are supposed to do it in a timely manner. You don't need to record the details of every expense on the day you incur it. It is sufficient to record them on a weekly basis. However, if you're prone to forget details, it's best to get everything you need in writing within a day or two.

Business Meals When Not Traveling

Meals and beverages you purchase other than while traveling on business are no longer subject to the strict substantiation rules described above. Instead, they are now subject to the same record-keeping rules as any business deduction. This means you are still supposed to have records of the amount and business purpose. But, if you lack adequate records, you can ask the IRS and/or Tax Court to permit you at least a partial deduction under the *Cohan* rule (see "What If You Don't Have Proper Tax Records?" below). Under this rule, taxpayers who lack all required records are permitted to make an estimate of how they must have spent the money. The IRS has discretion to allow such taxpayers to deduct all or part of the estimated amount. But, you must provide at least some credible evidence on which to base this estimate, such as receipts, canceled checks, notes in your appointment book, or other records.

Receipts to Keep

Type of Expense	Receipts to Save
Travel	Airplane, train, or bus ticket stubs; travel agency receipts; rental car; and so on.
Meals While Traveling	Meal check, credit card slip.
Lodging	Statement or bill from hotel or other lodging provider. Your own written records for cleaning, laundry, telephone charges, tips, and other charges not shown separately on hotel statement.

Listed Property

Listed property refers to certain types of long-term business assets that can easily be used for personal as well as business purposes. Listed property includes:

- cars, boats, airplanes, motorcycles, and other vehicles, and
- any other property generally used for entertainment, recreation, or amusement—for example, VCRs, cameras, and camcorders.

Because all listed property is long-term business property, it cannot be deducted like a business expense. Instead, you must depreciate it over several years unless you can deduct it in one year with the de minimis safe harbor, Section 179 expensing, or using bonus depreciation. (See Chapter 5 for more on deducting listed property.)

Special Record-Keeping Requirements

With listed property, the IRS fears that taxpayers might claim business deductions but really use the property for personal reasons instead. For this reason, you're required to document how you use listed property. Keep an appointment book, logbook, business diary, or calendar showing the dates, times, and reasons for which the property is used—both business and personal. You also can purchase logbooks for this purpose at stationery or office supply stores.

How Long to Keep Records

You need to keep copies of your tax returns and supporting documents in case you are audited by the IRS or another taxing agency. You might also need them for other purposes—for example, to get a loan, a mortgage, or insurance.

You should keep your records for as long as the IRS has to audit you after you file your returns for the year. These statutes of limitation range from three years to forever—they are listed in the table below.

To be on the safe side, you should keep your tax returns indefinitely. They usually don't take up much space, so this is not a big hardship. Your supporting documents probably take up more space. You should keep these for at least six years after you file your return. If you file a fraudulent return, keep your supporting documents indefinitely (if you have any). If you're audited, they will show that at least some of your deductions were legitimate. Keeping your records this long ensures that you'll have them available if the IRS decides to audit you.

Keep your long-term asset records for three years after the depreciable life of the asset ends. For example, keep records for five-year property (such as computers) for eight years.

You should keep your ledger sheets for as long as you're in business, because a potential buyer of your business might want to see them.

IRS Statutes of Limitations	
If:	The limitations period is:
You failed to pay all the tax due	3 years
You underreported your gross income for the year by more than 25%	6 years
You filed a fraudulent return	No limit
You did not file a return	No limit

What If You Don't Have Proper Tax Records?

Because you're human, you might not have kept all the records required to back up your tax deductions. Don't despair, all is not lost—you might be able to fall back on the *Cohan* rule. This rule (named after the Broadway entertainer George M. Cohan, involved in a tax case in the 1930s) is the taxpayer's best friend. The *Cohan* rule recognizes that all businesspeople must spend at least some money to stay in business and so must have had at least some deductible expenses, even if they don't have adequate records to back them up.

If you're audited and lack adequate records for a claimed deduction, the IRS can use the *Cohan* rule to make an estimate of how much you must have spent and allow you to deduct that amount. However, you must provide at least some credible evidence on which to base this estimate, such as receipts, canceled checks, notes in your appointment book, or other records. Moreover, the IRS will allow you to deduct only the least amount you must have spent, based on the records you provide. In addition, the *Cohan* rule cannot be used for travel, meal, entertainment, or gift expenses, or for listed property.

If an auditor claims you lack sufficient records to back up a deduction, you should always bring up the *Cohan* rule and argue that you should still get the deduction based on the records you do have. At best, you'll probably get only part of your claimed deductions. If the IRS auditor disallows your deductions entirely or doesn't give you as much as you think you deserve, you can appeal in court and bring up the *Cohan* rule again there. You might have more success with a judge. However, you can't compel an IRS auditor or a court to apply the *Cohan* rule in your favor. Whether to apply the rule and how large a deduction to give you is within their discretion.

Reconstructing Tax Records

If you can show that you possessed adequate records at one time, but now lack them due to circumstances beyond your control, you may reconstruct your records for an IRS audit. Circumstances beyond your control would include acts of nature such as floods, fires, or earthquakes or theft. (Treas. Reg. 1.275.5(c)(5).) Loss of tax records while moving does not constitute circumstances beyond your control. Reconstructing records means you create brand-new records just for your audit or obtain other evidence to corroborate your deductions—for example, statements from people or companies from whom you purchased items for your business.

Accounting Methods

An accounting method is a set of rules used to determine when and how your income and expenses are reported. Accounting methods might sound like a rather dry subject, but your choice about how to account for your business expenses and income will have a huge impact on your tax deductions. You don't have to become as expert as a CPA on this topic, but you should understand the basics.

You choose an accounting method when you file your first tax return. If you later want to change your accounting method, you must get IRS approval. The IRS requires some types of businesses to use the accrual method. If your business doesn't fall into this group, you are free to choose the method you want, as long as it clearly shows your income and expenses.

The two basic methods of accounting are cash basis and accrual basis. Any business can use the accrual method, but not all can use the cash method.

Cash Method

The cash method is used by most small businesses and is based on this commonsense idea: You haven't earned income for tax purposes until you actually receive the money, and you haven't incurred an expense until you actually pay the money. Using the cash basis method, then, is like maintaining a checkbook. You record income only when the money is received and expenses only when they are actually paid. If you borrow money to pay business expenses, you incur an expense under the cash method only when you make payments on the loan.

The cash method is by far the most popular because it is the simplest and easiest to understand and apply. It can also save on taxes because taxable income can be deferred by postponing billings to the following year. Deductions can be speeded up by buying things before year end. For these reasons, the IRS has not been in favor of the cash method. Before 2018, there were restrictions on the ability to use the cash method by C corporations and businesses that produced, bought, or sold merchandise and were required to maintain an inventory. However, the Tax Cuts and Jobs Act greatly expanded the number of businesses that may use the cash method. Any business with no more than $26 million in average gross receipts during the prior three tax years can use the cash method. Businesses other than regular C corporations can use the cash method even if their gross receipts exceed $26 million provided that the method clearly reflects their income.

The Cash Method of Paying Expenses

Although it's called the cash method, this method for paying business expenses includes payments by check, credit card, or electronic funds transfer, as well as by cash. If you pay by check, the amount is deemed paid during the year in which the check is drawn and postal mailed or emailed—for example, a check dated December 31, 2021 is considered paid during 2021 only if it has a December 31, 2021 postmark or it's electronically paid by that date.

Constructive Receipt

Under the cash method, payments are "constructively received" when an amount is credited to your account or otherwise made available to you without restrictions. Constructive receipt is as good as actual receipt. If you authorize someone to be your agent and receive income for you, you are considered to have received it when your agent receives it.

> **EXAMPLE:** Interest is credited to your business bank account in December 2021, but you do not withdraw it or enter it into your passbook until 2022. You must include the amount in gross business income for 2021.

No Postponing Income

You cannot hold checks or other payments from one tax year to another to avoid paying tax on the income. You must report the income in the year the payment is received or made available to you without restriction.

> **EXAMPLE:** On December 1, 2021, Helen receives a $5,000 check from a client. She holds the check and doesn't cash it until January 10, 2022. She must still report the $5,000 as income for 2021, because she constructively received it that year.

No Prepayment of Expenses

The general rule is that you can't prepay expenses when you use the cash method—you can't hurry up the payment of expenses by paying them in advance. An expense you pay in advance can be deducted only in the year to which it applies.

> **EXAMPLE:** Helen pays $1,000 in 2021 for a business insurance policy that is effective for one year, beginning July. She can deduct $500 in 2021 and $500 in 2022.

However, there is an important exception to the general rule, called the 12-month rule. Under this rule, you may deduct a prepaid expense in the current year if the expense is for a right or benefit that extends no longer than the earlier of:

- 12 months, or
- until the end of the tax year after the tax year in which you made the payment.

EXAMPLE: You are a calendar year taxpayer and you pay $10,000 on July 1, 2021 for a business insurance policy that is effective for one year beginning July 1, 2021. The 12-month rule applies because the benefit you've paid for—a business insurance policy—extends only 12 months into the future. Therefore, the full $10,000 is deductible in 2021.

There is one small catch: If you previously followed the old rule under which expenses prepaid beyond the calendar year were not currently deductible, you must get IRS approval to use the 12-month rule. Approval is granted automatically by the IRS upon filing of IRS Form 3115, *Application for Change in Accounting Method.* You should attach one copy of the form to the return for the year of change and then send another copy to the IRS national office (not the service center where you file your return). The address is on the instructions for the form.

It is a good idea to get a tax pro to help you with this form because it may require some adjustment of the deductions you've taken for prepaid expenses in previous years under the old rule.

Accrual Method

In accrual basis accounting, you report income or expenses as they are earned or incurred, rather than when they are actually collected or paid. The accrual method can be difficult to use because there are complex rules to determine when income or expenses are accrued. You recognize income when it is earned, due, or received—whichever is earlier. Expenses are deductible only when liability is fixed, the amount can be determined with reasonable accuracy, and economic performance has occurred.

Obtaining IRS Permission to Change Your Accounting Method

You choose your accounting method by checking a box on your tax form when you file your tax return. Once you choose a method, you can't change it without getting permission from the IRS. Permission is granted automatically for many types of changes, including using the 12-month rule to deduct prepaid expenses. You must file IRS Form 3115, *Application for Change in Accounting Method,* with your tax return for the year you want to make the change (if the change is automatically granted).

Automatic approval can also be obtained to change to the cash method if you've been using the accrual method and come within one of the exceptions discussed above. However, changing your accounting method can have serious consequences, so consult a tax professional before doing so.

Tax Years

You are required to pay taxes for a 12-month period, also known as the "tax year." Sole proprietors, partnerships, limited liability companies, S corporations, and personal service corporations are required to use the calendar year as their tax years—that is, January 1 through December 31.

However, there are exceptions that permit some small businesses to use a tax year that does not end in December (also known as a "fiscal year"). You need to get the IRS's permission to use a fiscal year. The IRS doesn't like businesses to use a fiscal year, but it might grant you permission if you can show a good business reason for it.

One good reason to use a fiscal year is that your business is seasonal. For example, if you earn most of your income in the spring and incur most of your expenses in the fall, a tax year ending in July or August might be better than a calendar tax year ending in December because the income and expenses on each tax return will be more closely related. To get permission to use a fiscal year, you must file IRS Form 8716, *Election to Have a Tax Year Other Than a Required Tax Year.*

Staying Out of Trouble With the IRS

Most taxpayers have at least some concern about the possibility of facing an IRS audit. You might be wondering how the IRS decides to audit, how likely it is that you'll be audited, and what you can do to avoid being one of the unlucky ones. This chapter explains IRS audits and provides tips and strategies that will help you avoid attracting the attention of the IRS—or come out of an audit unscathed, if you find yourself in the government's crosshairs.

RESOURCE

Need more information on dealing with the IRS? For a detailed discussion of audits and other IRS procedures, see *Stand Up to the IRS*, by Frederick W. Daily and Stephen Fishman (Nolo).

What Every Business Owner Needs to Know About the IRS

Just as you should never go into battle without knowing your enemy, you should never file a tax return without understanding what the IRS plans to do with it.

Anatomy of an Audit

You can claim any deductions you want to take on your tax return—after all, you (or your tax preparer) fill it out, not the government. However, all the deductions you claim are subject to review by the IRS. This review is called a "tax audit." The three types of audits are correspondence audits, office audits, and field audits:

- **Correspondence audits.** As the name indicates, correspondence audits are handled entirely by postal mail. These are the simplest, shortest, and by far the most common type of IRS audit, usually involving a single issue. In 2019, 75% of all IRS audits were correspondence audits. The IRS sends you written questions about a perceived problem, and may request additional information and/or documentation. If you don't provide satisfactory answers or information, you'll be assessed additional taxes. Correspondence audits are often used to question a business about unreported income—income the IRS knows the taxpayer received because an IRS Form 1099 listing the payment has been filed by a client or customer.

- **Office audits.** Office audits take place face-to-face with an IRS auditor at one of the 33 IRS district offices. These audits are more complex than correspondence audits, often involving more than one issue or more than one tax year.

- **Field audits.** The field audit is the most comprehensive IRS audit, conducted by an experienced revenue officer. In a field audit, the officer examines your finances, your business, your tax returns, and the records you used to create the returns. As the name implies, a field audit is normally conducted at the taxpayer's place of business, which allows the auditor to learn as much about your business as possible. Field audits are ordinarily reserved for taxpayers who earn a lot of money.

How Small Business Owners Get in Trouble With the IRS

When auditing small business owners, the IRS is most concerned about whether you have done one of the following:

- **Underreported your income.** Unlike employees who have their taxes withheld, business owners who are not employees have no withholding—and many opportunities to underreport how much they earned, particularly if they run a cash business.

- **Claimed tax deductions to which you were not entitled.** For example, you claimed that nondeductible personal expenses, such as a personal vacation, were deductible business expenses.

- **Improperly documented the amount of your deductions.** If you don't have the proper records to back up the amount of a deduction, the IRS may reduce it, either entirely or in part. Lack of documentation is the main reason small business owners lose deductions when they get audited.

- **Taken business deductions for a hobby.** If you continually lose money, or you are involved in a fun activity, such as art, photography, crafts, or writing, and don't earn profits every year, the auditor may also question whether you are really in business. If the IRS claims you are engaged in a hobby, you could lose every single deduction for the activity. (See Chapter 2 for more on the hobby loss rule.)

Records Available to Auditors

An IRS auditor is entitled to examine the business records you used to prepare your tax returns, including your books, check registers, canceled checks, and receipts. The auditor can also ask to see records supporting your business tax deductions, such as a mileage record if you took a deduction for business use of your car. The auditor can also get copies of your bank records, either from you or your bank, and check them to see whether your deposits match the income you reported on your tax return. If you deposited a lot more money than you reported earning, the auditor will assume that you didn't report all of your income, unless you can show that the deposits you didn't include in your tax return weren't income. For example, you might be able to show that they were loans, inheritances, or transfers from other accounts. This is why you need to keep good financial records.

The IRS: Clear and Present Danger or Phantom Menace?

A generation ago, the three letters Americans feared most were I-R-S. There was a simple reason for this: The IRS, the nation's tax police, enforced the tax laws like crazy. In 1963, an incredible 5.6% of all Americans had their tax returns audited. Everybody knew someone who had been audited. Jokes about IRS audits were a staple topic of nightclub comedians and cartoonists.

In 2019, only 0.4% of all Americans were audited (one-fourteenth as many as in 1963), and an IRS audit was a rare event. The decline in audits was primarily due to reductions in the IRS workforce because of budget cuts and hiring freezes while at the same time the agency's workload vastly increased due to:

- increases in the overall number of tax filings each year
- the increasing complexity of the tax code
- frequent changes to the tax code, and
- the IRS's increasing responsibility for administering economic and social policies, including the health care law.

According to the IRS Oversight Board, the IRS does not have the resources to pursue at least $30 billion worth of known taxes that are incorrectly reported or not paid. The nation's tax gap—the total inventory of taxes that are known and not paid—is estimated at $600 billion.

Is Help Coming for the IRS?

In an effort to increase audit rates and help close the tax gap, the Biden Administration has announced plans to increase IRS funding by $80 billion over ten years, an increase of over 50% that would double the IRS workforce. Roughly three-quarters of the new funding would be allocated to enforcement, particularly audits of the wealthy and businesses. It is hoped that increased enforcement could raise an additional $300 billion in taxes during 2022 through 2031. It remains to be seen, however, how much of this plan Congress will adopt.

However, the fact that audit rates are low and likely going lower doesn't necessarily mean that you can easily get away with wholesale cheating. The IRS has sophisticated software in place that searches for anomalies in tax returns that can signal cheating. If anything in your return looks out of place, your chances of getting flagged for an audit go way up. This includes, for example, deductions that seem out of line with your income or type of business. Nevertheless, the chances that the average person will be audited are low.

Aggressive or Dishonest?

Given the relatively low audit rates in recent years, many tax experts say that this is a good time to be aggressive about taking tax deductions. In this context, "aggressive" means taking every deduction to which you might arguably be entitled. If a deduction falls into a gray area of law, you would decide the question in your favor. This is *tax avoidance*, which is perfectly legal.

However, being aggressive does not mean being dishonest—that is, taking phony deductions that you are clearly not entitled to take or falsely increasing the amount of the deductions to which you are entitled. This is *tax evasion*, which is a crime.

You Are a Prime IRS Target

Although the IRS is a troubled agency and audit rates are low, thousands of people still get audited every year. In 2019, the IRS audited 126,711 of the 16,848,093 tax returns filed in 2018 by Schedule C filers— the category that includes most small business owners. This category accounted for 16% of all IRS audits. Every year, the IRS releases statistics about who got audited the previous year. Here are the most recently available audit statistics.

This chart shows that in 2019, 1.6% of sole proprietors earning $100,000 to $200,000 were audited. Not even corporations with assets worth between $5 million and $10 million were audited as often.

These statistics undoubtedly reflect the IRS's belief that sole proprietors habitually underreport their income, take deductions to which they are not entitled, or otherwise cheat on their taxes. The lesson these numbers teach is that you need to take the IRS seriously. This doesn't mean that you shouldn't take all the deductions you're legally entitled to take, but you should understand the rules and be able to back up the deductions you do take with proper records.

IRS Audit Rates		
	2018 Audit Rate	2019 Audit Rate
Sole Proprietors		
Income less than $25,000	0.9%	0.6%
$25,000 to $100,000	0.9%	0.8%
$100,000 to $200,000	2.4%	1.6%
More than $200,000	1.9%	1.4%
Partnerships	0.2%	0.2%
S Corporations	0.2%	0.2%
C Corporations		
Assets less than $250,000	0.4%	0.3%
$250,000 to $1 million	0.9%	0.8%
$1 million to $5 million	0.8%	0.8%
$5 million to $10 million	1.1%	1.1%

How Tax Returns Are Selected for Audits

It's useful to understand how tax returns are selected for audit by the IRS. (By the way, if you are audited, you are entitled to know why you were selected. You ordinarily have to ask to find out.)

DIF Scores

One way the IRS decides whom to audit is by plugging the information from your tax return into a complex formula to calculate a "discriminate function" score (DIF). Returns with high DIFs have a far higher chance of being flagged for an audit, regardless of whether or not you have done anything obviously wrong. Anywhere from 25% to 60% of audited returns are selected this way. Exactly how the DIF is calculated is a closely guarded secret. Some of the known factors the formula takes into account are:

- **The nature of your business.** Businesses that deal with large amounts of cash are scrutinized more closely than those that don't.

- **Where you live.** Audit rates differ widely according to where you live. In 2000, for example, taxpayers in Southern California were almost five times more likely to be audited than taxpayers in Georgia. The IRS no longer releases information on audit rates by region, but according to the latest available data, the state with the highest audit rate is Nevada; other high-audit states include Alaska, California, and Colorado. Low-audit states include Illinois, Indiana, Iowa, Maryland, Massachusetts, Michigan, New York (not including Manhattan), Ohio, Pennsylvania, and West Virginia.

- **The amount of your deductions.** Returns with extremely large deductions in relation to income are more likely to be audited. For example, if your tax return shows that your business is earning $25,000, you are more likely to be audited if you claim $20,000 in deductions than if you claim $2,000.

- **Hot-button deductions.** Certain types of deductions have long been thought to be hot buttons for the IRS—especially auto, travel, and entertainment expenses. Casualty losses and bad debt deductions might also increase your DIF score. Some people believe that claiming the home office deduction makes an audit more likely, but the IRS denies this.

- **Businesses that lose money.** Businesses that show losses are more likely to be audited, especially if the losses are recurring. The IRS might suspect that you must be making more money than you are reporting—otherwise, why would you stay in business?

- **Peculiar deductions.** Deductions that seem odd or out of character for your business could increase your DIF score—for example, a plumber who deducts the cost of foreign travel might raise a few eyebrows at the IRS.

- **How you organize your business.** Sole proprietors get higher DIF scores than businesses that are incorporated or owned by partnerships or limited liability companies. As a result, sole proprietors generally are most likely to be audited by the IRS. Partnerships and small C corporations are ten times less likely to be audited than sole proprietors.

IRS Matching Program

Whenever a client pays you $600 or more for your services during the year, it must report the payments to the IRS on IRS Form 1099-MISC (Form 1099-NEC for 2021 and later). IRS computers match the information on 1099s with the amount of income reported on tax returns using Social Security and other identifying numbers. Discrepancies usually generate correspondence audits.

Groups Targeted for Audit

Every year, the IRS gives special attention to specific industries or groups of taxpayers that it believes to be tax cheats. Businesses that receive a lot of cash are a perennial audit favorite. Other IRS favorites include doctors, dentists, lawyers, CPAs, and salespeople.

The IRS also targets taxpayers who use certain tax shelters or have offshore bank accounts or trusts. But you don't have to be rich to be an audit target. The IRS also heavily audits low-income taxpayers who claim the earned income tax credit.

Tips and Referrals

You could also get audited as a result of a referral from another government agency, such as your state tax department. The IRS also receives tips from private citizens—for example, a former business partner or an ex-spouse.

Bad Luck

A certain number of tax returns are randomly selected for audit every year. If you find yourself in this category, you can't do much about it. As long as you have adequate documentation to support your deductions, you should do just fine.

State Tax Audits Grow Increasingly Common

Although most people (and books) focus on IRS audits, audits by state income tax agencies are becoming increasingly common. Many states have increased fines and late-payment penalties. Others have adopted severe—and highly effective—punishments against delinquent taxpayers. For example, some states refuse to issue driver's licenses to people who owe back taxes. Others are hiring private tax collectors and publishing names of tax evaders online.

Eight Tips for Avoiding an Audit

Here are eight things you can do to minimize your chances of getting audited.

Tip #1: Be Thorough and Exact

Submit a tax return that is thorough and exact; this will help you avoid unwanted attention from the IRS. Your math should be correct. Avoid round numbers on your return (like $100 or $5,000). This looks like you're making up the numbers instead of taking them from accurate records. You should include, and completely fill out, all necessary forms and schedules. Moreover, your state tax return should be consistent with your federal return. If you do your own taxes, using a tax preparation software will help you produce an accurate return.

Tip #2: Don't File Early

Unless you're owed a substantial refund, you shouldn't file your taxes early. The IRS generally has three years after April 15 to decide whether to audit your return. Filing early just gives the IRS more time to think about whether you should be audited. You can reduce your audit chances even more by getting an automatic extension to file until October 15. (Partnerships and S corporations receive an automatic extension only until September 15—five months, instead of six.) Note, however, that filing an extension does not extend the date by which you have to pay any taxes due for the prior year—these must be paid by April 15.

Tip #3: Form a Business Entity

The IRS audit rate statistics, discussed above, show that partnerships and small corporations are audited far less often than sole proprietors. In 2019, for example, the IRS audited 0.2% of partnerships, 0.2% of S corporations, and only 0.3% of regular C corporations with assets worth less than $250,000. In contrast, 1.6% of sole proprietors earning $100,000 to $200,000 were audited. The majority of small business owners are sole proprietors, but no law says they have to be. Incorporating your business or forming a limited liability company will greatly reduce your audit risk. However, you must balance this against the time and expense involved in forming a corporation or an LLC and having to complete more complex tax returns. Moreover, in some states—most notably California—corporations and LLCs have to pay additional state taxes.

Tip #4: Explain Items the IRS Will Question

If your return contains an item that the IRS might question or that could increase the likelihood of an audit, include an explanation and documentation to prove everything is on the up and up. For example, if your return contains a substantial bad debt deduction, explain the circumstances showing that the debt is a legitimate business expense. This won't necessarily avoid an audit, but it might reduce your chances. Here's why: If the IRS computer gives your return a high DIF score, an IRS classifier screens it to see whether it warrants an audit. If your explanations look reasonable, the screener may decide you shouldn't be audited after all.

Such explanations ("disclosures" in tax parlance) can be made on plain white paper and attached to your return if you file by postal mail, or you can use special IRS forms. IRS Form 8275, *Disclosure Statement*, can be used to explain or disclose any information that there isn't room to include on your other tax forms. Another IRS form, Form 8275-R, *Regulation Disclosure Statement*, must be used to disclose tax positions that are contrary to IRS regulations or other rules. You shouldn't file Form 8275-R without professional help.

Tip #5: Avoid Ambiguous or General Expenses

Don't list expenses under vague categories such as "miscellaneous" or "general expense." Be specific. IRS Schedule C lists specific categories for the most common small business expenses. If an expense doesn't fall within one of these classifications, create a specific name for it.

Tip #6: Report All of Your Income

The IRS is convinced that self-employed people, including many home business owners, don't report all of their income. Finding such hidden income is a high priority. As mentioned above, IRS computers compare 1099 forms with tax returns to determine whether there are any discrepancies. Not all income business owners receive is reported to the IRS on Form 1099—for example, if you sell a product to customers rather than providing a service, your receipts will not be reported on Form 1099. However, if you are audited, the auditor may examine your bank records to see whether you received any unreported income.

Tip #7: Watch Your Income-to-Deduction Ratio

Your income-to-deduction ratio can be an important audit flag. One statistical study of more than 1,200 returns that were audited concluded that if your total business expenses amount to less than 52% of your gross business income, you are not very likely to be audited. If your business expenses are 52% to 63% of your business income, there is a relatively high probability that the IRS computer will tag you for an audit. Finally, if your expenses are more than 63% of your income, the study found that you are certain to be computer tagged for audit. Of course, this doesn't necessarily mean that you *will* be audited. Less than 10% of returns that are computer tagged for audit are actually audited. But being tagged considerably increases the odds that you'll be audited.

Whether these precise numbers are correct or not is anyone's guess. However, the basic conclusion—that your income-to-deduction ratio is an important factor in determining whether you'll be audited—is undoubtedly true.

Tip #8: Beware of Abnormally Large Deductions

It is not just the total amount of your deductions that is important. Very large individual deductions can also increase your audit chances. How much is too much? It depends in part on the nature of your business. A $2,000 foreign travel deduction might look abnormal for a plumber, but not for a person in the import-export business.

Index

taken the year it is placed in service, 79–80

tax basis and, 80

tax preparation and other software for tracking, 100

tax reporting, 99–100

used vehicles and, 170

See also Accelerated depreciation; Actual expense method (for local transportation expenses), and depreciation of vehicle; Amortization of intangible assets; Depreciation periods

Depreciation periods

  bonus depreciation and class-wide requirement, 85

  for buildings, 95–96

  defined, 90

  for improvements to buildings, 96–97

  method chosen as class-wide requirement, 93

  recovery classes, 90

  routine maintenance safe harbor and, 88

  Section 179 expensing and ability to pick and choose within classes, 87

  table of, 91

DIF (discriminate function) score, 399–401, 404

Digital cameras, as listed property, 82, 83, 94

Disability, and nonmedical withdrawals from health savings accounts (HSAs), 322

Disability insurance, state

  overview, 238

  benefits of, included in taxable income, 299

  deduction of premiums as business expense, 299

  parental leave, 239

Disaster relief payments to employees (COVID-19 related), 251–252

Disasters. *See* Casualty losses

District of Columbia, mandate for health insurance, 286

Dividends

  capital gains taxes on, 15

  as child's unearned income, 255

  effective tax rates on, 15

  Medicare tax on, 15

  as not deductible, 15

  and spouse co-owners electing sole-proprietorship status, 17–18

Documentation. *See* Record keeping

Double declining balance depreciation method, 93–94

Double taxation, C corporations and, 14–15, 16

Dry cleaning, 343

Dues (fees) for professional organizations, 343

Dues for club memberships, 62

E

Earned income credit, and audit risk, 401

Earthquakes. *See* Casualty losses

Education expenses

  continuing professional education as deductible, 344–345

  employee training as deductible, 345

  as exception to early withdrawal penalty for IRAs, 273

  lifetime learning tax credit, 344

  local transportation for deductible education, 346

  MBAs, deductibility of, 345

Q

QBI (qualified business income)
definition and requirement for pass-through deduction, 210
established by the Tax Cuts and Job Act, 208
and sale of business property taxed as ordinary income, 81
underreporting, and audit risk, 395, 404
See also Income; Pass-through deduction
Qualified employee benefits plans, 240
See also Employee fringe benefits
Qualified improvement property (interiors of commercial buildings), 97–98
Qualified small employer HRA (QSEHRA)
overview, 313
all eligible employees must be offered the HRA, 314
eligible employers/employees, 313–314
establishment and notice of, 314–315
health insurance must be individually purchased by employee, 313
limits on allowances, 313
penalty for failure of employer co provide notice, 315
S corporation shareholder-employees eligibility for, 314
tax reporting of, 314
QuickBooks, 100, 238, 371, 375
QuickBooks Online, 372
QuickBooks Self-Employed, 372
Quicken, 100, 370–371, 372, 375
QuickPay, 238

R

Real property
buildings, depreciation of, 68, 95–96
buying an outside workplace, 142
excluded from bonus depreciation, 83, 95
excluded from de minimis safe harbor, 70
excluded from Section 179 expensing, 95
first-time home buyers' exception to penalties for early withdrawals from IRAs, 273
improvements that can be deducted in one year, 96–98
improvements to, 96
land as not depreciable, 95
land cost, clearing and other preparations, 95
land cost deducted from sale price to determine gain, 95
mortgage interest deduction limitations, 358
resource for, 96
sale of, and property taxes, 363
Recapture of depreciation, sale of home and home office deduction, 133–134
Recapture of depreciation when business use of property falls below 50%
improvements to property and, 88
listed property, 83, 94–95
Section 179 expensing and, 86, 165
and self-employment taxes, 95
vehicles, 165